STRUGGLE FOR AFRICA

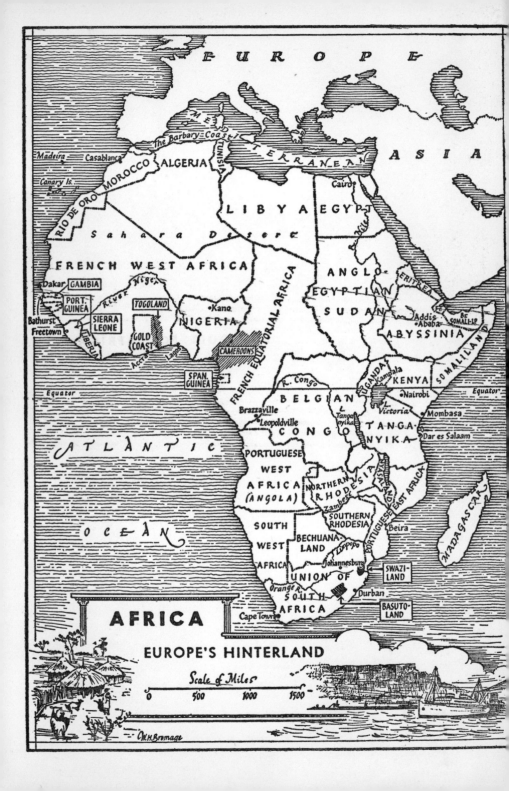

AFRICA

EUROPE'S HINTERLAND

STRUGGLE

FOR AFRICA

VERNON BARTLETT

FREDERICK A. PRAEGER, NEW YORK

BOOKS THAT MATTER

Published in the United States of America
in 1953 by Frederick A. Praeger, Inc.,
Publishers, 105 West 40th Street,
New York 18, N. Y.

Copyright, Vernon Bartlett, 1953
Library of Congress Catalog Card Number: 53-11083

Manufactured in the United States of America
by H. Wolff, New York, N. Y.

CONTENTS

FOREWORD

This is not a book for the expert. The reason for its existence is that three visits to different parts of Africa since the war have impressed upon me that this continent is the natural hinterland of Europe, that its primitive peoples are making an amazing effort to leap across the centuries, that every European who goes to Africa has an opportunity of making history such as have come to few men in history. All the elements of drama are there—love and devotion, jealousy, greed, fear— above all, fear. And it seemed to me that it might be useful if I were to pass on my rather superficial knowledge and impressions to others with less opportunity to travel than myself.

I had not realized until I went there how much the events in one part of Africa would influence those in another. It was impossible, for example, to give a balanced description of the Union without also describing the Gold Coast, since the black man's accession to power in West Africa makes Europeans so much more anxious to prevent a similar achievement in the very different circumstances of South Africa. But it was also unsatisfactory to write of British rule in West and East Africa without referring to the ways in which other governments were dealing with their analogous problems. I found myself straying farther and farther from the few paths in Africa which I knew fairly well.

That is why I repeat that this is not a book for the expert—he would find too much to criticize in it. On the other hand I hope that my picture is more or less in proportion, and may therefore stimulate a sane interest in and curiosity about this amazing continent. I have received much help, direct or indirect, in its preparation, and there are some authors, authorities and advisers to whom I should like to express my particular gratitude.

Thanks, then, to C. Y. Carstairs and J. A. Hutton at the Colonial Office; to Perry Fellowes at the Foreign Office; to H. H. H. Biermann, Director of Information at South Africa House; to Comte Bertrand de La Salle at the French Embassy; to Charles Wilmot of the British Council. It should go without saying that none of these gentlemen bears the slightest responsibility for the opinions I have expressed. Thanks, also, to Mrs. Irwin Schuller, E. B. Dawson and Joel Mervis, of Johannesburg (who kindly corrected some of my grosser errors); to Senator and Mrs. Ballinger for their advice. I have learned a lot from the writings of my friends, Basil Davidson, Elspeth Huxley, Charles d'Ydewalle and Negley Farson, and, above all, from *Afrika*, a book by a German writer, Dr. Anton Zischka.

I must also thank Robin Cruikshank, Editor of the *News Chronicle*, and S. Mervyn Herbert, until recently its Foreign Editor, partly because some material in the book has already appeared in that paper, but still more because, but for them, I should not have got to Africa at all. The Editor of the *Spectator* has also kindly allowed me to use material that had appeared in his paper. Then I must express my gratitude to Miss Pamela Young, whose encouragement is all the more admirable in view of the puzzling scribble which she has been called upon to convert into an intelligible typescript. Lastly, I apologize to those others whom I have omitted to thank by name. This portmanteau expression of gratitude applies in particular to the many officials and journalistic colleagues in the Union and the various colonies, without whose help I could not have collected the material for this book, and without whose hospitality I should have been a much less happy man.

This book is dedicated to my wife, with deep gratitude for her courageous and even humor on two difficult African journeys and with apologies for the way in which the writing of it has made my company so nearly intolerable for so many months.

VERNON BARTLETT

1

CONTINENT WITHOUT HISTORY

Africa the Unknown. Look at an old map of the Continent. At a time when the other continents were charted with considerable accuracy, great areas of Africa were still left empty. Sometimes the cartographer put in a great lake or a range of mountains, but they existed only in his fancy. Sometimes there were pictures of strange beasts. Dean Swift wrote:

> "Geographers, in Afric's maps,
> With savage creatures filled the gaps;
> And o'er unhabitable downs
> Placed elephants for want of towns."

The human inhabitants, it was widely believed, had their faces where their chests ought to be, or single eyes in the middle of their foreheads. Gorillas must have given rise to the strangest legends, and there are at least four animals in Africa so

1

improbable that they would surpass all conceptions of the explorer's most fevered imagination—the hippopotamus, the rhinoceros, the giraffe and the crocodile. Quite obviously, such beasts cannot be true.

One is amazed by the courage of the early explorers. They had no idea, of course, that malaria was carried by an insect—its name is a reminder of their ignorance—and malaria is so prevalent that almost every white man between the Tropics of Cancer and Capricorn takes his daily dose of preventive drug. They were attacked by any number of parasites of which they could not even suspect the existence. Feverish and ill, they had also to deal with the larger and more obvious dangers —suspicious native chiefs and wild animals. By their pertinacity, they opened up Africa, but so recently that many Africans can still remember the sale of slaves, and tribal warfare still flares up from time to time. Even to-day the only thick clusters of railways are to be found in the extreme south and extreme north-west, and their mileage amounts to less than six per cent of the world's total. The Great North Road, through the Rhodesias, Tanganyika and Kenya sounds impressive, but only a fool would drive along it in the rainy season without chains on his wheels, and at any time without the constant fear of breaking a spring on its corrugated laterite surface.

And yet, for thousands of years, Africa has had contact with the civilizations that have so drastically influenced the other continents. Herodotus describes how Egyptian ships sailed down the Red Sea in 600 B.C. and returned three years later through the Straits of Gibraltar. Mombasa, then called Tonike, existed in the first century A.D. Phœnicians, who are supposed to have come to Cornwall for its tin, sailed down the West Coast of Africa in search of gold and ivory. The Romans turned the land north of the Sahara into an immense and prosperous granary. The Egyptians spread their luxurious civilization up the Nile Valley far into the interior. Persian dhows sailed to the East Coast before one monsoon and home again before the other monsoon, as they still sail to-day. All round the coasts you may find old Dutch and Portuguese fortresses, and the Governor of the Gold Coast to-day lives in a magnificent Danish castle, the Christianborg.

But Africa bears practically no traces of an indigenous civilization. In the jungle of Northern Ceylon, or of Indo-China, or of Central America, there are ruins recalling ancient splendor. The desert sands of the Middle East yield rewards year after year to the archæologist. I recall one place in Cyprus where almost every stone you pick up is, in fact, a piece of broken tile or pottery made many centuries ago. The Chinese, the Aztecs, the Incas and so many others have left enough traces to enable one to picture their lives. Europe can plot its history back to the beginning of historical times.

There are the bronze heads and terracotta that have been dug up at Ife in West Africa, but these are believed to have been the work of the earlier Egyptian or Arab tribes that crossed the Sahara from the north or came along its southern border from Sudan and the Upper Nile. For a time the splendid ruins of Zimbabwe, in Southern Rhodesia, were attributed to black men; now they are considered to be the ruins of an Arab stronghold built to facilitate the trade in black slaves. There is a fascinating and very striking similarity between the rock paintings attributed to the early Bushmen in South Africa and those discovered in caves in Spain and France, but these serve merely to emphasize the lack of details about the people who painted them. The bones and other human relics found in Rhodesia and Kenya prove that men have lived in Africa from very early times, but they tell us very little about them.

Africa covers one-fifth of the land surface of the globe, but it has considerably less than one-tenth of the population. So little known is this continent that there is still no agreement among the experts about the number of people who live on it. In his famous *African Survey*,[1] Lord Hailey writes: "In the last hundred years estimates of the population . . . have been as low as 28,000,000 and as high as 205,000,000; expert authority now limits itself to the view that the present total

[1] *An African Survey* (Royal Institute of International Affairs).

may lie between 138,100,000 and 163,300,000." But Dr. Anton Zischka[2] gives the population as 180,000,000, and then himself quotes another authority for the statement that the population has risen in the last three hundred years from 100,000,000 to 190,000,000, during which time the people of Europe, roughly one-third the size of Africa, increased from 100,000,-000 to 520,000,000. The United Nations went one better, and gave the population in 1950 as 198,000,000. You pay your money and you take your choice.

This confusion arises, of course, from the fact that the opening up of Africa, as distinct from the settling along its coasts, only began some sixty years ago. And the conditions at that time were unbelievably primitive. I know of no more concise description of them than that to be found in an already well-known passage from a report by Sir Philip Mitchell, until recently the very successful Governor of Kenya.[3]

"They had no wheeled transport and (apart from the camels and donkeys of the pastoral nomads) no animal transport either; they had no roads nor towns; no tools except small hand hoes, axes, wooden digging sticks and the like; no manufactures, and no industrial products except the simplest domestic handiwork; no commerce as we understand it and no currency, although in some places barter of produce was facilitated by the use of small shells; they had never heard of working for wages. They went stark naked or clad in the bark of trees or the skins of animals, and they had no means of writing, even by hieroglyphics, nor of numbering except by their fingers or making notches on a stick or knots in a piece of grass or fibre; they had no weights and measures of general use. Perhaps most astonishing of all to the modern European mind they had no calendar nor notation of time, and reckoned by the moons and seasons and the rising and setting of the sun. Before European occupation there was no way of saying '1st January, 1890' or '2.30 p.m.' or their equivalents in any language spoken

² *Afrika*, by Anton Zischka (Stalling Verlag, Oldenburg).
³ *The Agrarian Problem in Kenya* (Government Printer, Nairobi).

from Abyssinia to the Transvaal, except Swahili on the coast. There was a great variety of language or dialect, largely within the great linguistic group now called 'Bantu' by European scholars, and it was common, as it is to-day, for an area the size of an English county to contain several groups speaking different languages. They were pagan spirit or ancestor propitiators, in the grip of magic and witchcraft, their minds cribbed and confined by superstition . . . they are a people who in 1890 were in a more primitive condition than anything of which there is any record in pre-Roman Britain."

This description is much less applicable to West Africa than to the East. But even to-day, you may drive many hundreds of miles through any part of black Africa and find no means of transport but lorries and women. A few rattling old lorries and a great number of tired but cheerful women. Every visitor admires their stately and graceful walk, but one does not always realize the price paid for this gracefulness. The chief strides along with no encumbrance except his spear or his stick, but his wives follow him with all kinds of burdens balanced on their heads, and doubtless they would willingly forego some of their grace if their burdens could be less heavy. It was at Nongoma, in Zululand, that I noticed a Native girl buying a bottle of oil. That she should carry the bottle upright on her head no longer astonished me, but, although her hands were empty, even the money for it was balanced on her crinkly hair. In Kenya, the Kikuyu women carry their loads on their backs, but with the weight dependent on a strap across their shaven skulls, with the horrible result that by the time they reach middle age they have pronounced grooves across the tops of their heads—to the bewilderment, no doubt, of the anthropologist in the remote future.

The absence of an African history must always remain a mystery. The original inhabitants seem to have been small men who lived entirely by hunting and whose skins were yellow rather than black. They probably resembled the Pygmies of the Belgian Congo and French Equatorial Africa, or the Bushmen who now live in such inhospitable regions as the Kalahari Desert. There is evidence that these Bushmen used to live as far north as Lake Tanganyika.[4] But they were pushed farther and farther southward by two main forces of invaders from the north-east. One of these forces, consisting of men with negroid features, seems to have advanced up the Nile Valley to Lake Victoria, with a branch swerving westward, just south of the Sahara, until it reached what is now known as West Africa. The other force, consisting of men with finer, Hamitic features, either followed much the same path or crossed the Red Sea from Asia Minor. They were, and still are mainly pastoralists and warriors—the Zulus in South Africa, for example, the Masai in Kenya and Tanganyika, the Matabele in Southern Rhodesia, the Fulani in Northern Nigeria; the Negroes were, and still are, primitive agriculturists.

In course of time most of these black-skinned men who pushed southward have become known as Bantu—a word which means merely "the People." The vanguard of them drifted on in three main streams—one along the east coast, one, roughly, through the Rhodesias and Bechuanaland, and one toward the west coast—whenever they needed to cultivate fresh land or to provide pasture for their cattle. Within the last three hundred years this southward movement of the black men has been temporarily checked by another migratory movement in the opposite direction—that of the Dutch and British moving up from the Cape of Good Hope. Between the two, the unfortunate Bushmen and Hottentots have been practically obliterated—sometimes in the past they were hunted and shot like wild game.

The Bantu are now to be found over all Africa south of the Equator, and their many languages are clearly related. Their long migration has come to a degrading end, for, within the last few years, they have reached the south-west corner of their

[4] Cf. "Africa; Ethnology," by T. Athol Joyce, *Encyclopædia Britannica*.

continent—more and more of them are filtering into Windermere which, despite its name, is a hideous and abominable shanty location just outside Cape Town.

The other black men who turned westward—the real Negroes—have no such links between their languages, and in parts of Nigeria half a dozen completely different tongues may be spoken almost in neighboring villages. Another wave of migrants, the Libyans (Berbers) came southward across the Sahara, which helps to explain both the Moslem religion and the fine-cut features of many of the Negroes in the inland territories of West Africa.

And all these migrants have passed on their way without leaving a single monument behind them. Recent discoveries in Uganda, Kenya and the Transvaal support the theory that Africa, and not Asia, was the cradle of the human race. The "missing link," about which there were so many silly jokes during my schooldays, is unlikely ever to be found, but the Transvaal has produced remains of half a dozen creatures that were man-like apes or ape-like men—the change having occurred when these creatures learned to make rough tools to preconceived designs. Pebbles that were undoubtedly chipped for some such purpose have been found in Uganda in geological deposits nearly one million years old.

But these traces make the absence of any historical and architectural record all the more amazing. Except in parts of the west, where you may find the most primitive Africans living side by side with the most advanced, and along the Mediterranean Coast where the people are much more closely related to Asians than to indigenous Africans, you can travel in Africa east to west and north to south—five thousand miles either way—and find very little in the way of African dwelling houses except round huts of wattle and daub or sun-baked mud bricks. Most of these huts have conical thatched roofs. There are slight variations in shape or material. In Zululand, for example, the huts are shaped like rather flattened beehives, with such low entrances that you have to crawl in on all fours, like the wild beasts these low entrances are designed to discourage. The thatched roofs may be of palm leaves or straw or some other material, generally so inflammable that one is no longer surprised by the absence of old villages. But, such small differences apart, almost all the black men live in little primitive round huts that are built to last only for the few years that elapse before the soil around them is exhausted, and the time comes to move elsewhere.

Many of the stone implements found in South Africa provide very little clue to the past, for they lie on the surface of the ground. There has been no time for them to be buried in geological strata since they were still being used by the Bushmen less than a century ago. These primitive implements are significant, not because they are old, but because they are so new.

The fact that civilization has only begun to influence the Africans in the last sixty years or so is in many ways unfortunate. The villages, when you see them—for many of them are carefully concealed from the main roads—appear to be camps, rather than groups of permanent homes. The towns are entirely European or Asian. They consist mostly of one-storied, open-fronted stores such as you find all through Asia, but the residential quarters are British, French and so on, according to the European allegiance of the particular territory, with the necessary modifications to cope with the heat, the rain and the white ants. There is therefore nothing specifically African about them, and, since few of them are as much as fifty years old, you get the very false impression that you are crossing a continent that has only recently become inhabited.

And one result of this lack of visible evidence of Negro civilization may be to make the Europeans more contemptuous than they ought to be of African customs and laws, which are often much more suitable for Africans and their climate and their way of living than are the rules and regulations which we tend to impose upon them. One wonders, for example, which system of law they respect the more. In a Native court the village chiefs and elders, seated, perhaps, on kitchen chairs to give them dignity, listen to plaintiff, defendant and witnesses crouching on the floor and putting down short lengths of stick to emphasize each point they make. The verdicts are based on custom and equity, and are easily understood.

The contrast with the Supreme Court in one of the British African Colonies could scarcely be greater. The African plaintiffs and defendants, each giving evidence in his own particular language, must become incredibly confused by such fragments of the learned references to British law and discussions of precedents as may reach them through the Native interpreter. A man who wins his case against someone who has done him harm must leave the court bewildered and depressed to discover that the fine imposed upon his enemy is paid not to him, but to the court itself, or, in other words, to the government. This bewilderment may have its advantages, for one racial characteristic of the Africans is a passion for litigation, and the many Asian lawyers who already make a comfortable living by stimulating this passion would be multiplied if the plaintiff could more easily make money out of winning a case.

Professor Arnold Toynbee, in his *Study of History*, lists twenty-one civilizations, twelve of which have been those of the "white" races (including Egyptians, Persians, Hittites, and so on), and four, those of the "red" races in America. He can list no black civilization.

In these circumstances, it is easy—and silly—to put all the blame on the African, and to say that he's like a child, unable ever to do a responsible job, corrupt, lazy, and a liar. To a small extent all these things are true, but that does not mean that they will necessarily remain true. Still less does it mean— as it is generally intended to mean—that the black man is, in some peculiar way, permanently, biologically, the inferior of the white man, the brown man and the yellow man. In any case it is at least as dangerous to generalize about the black race as about the white, and yet the American feels himself very unlike the Russian, the Finn very unlike the Portuguese, the Scotsman very unlike the Sassenach. In Africa there are said to be twenty-six distinct ethnic groups, with upwards of 700 languages, some of which differ as widely as do the languages of Europe from those of Asia. Some are tonal languages, with the meaning dependent less upon the word than upon the intonation (and this, I am assured, is part of the explanation of the so-called "talking drums" since the different tones can convey fairly simple messages). Some Bantu languages in Natal and the Cape Province are still further complicated by a series of "clicks" inherited from the Hottentots and produced, with quite different meanings, in various regions of your mouth from the back of your teeth to the back of your throat.

But there are some racial peculiarities, and they are more pronounced perhaps in the black race than in others since until recently it has been relatively so unaffected by events elsewhere in the world. It may be worth while to consider these peculiarities one by one.

Lazy? And who would not be lazy with so many parasitic diseases and so much under-nutrition? According to Dr. E. B. Worthington,[5] over vast areas of Kenya "practically the entire population above one year of age harbor malaria parasites in their blood continuously." The damage done by sleeping sickness is difficult to estimate, since the presence of the disease is often not realized. "A victim may suffer for many years from general weakness, and, with resistance lowered, he may succumb to another disease." But it is estimated that there are nearly a million cases of sleeping sickness in Northern Nigeria alone.

Still worse are the ravages caused by parasitic worms, such as hookworm and bilharzia. Again according to Dr. Worthington, more than ninety per cent of the people in East Africa are infected with one or more kinds of these worms, and frequently as many as six kinds have been found in the same individual. And these diseases are not necessarily the result, as some non-Africans imagine, of uncleanly habits. Very few Af-

[5] *Science in Africa* (Oxford University Press).

ricans wear shoes. The hookworm takes advantage of the slightest cut or scratch to get into your blood stream and, through the blood stream, into your liver—I found the Lieu-tenant-Governor of the Western Region of Nigeria just re-covering from hookworm which he had acquired in some damp grass while he was bird-watching. Bilharzia attacks the Af-rican while he is wading or bathing in certain streams, and, in comparison with it, the hookworm is benevolent. Eighty per cent of all patients admitted to hospitals in Lower Egypt are found to have this disease, which produces "progressive de-bilitation and listlessness."

The spread of venereal diseases and tuberculosis are due in great part to ignorance. Tuberculosis came to Africa with the white man, and the African shows little more ability to resist it than did the Polynesians, who were almost obliterated by it. And it is, of course, linked with under-nourishment. But the African does not live on starchy foods because he wants to. Indeed, his desire for red meat encourages him to poach in a big way: he is wiping out the wild game of the continent far more quickly than white poachers in search of ivory, or white "sportsmen" determined to kill off every animal their expen-sive licenses authorize them to kill.

With one important reservation, the African would eat more meat if he could get it. The advent of the European, who has enclosed large tracts of good grazing territory, has put an end to the African's habit of moving to a new pasturage as soon as the old one showed signs of exhaustion. The European has still further aggravated this situation by putting an end to tribal wars and teaching the elements of hygiene and medical care, so that, in most areas, there are now far more Africans com-peting for far less land. Also, as they adopt European habits, they are apt to lose the knowledge of fruits and herbs which formerly must have helped to counteract the bad effects of a diet containing far too much tapioca and other starchy foods. A study of the primitive tribes in the Gold Coast, for example, showed that they included in their diet 114 species of fruits, 46 species of leguminous seeds and 47 species of greens.[6] Which sounds a lot healthier than the Englishman's diet of watery cabbage or the American's diet of stuff out of tins.

The important reservation, of course, is the African's widespread reluctance to eat cattle, even when he has them. In Zululand a Chief would rather go hungry than kill off some of his beasts. With cattle he can buy wives, and the more wives a man has the more he can sit outside his hut drinking Mabela beer and looking important. Spades do not exist in most parts of Africa; the earth is turned with the help of a heavy hoe, and the person wielding the hoe is a woman. If a plough is available, the man may deign to walk behind it, because a plough carries prestige. But the trouble is that he ploughs up the land too often and the thin topsoil blows away as dust. This reluctance to kill one's own cattle is to be found even in parts of Africa where brides are not bought by the transfer of so many cows. Beasts are just as important to the African as is the front garden or the motor car with which in England Mrs. Jones proclaims her social superiority over Mrs. Smith.

Perhaps the most serious reason for the backwardness of the Africans is that in so many parts of the continent they can keep no beasts at all. If all the Europeans were suddenly to return to Europe, it is very probable that immense areas with a large black population would go out of cultivation; even now, the efforts of scientists, research workers, administrators and agricultural and veterinary officers are insufficient to check the advances of the tsetse fly, which carries the dread sleeping sickness to humans and animals.

Driving along an African road, you may find yourself faced with a large barn with doors at either end. You are enclosed in this building while your car is fumigated, and an African with a small butterfly net apologetically peers around for an insect scarcely larger than our house-fly. It is this insect which is responsible for the absence or scarcity of domestic animals and, sometimes, of human beings over an area forty-five times as extensive as England, Scotland and Wales. And modern traffic spreads the scourge, for the tsetse fly will pursue any moving object, and even attach itself to passing trains. Ordinary cars usually travel too fast for it, but army convoys carried the disease into new areas during the war.

Antrycide? Was Britain not assured a few years ago, by an Under-Secretary at the Colonial Office, that this new drug was going to wipe out trypanosomiasis in cattle all over Africa? Would it not enable immense new areas of empty land to be brought into cultivation?

In the admirable veterinary research laboratories near Nairobi and at Vom and Kaduna, in Northern Nigeria, they talk rather bitterly about that Under-Secretary. The drug has done as much as the scientists working on it near Nairobi had expected, but this falls far short of what the British at home were told to expect. For cattle become reinfected if the concentration of antrycide in the bloodstream falls below a certain point, and yet over-frequent doses to keep the blood above that level are likely to develop "drug-fast" strains, in which resistance to the drug may be complete. Thus it has still to be proved that antrycide can be really effective except in the case of cattle being moved fairly quickly through a "fly" belt.

There is the additional difficulty that drugs of this kind have to be administered in the field, and many Africans are reluctant to carry out the instructions on the bottle. Instead of using the prescribed ampule on each beast, they think they are being clever and economical by using a quarter of the dose, and they may thus produce an antrycide-fast strain.

The trypanosomes that produce the human variety of sleeping sickness are found mainly in a variety of tsetse fly that lives near water. In many parts of Africa this fly has driven the people away to land that is too dry to provide good grazing or farmland, and that becomes so over-crowded that soil erosion and malnutrition both become inevitable. Much has been done by clearing vegetation away from the river banks. In some areas all wild animals, which are great carriers of "fly," have been destroyed. In others the "fly" has been kept back by clearing all vegetation along strips a mile wide. Sometimes the destruction of certain varieties of plants cleans a whole area of tsetse. Elsewhere there is a vicious circle— forests are destroyed to kill the fly, and the climate is altered; forests are planted again for rain and fuel and the fly returns.

In Nairobi and Kaduna, month after month, white and black research workers study the several varieties of tsetse in hundreds of glass tubes. Field officers all over Africa are clearing different types of bush and testing the distances the fly can cover in search of its prey. For this insect renders so much land uninhabitable that it is one of the most important political and economic factors in Africa.

The Africans, then, still suffer terribly from diseases, many of which were formerly common in Europe. They live mainly in tropical or semi-tropical countries, where violent effort is difficult, or even unwise. Even so, the Europeans who most readily accuse them of laziness are seldom able or willing to make as great physical efforts as they do. According to Dr. de Castro,[7] this is in part because Negroes lose less salt through perspiration than do people with light-colored skins, and they therefore suffer less physical fatigue from the same physical exertion. In consequence, the white man, generally with enough money (or beads, or cowries, or bars of iron) to pay others to work for him, has so tended to select for himself the administrative jobs that he now considers it beneath his dignity to make a hard physical effort, except for amusement. Rather than leave his arm-chair to get a book from the shelf, he will shout for his "boy" to come from the kitchen to get it for him; having read a few pages, he will go over to the Club to play a few hard sets of tennis or a round of golf on a course on which the African would dearly like to grow his maize or his manioc. Then, over his drink on the stoep, or

[7] *Op. cit.*

whatever he calls the veranda in his particular part of Africa, he will grumble about the laziness of his "boys."

I sometimes wonder whether this widespread belief that the white man loses caste by doing physical work does not constitute one of the gravest dangers to Africa. The desire to sit in an office and become a black-coated worker has a peculiar significance in Africa. For the African watches the European, copies the European, far more closely than the European himself is apt to realize. And he is rapidly coming to believe that, if he can learn to read, to write and to do simple sums, he will have acquired the magic whereby the white man is able to be rich and powerful by sitting in an office chair. Africa is in desperate need of engineers, artisans, agriculturists, veterinary surgeons; such openings seem much less attractive to the educated African than some job at an office desk. And infinitely less attractive, of course, than the law; I doubt whether any other people spend proportionately so much money on litigation.

This snobbish and almost mystical dislike of physical work must be an immense handicap to African development. For example, there are now well over 2,000 students from West Africa in Britain (as an indication of the growing wealth of the Africans, only one-third of them comes with scholarships or other official financial help). Many of them are violent nationalists, anxious to rid themselves of all dependence upon Britain at the earliest possible moment. But too few of them are studying those particular subjects which would enable them to achieve their ambition without disastrous results to their country. By far the largest number is that of the law students. Medical students come second, and engineering third. But those studying the two most important subjects for Africa, veterinary science and agriculture, are outnumbered by the would-be lawyers by more than twelve to one.

There is one more reason, apart from the bad health and undernourishment, which has to be taken into account before the African can be condemned as lazy. And that is the lack of adequate incentives. Most people who work hard do so for the

money or position that hard work will bring to them. But even
money loses much of its value if you cannot buy or rent a
house except in a stinking and overcrowded Native township.
And why make immense sacrifices to become a doctor or a
lawyer if you are allowed to practise either not at all or only
under all kinds of restrictions? The contrast between the activity of the Africans in the Union, where they are treated as a
helot race, and West Africa, where every kind of position is
open to them, is one of the most remarkable features of Africa.

The African is corrupt and a liar? In so far as these accusations are true, they can be explained to a great extent by the
sudden breakdown of his way of life. In most tribes, crime was
punished far more ruthlessly than it is in the more advanced
states. Is, not was, for we need not go back so very far in our
own history to read of people being hanged for stealing a sheep.
I have not the necessary experience to be dogmatic about these
matters, but most Europeans in Africa have had Native servants who showed the greatest devotion and loyalty, and most
of the lying seems to be due to the desire of a bewildered man
to say what he thinks his master would like him to say. Before
we can condemn the African for corruption we need to remember the contrast between, for example, the African townships
near Port Elizabeth, where housing conditions are good and
crime is uncommon, and the townships near Johannesburg,
where housing conditions and the incidence of crime are both
appalling. We need to consider cause and effect.

But in one respect the accusations against the African seem
to have more substance—this accusation of irresponsibility.
Europeans who have worked with and for the Africans for
many years, who put forward the highest claims for their ability, seem to agree that an African may do the same job day
after day for months or years, and then suddenly "go bush,"
omit some vital part of his routine, even say or do things which
he himself cannot remember or explain when the mood is over.

This is the basis for most of the arguments that the African will never hold his own in the modern world, and there are plenty of people who maintain that the African "has had his chips," that he will be no more able to adapt himself to western civilization than were the Red Indians. On the other hand, far too little allowance is made for the fact that he has to adopt utterly strange ideas and ways of reasoning, and must do so in at least one utterly strange language.

"It is easy to teach him a trade," writes André Siegfried,[8] "and he will usually become very skilled at it, provided always that nothing is expected of him beyond a certain level. It is this level which marks the real borderline between the primitive Native and the civilized White. . . . He grasps what is explained to him provided the explanation is concrete and practical and he is then made to repeat what he has learned. One must not demand initiative from him or reasoning, but only application and memory. . . . As long as his imagination is not called upon he will not complain that his work is dull or tedious. His patience is infinite and he can be more careful than the white man, particularly as his senses, younger and nearer to nature, have remained more acute. Through the microscope, for instance, he can see details which escape our European eyes."

This judgment may be unfair, for Africans who served in the army during the last war showed astonishing versatility and ability.[9] But these are matters for the sociologist and the anthropologist. As far as I am concerned, I can say only that I have never found a race of people more ready to respond to a smile, more anxious to meet a situation with laughter. I have suggested elsewhere that very primitive peoples laugh rather when they are happy than when they are amused. On that reckoning, the Africans are quite exceptionally predisposed to happiness. And civilization, rather than the African, would stand condemned if that predisposition were to be replaced by bitterness and malice.

[8] *African Journey,* by André Siegfried (Jonathan Cape).
[9] c.f. *Hope in Africa,* by C. J. M. Alport, M.P. (Herbert Jenkins).

2

BOER AND BRITON

The Dutch acquired South Africa in much the same haphazard way as the British acquired a lot of their Empire, with the authorities in Holland grumbling about increasing responsibilities just as much as the authorities in Britain grumbled when somebody like Rhodes or Raffles added territory and wealth to the British Empire.

Jan van Riebeeck, the ship's surgeon the tercentenary of whose landing in South Africa has recently been celebrated in Cape Town with enthusiasm that was not entirely divorced from politics, was a pioneer *malgré lui*. His job was to found a revictualling station for ships of the Dutch East India Company on their way to and from the East, and his masters at home were not interested in any ventures into the interior. He was, however, and many of the fruits and animals now common in South Africa were introduced by him. Also a few of his men showed an insubordinate initiative which later won for

18

them the title of "free burghers" (and whose descendants are now nearly as proud of themselves as are the British descendants of William the Conqueror). They settled down on small farms and fought a tough battle against the uncertainties of the Cape climate, the thieving capacity of the Hottentots and Bushmen, and the incomprehension of their Company. They had learned to resent interference from Holland long before the British conquered Cape Colony in 1795. Indeed, the farmers of the eastern districts had established the first independent republic a few months before the arrival of the British.

These Hollanders were not like the men who have gone at different times to North America in search of greater political or religious freedom. They had left Europe before they could be caught in the flood of angry and humane political opinion which produced, for example, the French Revolution and the British campaign for the abolition of slavery. It is true that the French Huguenots, who arrived in bulk in 1688, were in a different category since they were the victims of religious persecution. But they have become Afrikaners in everything but their names. Malan is only one of many French names to be found among the Afrikaner leaders of to-day.

But most of the Boers who set out in their ox-waggons in 1835 with their guns and their Bibles on the Great Trek, that notable journey across the harsh, hot and little-known plateau of South Africa, were driven onward not by a desire to spread new ideas, but rather to escape from them. They disliked all authority imposed from above, Boer or British. Above all, they were bitter against the British authorities for decreeing that there must be an end to slavery, and their bitterness was justifiably increased by the shabby way in which the British Government of the time failed to pay up the promised compensation for the liberation of their slaves. Compensation was offered to those South Africans who went to London to fetch it, which few of them could afford to do.

In the neighborhood of Cape Town the early settlers had come into conflict with the most backward of all Africans, the Bushmen and the Hottentots—whom van Riebeeck dismissed

as "stinking, black dogs." At one time the Company proposed
to institute segregation by digging a wide ditch—they were not
Hollanders for nothing—to separate the white men from the
black. But conflict with the African Native on a serious scale
began much later, when Europeans migrating eastward and
northward came into conflict with the Bantu migrating southward. Very roughly what is now Western Cape Province was
white man's territory; it was only when the Boers pushed farther east and north that they found themselves coming into
territory into which the Bantu had already penetrated. These
Boers were attracted to Bantu-occupied country, in the first
place, by the dislike of official interference from Cape Town;
in the second, by the desire for more land to accommodate their
increasing numbers; and, in the third, by the discovery that the
rainfall was heavier, and the soil richer, the farther they penetrated toward the east coast.

In the early days of European settlement, slaves had been
brought in from Malaya, Goa, West Africa and other places
to do work for which the white man was disinclined and the
Hottentots and Bushmen were inadequate. There was then not
much talk about miscegenation; white men, Boer or British,
produced babies by black women or brown women, and it is
in part from those alliances that are descended the Cape Coloreds, whose right to vote on the common roll—or rather, its
abolition—has recently caused the most acute crisis between
the two European races in South Africa since the days of the
Boer War.

But the color bar became much more pronounced as the
years went by. The Afrikaner might no longer call his black
servants slaves, but he never wavered in his conviction that
they had been ordained by God to be hewers of wood and
drawers of water. And some Predikants in the Dutch Reformed
Church still assure him that this is so. But the Synod has not
accepted the full policy of "apartheid," and the silent struggle
now being fought within the ranks of the Afrikaans-speaking
people is possibly more profound and important than that between them and the other Europeans.

Many writers have found a parallel between this Great Trek and the exodus of the Israelites from Egypt. The Boers called themselves farmers but few of them were, or are, interested in the diversities of agriculture. They, as much as the Bantu, were pastoralists whose cattle or sheep were moved on from pasture to pasture. It was not solely their character which made them feel that they were being overcrowded if they could see the smoke of a neighbor's homestead. By moving on they could feed their cattle with the least effort to themselves. A farmer demanded 10,000 acres as his right, and there was land enough for everyone in what then seemed the almost limitless territory of the Orange Free State and the Transvaal.

But not many years after the Boers had thus established themselves on the High Veld, diamonds were discovered in Griqualand West, then part of the Orange Free State. Within a few months, these men who had been through the hardships of the Great Trek in order to get away from the British and their interfering ways were overwhelmed by a crowd of greedy, noisy and unruly Englishmen or other non-Dutch Europeans. Then came the discovery of gold, and this crowd swarmed to the Witwatersrand—the Ridge of White Waters—and built Johannesburg. Their shacks and bars and brothels grew up on either side of what a few months before had been rough farm tracks.

Paul Kruger, President of the Transvaal, had his capital in Pretoria, a bare thirty-six miles away. The Boers were used to quarreling even amongst themselves, but they set aside their rivalries in their opposition to the British. One of the principal causes of, or excuses for, the Boer War was Kruger's determination to tax the newcomers but to give them no vote, no say in the running of his Republic. Within the last few years, Dr. Malan has followed President Kruger's example by extending from two to five years the period which must elapse before the white immigrant may be allowed to vote.

Few people in Britain to-day feel any pride over the Anglo-Boer War. It is doubtful whether a clash could have been avoided, but it was a shabby and unprofitable business. It was

mainly because the British were rather ashamed of it that it
was followed by an unusually generous peace settlement which,
they hoped, would wipe out the bitter memories; and the response by men like General Botha and General Smuts led them
to believe that it had done so. But the dispute in 1927 over
the introduction of a South African flag aroused even more
bitterness between Afrikaners and other South Africans than
the recent High Court of Parliament dispute has done. And
events in both world wars have shown how sensitive and sore
Afrikaner national feeling still is.

The fact, of course, is that Smuts, whom most people outside the Union considered as a great and wise patriot, was considered by many of his own people as an appeaser and a traitor.
He brought his country into the Second World War by so small
a Parliamentary majority that some Predikants of the Dutch
Reformed Church saw nothing immoral in excluding from religious rites young Afrikaners who had enlisted to fight against
Hitler. In most of the Nationalists the desperate plight of the
British Commonwealth roused a feeling not of sympathy or
anxiety, but of hope. Dr. Otto du Plessis, the present Director
of the State Information Office and one of Dr. Daniel Malan's
closest associates, wrote a pamphlet in the early days of the
war in which he declared that "Nationalist Afrikanerdom longs
for the death of that (the existing) system . . . Afrikanerdom
is fully determined that South Africa's destiny can be nothing
else but a free Republic; that South Africa will be completely
torn away from the British connection." And Dr. du Plessis to-
day is in the habit of expressing pained surprise if any visiting
journalists show distrust of his government's long-term motives.

Mr. Eric Louw, Minister for Economic Affairs and former
diplomatic representative in London, Paris, Washington and
Rome, said in 1948 that "we shall settle accounts with the
'Loyal Dutch,'" of whom Mr. Strydom, Minister of Lands, had
declared six years earlier that they were in the army "only to do
the dirty work of the British soldiers." In the same year—that
is to say, a long time after the successes of Hitler had ceased
to give some excuse and encouragement for the excesses of the

Nationalists—one of their well-known M.P.s said in the House of Assembly: "What is at issue is two outlooks on life, fundamentally so divergent that a compromise is entirely unthinkable except on superficial matters."

Probably even more important than statements by ministers are the declarations of policy emanating from the Broederbond, a secret society founded at the beginning of the First World War and now said to have some 3,500 most carefully-selected members, including three score members of the House of Assembly. Its Executive Council, known as the "twelve Apostles," issues directives which appear to be almost as imperative and as respected as those which go from the Potlitburo in Moscow to a somewhat different bunch of disciples. And, also in 1948, its chairman, Professor van Rooy, published a pamphlet on what—probably with no intention to blaspheme —he called Christian National Education. As one example of its Christianity he declared: "We will not have any mixture of languages, any mixture of cultures, any mixture of religions or any mixture of races."

One could fill pages with similar quotations, many of which date from after the war, and cannot therefore be explained by the universal desire of mankind to climb on any particular bandwagon that happens to be trundling by. Many of these Nationalist leaders, when you meet them, prove to be people of charm, culture and integrity. Even the former Commandant of the moribund "Ossewa Brandwag," the most extreme pro-Nazi organization in South Africa during the war, is a most amusing and attractive character. Nevertheless the events of the last few years have illustrated beyond reasonable doubt the Nationalist determination to destroy British influence in South Africa. It might be true, as most of these Nationalists explain, that their sentiments toward the rest of the British Commonwealth would be much more friendly if their country were an independent Republic. But there can be no illusions as to the inferior position to be reserved in such a Republic for those British South Africans who still talked and thought of Great Britain as "home."

The Nationalists have even longer memories than the Irish. "Concentration camps," to the Afrikaner of to-day, are not such places as Belsen or Dachau, but those barbed-wire enclosures in which Boer families were herded by the British during the Anglo-Boer War. I know one widow, closely related to Dr. Malan, who asserts with complete sincerity that the recent death of her husband was the direct consequence of his sufferings in one of these camps, and it is sad and surprising that the evil memories of the hardships they caused seem to grow more vivid and painful as they grow more distant in time.

But there are also other causes for Anglo-Afrikaner bitterness. There is, first, the question of language. When Englishmen proposed that Dutch—later Afrikaans—should be put on the same level as English as one of the two official languages, they considered they were acting with great magnanimity, and their proposal was received with acclamation by the Convention that was drawing up the constitution. After all, English was a world language, whereas Afrikaans was spoken nowhere outside the Union—although it is, of course, closely associated with Dutch and Flemish, and one of the greatest of Flemish scholars assured me recently that the best lyric poetry now being written in any of these three languages is in Afrikaans. An indication of the tough stubbornness of the Afrikaner may be the fact that his language is one of the very few languages with a double negative—"Do not smoke not." Even Russian has not this emphatic way of saying "No." Nor has Dutch, from which Afrikaans is derived.

But there are now about sixty Afrikaans-speaking South Africans to forty who speak English, and the proportion of Afrikaners is much higher among the children. Nor can it be denied that many of the British South Africans have tended to treat Afrikaans with contempt. There is therefore much the same kind of aggressive bitterness in the defense of Afrikaans as one finds in Belgium where even the explanations in the museums of Antwerp, which attract thousands of foreign visitors, are now confined to the Flemish language since there is an equivalent absence of Flemish in the French-speaking part of the country.

Again, because English is so much better-known, it is natural that most foreign newspaper correspondents in South Africa should have some link with one of the English newspapers there and this does undoubtedly mean that they are more likely to send abroad news that is favorable to the United Party, which is mainly English-speaking, than to the Nationalist Party, whose members nearly all prefer Afrikaans. The outside world thus gains the impression that the United Party must be very much more moderate than the Nationalists in its attitude toward the Non-Whites.

But the difference between the two parties is one rather of degree than of principle. The late Jan Hofmeyr, for many years General Smuts' right-hand man, spoke rather for himself than for his party when he claimed, in his Hoernlé Memorial Lecture in 1945, that the right course to take was "to refuse to abandon the firm ground of principle, to maintain the essential value of human personality as something independent of race or color." Hofmeyr was one of the few white South Africans to quote with approval Professor Hoernlé's own remark that "the price which the white caste pays for its domination is fear—fear for the continuance of its own domination, fear for its future." Neither European party in South Africa has a solution of the Native problem. The United Party tries to postpone it, in the vague hope that something will turn up. The "Nats" believe it is wiser to bring it to a head now by the introduction of "apartheid," which is the United Party's policy of segregation, only more so.

This rivalry between one section of the Whites and another will be discussed in greater detail in a later chapter. Here there is need only to point out that, despite the small difference of principle between them, the effect of their respective policies on the Natives has been immense. Perhaps, decisive. The Smuts policy was one of reluctant concession; it was more pliable and, above all, more human; it left the black man with some small hope of better times to come. The Malan policy has destroyed that hope, with the result that even those Europeans who have devoted their lives to the betterment of whiteblack relations are quickly losing the confidence of the African. For the first time the Natives tend to group all white men together. To group them together, and to condemn them all. Moderation on either side is at a discount.

It may be years, or decades, or even generations before the Natives will learn effectively to co-operate. Tribal warfare is still so fresh in their minds that it sometimes breaks out even in the compounds of the gold mines. Being themselves great lovers of long words and fine oratory, they have hitherto shown themselves to be terribly indiscriminating in their choice of leaders. But at least one in three Natives in the Union is urbanized—was born in a town or has spent most of his life in one—and the decision of the African Congress to institute civil disobedience in the summer of 1952 may prove to have been historic. Its campaign has been obeyed with greater discipline than most people had foreseen. Professor Z. D. Matthews, formerly of Fort Hare, one of the two Native University Colleges in the Union, once said something to the effect that the Africans were waiting for their Gandhi. And when he appears, the whole situation in the Union may change almost overnight.

This criticism of the Europeans in the Union, however, needs to be qualified. The critic from outside, in his distress that there should be any racial inequality at all, is very apt to underestimate what is, in fact, being done to raise the standard of life of the Africans. I shall later discuss the terrible inadequacy of the Native Reserves, which have to carry about eighty persons per square mile, compared with roughly two Europeans and eight Natives per square mile in the European rural areas. But within the limits of these Reserves, the Native Affairs Department does a job which cannot be overpraised. Expenditure in them on soil conservation and reclamation has increased from $172,550 in 1936 to $1,925,327.60 in 1949, but mere figures

convey no idea of the patient work of education in better methods of agriculture, to which the Africans are now responding
well. And yet some of the keenest members of this Department are equally keen supporters of the doctrine of "apartheid."

The amount spent on European education is now somewhere
about $84,000,000 a year, as against almost $22,400,000 spent on
four times as many Natives. Nevertheless, this is claimed to
represent a higher figure per head of the Native population
than is spent in the neighboring British colonies. This claim
is difficult to judge because much of the expenditure in the
Union is on salaries and buildings, often supplied by the missionaries in the Colonies with no direct charge to the State. In
any case, the expenditure on African education in the Union
is far higher than ever before and, thanks mainly to government
subsidies, an African can study for his degree at Fort Hare
University College at an all-in cost of about $210 a year. And,
admittedly for reasons which the Government deplores, there
has been a quite startling improvement in the standard of some
urban Africans in recent years. Nothing amazed me more,
while revisiting the Union in 1952, than the number of new
and prosperous hire-purchase stores catering entirely for the
Africans in Johannesburg. It is estimated by the *Bantu Press*
that the annual buying power of the Natives in South Africa is
now as high as $126,000,000. Pensions and workmen's compen-
sation for Africans exceed $2,800,000 a year. The tragedies of
Native health and housing will be dealt with later, but it
would be a great mistake to suppose that the Nationalists,
within the limits of their racial doctrine, are inactive in doing
good or devoid of a certain remote affection for the Natives
they control.

For those of us who do not live in a plural society, it is the
easiest thing in the world to condemn the inhumanity of the
Color Bar. But the frequency with which some African student in London is snubbed by some landlady—and thereby
pushed a little further toward the Communists who claim that
they have no color prejudice—should lead us to be careful in
our criticisms. In the United States the Negroes form about

twelve per cent of the population, and yet the white man's
fear of them leads to various injustices. But in the Union of
South Africa the Native proportion of the population is over
sixty, and the total Non-European about eighty per cent. The
white South Africans are probably just as sensible, as kindly,
as well-meaning as you or I, and to condemn them without
first trying to understand them is the surest possible way of encouraging them to continue a policy we may consider unjust,
cruel and suicidal.

Nor should one dismiss as hypocrisy the claim made by
many white South Africans that they are the defenders of Western civilization. It is tempting enough to point out that these
men themselves are bringing into disrepute the ideas of im-
partial justice and individual liberty which we have inherited
from Christianity and the civilizations of Athens and Rome.
But it would be folly to believe that anything like so many of
these ideas would survive if, by some miracle, the Natives were
suddenly placed in power. The crime of the Nationalists is less
that they want to maintain the dominance of the white man
than that they are doing so by destroying the hope and faith of
the black man. But to put the black man immediately on the
same electoral footing as the white man, because the fundamental ideas of democracy include universal suffrage, would be
a reprehensible act of folly; the torch of civilization cannot be
handed on to other races until they are more or less prepared
to carry it.

This belief that our own form of government is necessarily
a suitable article for export is the one point which the Europeans throughout Africa are justified in resenting. It was not
invented for a plural society. Some years ago I was working on
the terrace of a house in Northern Rhodesia, nearly four hundred miles from a railway. On a table near me were several
impressive volumes, including Trevelyan's *Social History of
England*, *The Grandeur that was Rome*, *Pericles and Athens*
and others that had been sent out for the benefit of African
readers by a benevolent British Council, the British propaganda
and information agency (which must occasionally do silly

things among its many sensible ones). The nearest African to me was a bright and lively young girl who was looking after my grandchildren, and she was studying a child's picture book upside down, being unable, like so many of her race, to understand that anything drawn on a flat surface could possibly represent anything she knew. Native custom, as I have already suggested, was in many ways sensible and well-suited to the people who were governed by it, but the claim that most of these people have yet succeeded in their ambition to adapt themselves to Western civilization is absurd, it is unjust to the African himself to expect him, in so short a time, to have caught up with the intervening centuries.

The problem of race relations has ceased to be a domestic issue for South Africa. It is now a major question of Commonwealth relations and one which, by implication, influences many of the discussions in United Nations committees. The initiative which has impelled white men—missionaries as well as traders—to set out on perilous explorations and to put up with hardships in establishing new colonies, is most certainly not one of which to be ashamed. That initiative has frequently been followed by abuses, but it is surely as unjust to condemn it as it would be to condemn the initiative of scientists because other men may abuse their discoveries. The development of nuclear fission should not destroy our admiration for Jenner, Ross, Faraday or Pasteur, nor should the injustices of some colonial administrations destroy our admiration for Livingstone, Rhodes, Lyautey or Mungo Park.

It is the misfortune of the Union that its colonies are, as it were, inside its own frontiers, with their surplus population spilling over from the Native Reserves into areas which the white man has taken as his own. The problems of a plural society, which never once touch the overwhelming majority of people in Europe and hardly affect people in the northern half of the United States outside the large centers of industry, are with the South Africans every day of their lives. Their country has become a laboratory for the study of this, one of the most important and difficult problems in the world to-day. That is their misfortune; it is not their fault—unless they are to be blamed because their ancestors put up with every kind of hardship in order to turn a harsh and almost empty country into a great modern state.

If their problem were not one of extraordinary difficulty it is at least probable that a simple and direct opposition to the Nationalist Government's policy would lead to its overthrow. Many people of goodwill in both the major political parties and in all four racial groups are doing practical work of an educational and social nature in an effort to mitigate conflict and to lessen the gap between the Native and the African of European origin. But no racial or language group is able to present a unified answer to the problem of this multi-racial society. My anger against obvious injustices may frequently lead me strongly to criticize the European, and particularly the Afrikaner, in South Africa; in these few paragraphs I have sought to suggest the need for that sympathy and humility we should feel toward someone who has to face a tragic situation which we are ourselves spared.

In one of the most charming houses on one of the most charming jacaranda-lined avenues of Pretoria, lives a British diplomat who is encouraged to develop schizophrenia. He is United Kingdom High Commissioner both in the Union of South Africa and in the "High Commission Territories," the three large areas inside the frontiers of the Union which are governed not from Cape Town and Pretoria, but from London. He has to win the confidence both of Dr. Malan and of the Africans in Basutoland, Bechuanaland and Swaziland who are so anxious not to come under Dr. Malan's control. The High Commissioner, as a matter of fact, has two lovely homes, for it has to be remembered that the administrative capital of the Union is in Pretoria and the legislative capital is in Cape Town, so that the government and the diplomats accredited to

it spend part of the year in one city and part in the other. Even
with his two homes, he is not to be envied; he has before him
a problem to which there can be no clear-cut solution.

Much against its will, the British Government accepted the
protection of these three territories. Moshesh, the chief of the
Basuto, wrote to Queen Victoria: "My country is your blan-
ket and my people the lice in it." The Swazi—who also wanted
protection from the Boers—assured the Queen in less picturesque phrases that they were her children. The Bechuana were
alarmed by Cecil Rhodes and his ambitions north of the Limpopo River, but they too said there was no other government
they could trust "as we can trust that of the great Queen."

When the Act of Union was drawn up, these three territories were kept out of it, although it was tacitly understood
that in time the responsibility for them would be transferred
from London to Cape Town. But two obstacles have appeared
since those optimistic days. One is that the Union is now a
Dominion, so that the safeguards for the Natives could no
longer be enforced by the United Kingdom; the other is that
the Nationalists have come into power in the Union, and,
rightly or wrongly, the Natives of these three territories are
much more bitterly opposed than before to any suggestion that
they should be absorbed. They fear, above all, that more of
their land would be taken away by the Europeans. No government in London, as things are at present, could possibly abandon the Protectorates. How could it do so, seeing that
the Governor of the Cape declared, when the Protectorate over
Basutoland was proclaimed, that henceforth the Basuto "shall
be, and shall be taken to be, for all intents and purposes, British subjects"?

But a casual glance at the map is enough to show what an
affront to South African national pride these territories provide.
Basutoland is entirely surrounded by Union territory. So, too, is
Swaziland, apart from a short frontier in common with Portuguese East Africa. Bechuanaland is a deep and wide wedge between the Transvaal and South-West Africa. No European may
farm in Basutoland, but many would like to do so for its soil

is fertile although the fertility is disappearing owing to the shocking overgrazing to which it is subjected—since the Natives have no other lands. Nearly half of Swaziland is in European occupation owing to the early concessions made by a dissolute Chief who was more interested in liquor than in land. Bechuanaland has an unoccupied area roughly the size of the United Kingdom, and the Colonial Development Corporation ranching scheme, despite the usual preliminary blunders, is beginning to show that much of this land can carry immense herds of cattle—the night before I visited it seven lion were poisoned, but the expense of wiring in such vast areas may possibly justify itself. Bechuanaland, in particular, might provide that extra territory which the "apartheid" policy pledges the Nationalists to provide for the Africans of the Union.

The Protectorates cannot exist without the goodwill of the Union, which provides the market for their products and their access to the outside world. If a large proportion of Basutoland's young men could not go into the Union to work in the mines the result in Basutoland would be catastrophic. It would, of course, also be very serious for the mine-owners, who have increasing difficulty in recruiting the necessary labor, but Basutoland's tragedy would be one of human lives, and not merely of dividends. The Union buys Basuto wheat and peas, and enables them to sell their wool. It buys asbestos, cattle and dairy produce from Swaziland. It buys cattle and hides from Bechuanaland.

There are now notable development plans for all three territories, which had hitherto in some ways lagged far behind the Union itself, but there is little sign of political progress. Although no British Government could hand over these peoples to the Union against their will, it is also obvious that no British Government is likely to train them for self-government, as it is doing with purely Native populations elsewhere in Africa; one or more autonomous black states inside the Union would certainly provoke the Union Government to take drastic action. The encouragement to such action is already provided in part by United Kingdom support of Central African

Federation a little farther north. The Nationalists can claim that the argument used against handing over the Protectorates to the Union—namely that we are pledged not to make any such change without the consent of the Natives—is precisely the argument which the United Kingdom tends to ignore in the case of Northern Rhodesia, which placed itself under the protection of Queen Victoria in much the same conditions as did the three High Commission territories. This fear of provoking the Union to action could easily lead to further incidents as discreditable to the United Kingdom as the Seretse Khama incident in Bechuanaland. And Dr. Malan has expressed his intention of demanding the transfer of these territories. That would cause a graver crisis than any yet known in Africa. But the answer to him is fairly obvious—certainly these territories can be transferred to the Union if he will accept the same representation of Africans in the central legislature and their same right of appeal to London as have been accepted by the governments in the Central Africa Federation.

3

"APARTHEID" IN ACTION

The time has now come to analyze the policy of the white South African toward his black compatriots. There are some three and a half million Natives in the Native Reserves which are nearly as large as England and Wales. Another three millions are now urbanized. Of the remaining two millions, most work on European farms and many are vagrants or squatters who cannot be traced in statistics.

These Native Reserves, in which in theory no white man or Indian may own land, represent only about 9.7 per cent of the territory of the Union. No Native may own any of the remainder. It is claimed, with complete truth, that the Native land is, or was, some of the most fertile in the country and that a great deal of the rest of the country is practically desert. Many of the Afrikaner farmers of the Karoo consider they are very lucky if they get five inches of rain in the year, and the soil in the country as a whole is so poor that, although two-thirds of the population live from the land, agriculture represents only about ten per cent of the national revenue. But it is also true that the Reserves are so overcrowded that roughly one-third of the Native families living there have no land of their own, and many others have too little land to keep them alive unless some members can leave the Reserves in order to add to the family income in other ways. It is also true that, despite all the efforts of the Native Affairs Department, the land is steadily losing its fertility.

For this there are two main reasons. One is that the African tribesmen have inherited even more wasteful methods of farming than have the Boers—both find it difficult to realize that there are limits to space, and that, after those limits have been reached, land must be rested if it is not to be exhausted. The Africans add to this an extreme reluctance to sell any of their cattle. The second reason is the failure of the Government to provide enough land for the Native population. Land hunger and soil erosion both increase year by year. The Land Act of 1913 operated in South Africa in ways similar to the English Enclosures and the Highland Clearances—it compelled the Native peasant to leave the country and to become an indentured mine worker. In 1916, the Beaumont Commission recommended that some 15,000,000 acres should be added to the existing Reserves, but the Native Trust and Land Act—which was one of the three acts by which the Natives in the Cape were to be compensated for their removal from the common roll of electors—was not passed until 1936, by which time the Native population had greatly increased. And the $28,000,000 with which the Native Affairs Department is supposed to buy the extra land is now totally inadequate in view of its greatly increased price, with the result that the land actually bought amounts to only about 9,000,000 acres. But if "apartheid" is to be enforced in the terms of a "Bantustan" for Africans, as the enthusiasts advocate, then even the full implementation of the promise of the 1936 Act, which would place thirteen per cent of the country in the Reserves, would be tragically and obviously insufficient.

In the circumstances it is remarkable that so many of the Natives in the Reserves retain their fine physique. The Zulu kraals, for example, still consist of a few circular huts inside a high stockade of the fiercest thorn branches to keep out wild beasts. Much of their country resembles Salisbury Plain, with the hawthorn and yew trees replaced by aloe and mimosa. As in the old days, the women do almost all the work, with their babies carried pick-a-back, strapped into place by a long strip of cotton cloth. The mother thus has her hands free, but the child sometimes has its head jerked about so amazingly that one fears its spine must snap. This way of carrying children is also found, of course, in South-East Asia, China and Japan. I have seldom seen finer-looking people than these Zulus—father striding in front, dressed fore and aft in skins, and carrying his assegai; mother, bare-breasted and proud, with her hair stiffened with red mud into a kind of rimless top-hat to show that she is married; the piccanins following behind, stark naked and precociously quick and lively. The very small African child is among the brightest of God's creatures.

Whatever may have been the growth of the Native population during the past few decades, the introduction of "apartheid," whether by design or not, is likely to check it, and to do so very abruptly. For "apartheid" as a policy is disastrously different from "apartheid" as a theory, and the most depressed-looking man I met in the Union on my last visit there was Dr. W. M. Eiselen, Secretary of the Department of Native Affairs, and principal exponent of the theory. For Dr. Eiselen believes that, under "apartheid," the European in the Union should learn to do his own menial work, as in the continent of his origin, and that the Native should be given enough land to develop his own personality to the full. Two races, one white and one black, growing up side by side within the frontiers of the Union. But the politicians would not dare do anything so desperately unpopular as to share this belief. "Apartheid," as the theorists see it, would give the Natives the chance to es-

cape from a position of permanent inferiority to the Europeans;
some of the Native leaders, indeed, have welcomed the theory,
since logically it would enable them to invite foreign capital for
the development of the Reserves and, above all, would enable
them to withhold their labor from the white man. "You've
insisted on separation," their argument runs. "Very well, you
shall have it."

But Dr. Malan and other Nationalist leaders have rejected
the theory, and have adopted an interpretation of "apartheid"
which, to the foreign inquirer, seems very closely related to
serfdom. For one thing, there is no sign that Afrikaner farmers
will be compelled to sell land at a reasonable price so that the
Native Reserves can carry a Native population independent of
the extra income the sons now earn in the Johannesburg mines.
In the second place, these *platteland* farmers, who are the back-
bone of the Nationalist Party, have no intention whatsoever of
losing their Native workers. In the third place, for reasons that
will be discussed later, the stream of Natives from the Reserves
to the cities has now become almost irresistible—as irresistible
as was the stream from the English countryside to the cities
during our own industrial revolution.

According to the theory, even the present Reserves could
carry a larger population if the Europeans would provide the
capital to start industries to absorb Natives who now crowd to
the white man's cities. But, again, there is no sign that the Nationalist Government is prepared to supply the capital, and in
any case it is almost inconceivable that workers in these Reserves, which in almost every case are remote from large centers of population and are connected with them by the most
indifferent lines of communication, could compete successfully
with the white man's products. It is equally improbable that
the white man would be willing to lose the Native market which
is too valuable to be sacrificed to a theory.

So now the theory is being changed to meet the demands of the "realists," and the changes are all to the disadvantage of the Native. Those black men whom the Europeans
need will be allowed to remain near the Europeans' cities. But

they will be more ruthlessly segregated than ever. In a few cases Natives own freehold land—in Sophiatown, one of the Native locations near Johannesburg, for example. Under the Group Areas Act, which is one of the instruments of the "apartheid" policy, this will no longer be allowed. There is a great campaign to use the same act in order to send to a more remote area all Natives from the western outskirts of Johannesburg, which were originally set aside for the Natives, but upon which the poorer Whites have encroached more and more during the last two decades. Under this same act, the Native locations would become Second Class Reserves, in which the Natives would not be anything like as near to independence as in the rural Reserves. But even in the rural Reserves the present tendency is rather to limit the Native's liberty than to extend it. For example, many of the villages are now classified as urban areas—an absurdity if ever there was one—and under the Urban Areas Act, another instrument of "apartheid," all Natives are declared to be temporary residents, to be harassed by restrictions about passes and curfews. It would almost seem that the authorities had gone deliberately out of their way to anger the people who constitute the immense majority in the Union.

The present policy is to limit the number of Africans in the cities to the European's requirements, but not to encourage their return to the Native Reserves, where their presence would aggravate the existing hunger for land. Above all, the Native must be induced to work on the white man's farms.

To carry this policy out, a Native in Johannesburg who earns less than $509.60 a year—as most of them do—gets no unemployment assurance money. He is told he could always find work either in the mines or on a farm, and, should he refuse such jobs, he is given an "endorsement out" form, which means that he is no longer entitled to stay in the city; any employer who gives him a job after he has been "endorsed out" is himself committing an offense. The Native has to leave, with his family and at his own expense. The probability is that he cannot return to his Native Reserve, for there will be no work for him there, even if his sojourn in Johannesburg has not been so long as to break all his old contacts with his kraal. Either he ends up on some white man's farm, at almost any wage the farmer cares to pay, or he becomes a vagrant, in constant fear of the police who may send him, as a prisoner, to farm work of this kind. The chances are that, in a few days or weeks, he will be back in Johannesburg, living there illegally. It is reckoned that there are some 200,000 such illegal inhabitants in the City of Gold at the present time.

The co-operation between the police and the farmers, who find it increasingly difficult to get Native workers (owing to the attraction of the mines) deserves a paragraph to itself. For decades prison labor has been "hired out" to private employers. There are now a dozen farm jails in rural areas. In 1952 there was a new development. The first private prison was opened by the Minister of Justice. A group of farmers built a jail on condition that the government kept it full of prisoners. The State gets 25 cents a day for the work done by these prisoners on the local farms. The farmers get their cheap labor. The prisoners, of course, get nothing, but the Minister claims that they are first offenders who in this way are kept out of contact with hardened criminals.

There are other, and harsher, laws to enforce "apartheid," and one—the Suppression of Communism Act, which must be dealt with separately—which can be used to silence anybody who ventures to criticize its enforcement. There is, for example, the Prohibition of Mixed Marriages Act, which is one of the cruellest acts ever placed on any statute book, even though mixed marriages of this kind are much less frequent than were those between Jew and Aryan in Germany before Hitler showed Malan the way. This Act is much less likely to affect Natives than Coloreds, so many of whom could be mistaken for Whites, but it must be mentioned; there is already enough social prejudice in these matters to make the law unnecessary unless it is required as a sop to sadists. No European in South Africa may now marry a person classed as being of a different color, such people are imprisoned if they live together without marriage, and a priest who marries two such people is liable to prosecution.

The Group Areas Act, already referred to, will not only mean that the Governor-General—in other words, the Government—can allocate any area for the exclusive occupation of one of the four groups in the Union, namely the Europeans, the Coloreds, the Indians or the Natives, but also that inspectors will be entitled "without previous notice, and at any time during the day or night, to enter upon any premises whatsoever" in order to see that people of the wrong race are not living there. This extends the interference with private lives which is already permitted to the police in search of illicit Native liquor, and which is doing more than anything else to arouse the black man's hatred of the white. In 1953 two more laws—the Criminal Law Amendment Bill, which makes it dangerous to organize resistance against existing laws, and the Public Safety Bill, which gives the Government most unusual powers to declare a state of emergency—have been added to the difficulties placed in the way of Africans' progress.

Such, then, are some of the measures that have been introduced by the Nationalist Government under the cloak of "apartheid." It will be seen that they give the Native relatively little help in building up his own separate community, and the European every possible help in using the Native labor force to his own greatest—immediate—advantage. Subsequent chapters will, I think, show that this policy must fail.

Somewhere recently I came across a sentence about the Boers written a century ago by Dr. Livingstone. They were, he wrote, "determined to erect themselves into a Republic in which they might pursue without molestation the 'proper treatment of the Blacks.'"

I would end this chapter by repeating that the men who impose this cruel legislation are not themselves necessarily cruel men. Their problem is itself a cruel one. It is generally expected that Mr. Strydom will succeed the ailing Dr. Malan—who, as an ex-Predikant of integrity, very probably shrinks from the consequences of his own policy. And it was Mr. Strydom who gave me the most significant explanation of "apartheid."

Like the other Nationalist leaders whom I met, he received me with impeccable courtesy and admitted the validity of many of my criticisms. He is thin-lipped, uncompromising, determined at all costs to maintain white supremacy. Surely it was foolish, I suggested, to destroy the Native's hope. In Southern Rhodesia, the Native who could satisfy certain conditions about finance or literacy could be on the common roll of electors. Even though the Southern Rhodesian Government had kept the number of black voters down by raising these qualifications, the basic principle of racial equality was admitted, and gave the Native something for which to hope and to work.

In the case of South Africa, said Mr. Strydom, no such compromise was possible. If the obstacles in the way of the voter were low enough to allow every white man to be on the register, the number of qualified Native voters would become dangerously high; if the obstacles were high enough to keep the number of Native voters insignificant, then a lot of white voters would fail to qualify. And no government could remove men from the electoral register. It would not even be democratic, Mr. Strydom added with a slight twinkle in his eye.

It is because the most efficient of the Natives have achieved a higher standard than the least efficient of the Europeans that the color problem in South Africa has become so acute and has compelled the Nationalists to antagonize every other group in the Union—the Natives themselves, the Cape Coloreds, the Indians, and what is probably the majority of their fellow-Europeans.

4

BLACK AND GOLD

Every Native in the Reserves who visits his nearest township to buy goods from the general store run, in most cases, by Indians who work outside it all day long at their sewing-machines —passes an impressive recruiting office for the mines, with pictures as tempting as the recruiting posters that urge our own young men to join the fighting services and see the world. The demands of the gold mines are insatiable, and workers are drawn to them not only from every part of the country, but also from the Rhodesias, the Portuguese colonies and elsewhere. Sixty per cent of them come from outside the Union. In the old days, no young Native could win the admiration of the opposite sex until he had drawn blood in battle or killed his lion; now he must have visited Johannesburg.

Every book on Africa has its chapter on the City of Gold, for it is the most frightening, the most hospitable, the most

vulgar, the most exciting, the most prosperous, the poorest city
in the world. It is at the same time the largest white city and
the largest black city in Africa south of the Sahara. Within a
few minutes from the most luxurious Country Club I have seen
outside the United States is the degrading poverty of Sophiatown, one of the African locations. By day, it is a busy, bus-
tling, bumptious white man's city; after dark, although the
great majority of Natives live outside in their locations and
others must have special passes if they are in the streets after
nine o'clock, it becomes a city for black men, and one is sol-
emnly warned not to wander far from the main streets. It is
surrounded by golf courses, the sacrifice of any one of which
could save tens of thousands of Natives from spending some
four hours a day on their journey to and from their work.
There is a lot of noise and laughter in the villas as splendid as
those of Washington, D.C., but one nevertheless has the impression that the people who get most enjoyment out of life
are the Natives themselves. Despite the conditions in which
many of them live, at least 400,000 of them—quite apart from
another 400,000 who come temporarily to work in the mines
—look upon Johannesburg as *their* city. And on Saturday afternoons and Sundays, when the white men are away in their cars,
these black men wander contentedly through the streets—*their*
streets—plucking nostalgic little melodies out of their home-
made musical instruments.

It was one such instrument in a Johannesburg street that,
more than anything else in any remote part of Africa, helped
to convince me of the immense gap between white men and
black. The instrument was made principally of empty tobacco
tins, with a strip of wood as a sounding board, and from it an
old Native was producing a tuneless rhythm with infinite and
subtle variations. In a few minutes he was surrounded by some
thirty or forty Natives, each responding to these changes far
more quickly than I could do. In their eyes was an expression
of mingled exaltation and longing, as though they were receiving some inspiring message from long, long ago. I had
almost the feeling that I had accidentally stumbled into the

middle of some religious ceremony uniting all these shabby, humble black men, and giving them an immense dignity.

There are thus two entirely distinct Native communities in Johannesburg—the mine-workers, who live in compounds, and the city workers, who live in native locations. The latter, despite the terrible poverty of the homes, are slowly developing a normal urban life; the former are the victims of a scheme which, introduced by the Europeans for reasons of economy, may prove in the long run to have been disastrously extravagant.

For this system brings only the young workers from the kraal. They sign on for roughly one year in the mines, where each man is well-fed and well-doctored, but has no more home than a concrete bed bunk in a large dormitory. He leaves his wife and children back in the Reserve so that she can continue to look after their little plot of ground. After his term of service, the miner goes back to his kraal, generally taking with him a pathetic collection of flashy and worthless junk and a contempt for the old tribal customs which destroys the influence of the chiefs.

Superficially this system has much to be said for it. It costs the mine-owners less to feed one man living in a compound than one man settled in a town, complete with wife or wives. And the worker receives better medical care under this close control. Most of these miners put on weight, despite an eight-hour shift a mile or a mile and a half underground, and many of them return time after time for further periods of service in the same mine. But the moral and social disadvantages outweigh the economic advantages. At Odendaalsrus, the great new goldfields in the Orange Free State, Mr. Harry Oppenheimer and other mine-owners are breaking away from the tradition of the compound and are building entire villages for the Native workers and their families, as has been done in the copper mines of Northern Rhodesia. But it is significant that this change has so far been unsuccessful mainly because the

Natives do not like to bring their wives to the corrupt atmosphere of the cities.

It is now some years since I went down a Johannesburg gold mine, but I still remember the thirst with which I returned to the surface. I had first to take off all my clothes and to replace them by a thick vest, thick socks, heavy overalls and boots. The invitation to visit the mine, which came on a card like an invitation to a cocktail party, had these words printed on it in red type: "Persons who are not in robust health should on no account go underground," and "robust" sounded so very strong and vigorous. The letter accompanying the invitation had warned me in genteel language that "the mine is warm and induces free perspiration," and, although this particular mine was not one of the deeper ones, the warning was an understatement. I sweated like a pig.

The gold-bearing reef was in most cases about a foot thick, and the most impressive part of the mining operations was that they were carried out almost entirely by Native workers. They handled pneumatic drills to bore holes for the explosive charges. They managed the mechanical scoops that scraped up the ore and dropped it into trucks that rattled and banged their way along to the hoists. They revealed the basic tragedy of the European's policy in South Africa. For these Natives were skilled laborers in all but name and pay, and the more skilled work they did, the more the European miner was pushed upwards into the grade of supervisor. All over the Union Europeans are losing their pride and ability as craftsmen because they must not do the same work as a Native, and the Native costs so much less to employ. The Native miner is paid 50 cents a shift and his food and lodging; the European is probably paid $50 a week.

The process of separating the gold is wearisome and very costly. Each ton, after prolonged crushing and washing, produces about enough gold to cover one's small finger-nail. Furthermore, gold is one of the very few products the price of

which has of late years remained fairly stable in a world of
rising prices. But at present the whole economy of South Africa depends upon this one asset. Sooner or later the wages of
the Natives must rise—perhaps to a point when it will no
longer pay to mine such low-grade ore. Uranium from
the "slime" that is left over after the gold has been extracted
may give the mines a fresh value. Nevertheless, the obvious
safeguard is to develop other industries, but this can be done
only by training the Natives to do skilled jobs. That is the dilemma facing the Nationalists—they demand "apartheid," but
"apartheid" would prevent the only policy which could free
South Africa from this dangerous dependence on gold.

But the Native of the locations is a still graver menace to
the present system. Conditions in some of these locations are
so bad that after dark even the police dare not enter them except in strength, and the Whites find it advisable to leave the
maintenance of order to Native constables. There is an urgent
need for over 71,000 Native houses in Johannesburg and along
the Reef. In 1951 only 83 of them were built in Johannesburg and 1,763 in other towns in the area. This need will be
immensely enlarged if the Government carries out the plan
under the Group Areas Act, to remove all Natives from the
present location of Sophiatown in order that it may become
a European area.

For this, the Nationalists are not to blame, except in so far
as they, and the United Party before them, have failed to face
up to the problem of housing the urban Native. There is no
adequate demarcation of responsibility between the State, the
provinces and the municipalities, and each has tended to leave
the problem to the others. The State is implicated, since its
policy of "apartheid" affects the siting and construction of Native locations. The province is implicated, since the insistence
on segregation sometimes means that Natives are expected to
settle on land well outside the city limits. The municipality is

implicated since it has to find the money for building and is expected to supply drains, water and other amenities. And in several of the locations, even in some of long standing such as Alexandra, the municipality has done nothing of the kind. Those others, where small brick-built houses are replaced by "pondokkies"—miserable sheds made out of kerosene tins, odd bits of boarding, sacking and an occasional piece of rusty corrugated iron—conditions are far worse. But the Nationalists can point to the fact that the cities, which must bear the responsibility for such locations as Windermere near Cape Town, Cato Manor near Durban, and Moroka near Johannesburg, are the strongholds of their political enemies, the United Party.

For the squalor of these locations there are three reasons that are often overlooked. One is that, when a municipality has done a reasonably good job in the supply of houses and amenities, this very fact proves an irresistible attraction to other Natives. They crowd into the place, squat round its periphery, put up their shacks on every yard of open space. The amenities at once become hopelessly inadequate. A second reason is that the drift to the cities is now of such proportions that even the most vigorous building program would hardly be adequate to house the newcomers. So houses designed for the members of one family in very cramped conditions end up by housing twice or three times that number of people—every available square yard is let to tenants, and often at profits which would shock even the most grasping white profiteer. Somehow, at whatever cost, the worker must find a place to live in, and the scarcity of public transport limits the distance he can put between himself and his work.

But the third reason is perhaps the most important of all. Until very recently such houses as were built for the Natives were built by white men, and white man's wages at once so raised the cost that the house could not be let at an economic rent. All the Native houses were sub-economic, and no municipal council on earth willingly puts up its rates by building sub-economic houses. For years, Natives have wanted to build their own houses, but the Europeans have objected to this encroachment on a field of skilled employment, since skilled jobs must be reserved for the privileged man with a white skin.

Here, again, force of circumstance is breaking down the barriers. In many Native areas, the authorities now buy the materials for Native contractors to build houses. The Rand consists not of Johannesburg alone, but of a number of other towns stretching for roughly a hundred miles. In some of these satellite towns—in Springs, Germiston and Benoni, for example —some of the more enlightened Europeans are thinking of the day when the gold mines which brought their towns into existence will no longer be profitable. They are therefore planning the development of other industries and the establishment of a contented labor force to operate them. In Germiston a Native can get $210 of building material on loan and further material at cost price. He repays the loan in ten years. And more important still, Native contractors are now building these houses, although still under European supervision. Springs now has a team of ninety-five keen Native builders who are putting up houses that can be let at an economic rent, and it has been found that these builders respond to the award of badges and other incentives that appeal to a man's pride rather than to his pocket. They are building houses of various grades, with a park, a swimming pool and other attractions which must seem bewildering to people who are so dreadfully accustomed to seeing the words "Europeans Only" painted on every park bench. One of the first things a Non-European child has to learn is that it must not sit on a public bench.

Other cities in the Union, with Port Elizabeth as the best of them, are making efforts to keep pace with their Native housing problem. And their greatest reward is that they have virtually no crime, although Port Elizabeth has recently been the scene of some of the worst racial riots in the country. The "tsotsi" of the Johannesburg locations—gangs of flashy youngsters who terrorize white and black people alike—have no parallel in these newer townships, where some kind of family life becomes a possibility.

There is one area in which even the policy of segregation, and still more that of "apartheid," breaks down. There are now probably more Blacks than Whites living in the select suburbs of Johannesburg. These Blacks, of course, are the domestic servants, and they constitute a third Native community. They are spared the misery of the long wait to return to the over-crowded and unhealthy locations, and, by the nature of their work, they live on terms of common humanity with their European employers, although on a footing far inferior to the "below stairs" footing of the domestic servant in Victorian England.

Their number cannot be estimated with any accuracy. "I pay two Natives to work for me," a Johannesburg friend said to me, "but three more live in my back yard." They are presumably the most fortunate of the urbanized Natives to-day. They are likely to receive better food and medical attention than any other Natives, and their wages have risen in such a sensational fashion that a good cook in the luxury suburbs of Johannesburg will probably be getting $22 a month. But even in this narrow stratum of society where white people and black can learn to like and respect each other—because the Whites find it convenient to have somebody to do their housework and to look after their children—this curse of color is always present. One of the most enlightened women I know, who lives in a charming house well away from a main road, told me that she seldom dared give her Native cook a lift in her car from the bus stop a mile and a half away. It would be much more convenient for her thus to shorten her cook's absence and to lessen her cook's fatigue. But—well, neighbors would talk! And in an even more luxurious house, of the kind inhabited by Hollywood film stars on Beverly Hills, my host told me he always "toted a gun."

And he totes a gun because he and his fellow-Europeans have not sought to solve the problem of the one million Non-Europeans who now live along the Rand. The Native death-rate from tuberculosis there is probably seven times that of the Europeans. Thirty-five per cent of Natives die in their first

year, and thirty-five years is the Native's expectation of life.
At least half the births in locations are illegitimate and, however much the police raid people's homes at night, they cannot
check the brewing of filthy liquor.

With so much lawlessness about, the insistence on the Pass
Laws is understandable, even though it accentuates the spirit
of revolt which is partly responsible for the crime. Each Native
must have four passes in order to be comparatively safe. One
shows that he has a job, and is therefore entitled to be in Johannesburg at all. Another is his "Night Special," or Curfew,
pass. He also needs a travel pass and a paper to show that he
has paid his poll tax, varying from £1 ($2.80) for a man living
alone to £3 (8.40), according to the number of wives. Yet
another is needed if he is looking for a job, and its duration
is for one week only. To get it renewed he may have to hang
about for very many hours at that most tragic of buildings,
the Pass Office, and if the officials there do not choose to renew
it, his papers are "endorsed out" and, as explained in an earlier
chapter, he has to leave the city.

Despite all this misery, despite the danger of the destruction
of Native confidence even in such Europeans as Mrs. Margaret
Ballinger, one of their three representatives in the South African Parliament, despite the firm and ruthless determination
of the Nationalists to prevent "any mixture of language, any
mixture of cultures, any mixture of religions or any mixture of
races"—despite all such items on the debit side of the balance
sheet, one has the impression that "apartheid" will fail far
more rapidly than most of its enemies yet realize. If the failure
is to be brought about by Native revolt, then it will be accompanied by much bloodshed and the prospects of reasonable co-
operation between white men and black may be destroyed
throughout Africa. But I believe it will fail because the white
man's economy cannot support so extravagant a policy.

"Have you noticed," a friend asked me on my last visit to
Johannesburg, "that the telegraph boys are now Natives?" This

was passed on to me as an item of significance because the Government—each government—hitherto has done its best to avoid employing Natives except in the most humble capacities, and the percentage of Europeans employed by the State is far higher than the percentage engaged by private employers. In other words, the State has reserved for the Poor Whites—mostly Afrikaners for whom there is no longer room on the farm—a whole lot of jobs that could be done, and done more economically, by Natives. But the labor shortage is now sufficiently acute not only to have absorbed most of these Poor Whites, despite their lack of training and skill, but also to have compelled a government dedicated to "apartheid" to employ more Natives.

This is, in part, the result of the industrial revolution through which the country is passing. At the outbreak of the war the gross value of manufactures was just under $560,000,000; it has since risen to nearly three times that amount. The contribution of mining to the national income during 1947–8 was only about half the amount contributed by the manufacturing industry. And this leads to four conclusions. One is that the demand for skilled labor must be increasing very rapidly. A second is that, whether for skilled or unskilled jobs, the demand for urbanized Native workers—as apart from temporary workers living in the mine compounds—is also increasing. The third is that the needs of industry cannot be met unless some of these Natives are allowed to rise from the unskilled category to that of the skilled. And a fourth is that the whole industrial development depends upon the flow of foreign capital, and already United Kingdom capital is fighting shy of a country in which racial relations are so bad.

"Two of the greatest drawbacks to the development of industry," in the words of *Africa South of the Sahara*,[1] "are: (a) the wide gap in wages paid to the unskilled worker and those paid to the skilled worker; the gap is much wider in the Union than in other important manufacturing countries. (b) The small percentage of skilled workers to the total population; this does not exceed one per cent." All European groups agree that

[1] Oxford University Press.

there should be no encouragement to unskilled immigrants, but this negative measure does nothing to right the balance between skilled and unskilled workers already in the country.

The deduction would seem to be fairly obvious—the industrial development of South Africa cannot continue unless a far greater proportion of the Natives is allowed, and even encouraged, to become skilled or semi-skilled. I have already mentioned the way in which they do jobs in the gold mines which would be at least in the semi-skilled category, if that would not involve more money in the form of wages and more humiliation for the European workers. So the convention holds that there are no skilled Natives in the mines. In industry in general there is no legal ban of this nature, but hitherto the white trade unions have managed to enforce one. And, color prejudice apart, the employers have no desire to make the change, since wages for skilled labor are so much higher than those of the unskilled. But the Union's industrial revolution is forcing their hands, just as surely as it forced the hands of the employers in Britain. Already some sixty per cent of the industrial workers are Non-Europeans, and, although it is true that industry as a whole favors the United Party, it seems doubtful whether the racial fanaticism of the Nationalists will extend to industrial suicide.

5

MALAN CONTRA MUNDUM

Some reasons have already been given for the bitterness of the
Afrikaner against the British South African. Of some Afrikaners. Many thousands of them enlisted in the last war, fought in
Abyssinia or Egypt side by side with the British, and developed
a liking and a respect for them which is one of the few hopes
at the present time of a peaceful settlement in the Union. And
there are some twelve hundred families with British names
whose members speak Afrikaans in the home. The Afrikaners
argue that, unlike the British South Africans, they have no
home, or possibility of a home, outside the Union (and they
might do well sometimes to ask themselves why this is so) but
very many British South Africans are just as loyal, just as devoted, as are the Afrikaners to their home in the Southern
Hemisphere. Time after time I have guessed, and guessed
wrongly, the language that some couple in the street would be

talking; the Union is producing a South African type that is neither British nor Dutch.

But the Nationalists appear to want a kind of wolf and lamb fusion of the two races, an Afrikaner absorption of the British as complete as was the Dutch absorption of the two hundred Huguenots who found refuge in South Africa after 1688. Instead of encouraging a blending of the two main races, there is so much evidence of a desire to subordinate the one, the British, to the other, the Afrikaner.

This separation now begins in the schools. Parents used often to send their children to a school in which the predominant language was not the language spoken in the home. After all, the two official languages are English and Afrikaans, and each child is expected to know them both. But now, apparently on the advice of leading educationalists, there are to be no more "parallel-medium" schools, at least in the Transvaal. A Language Ordinance enacted by the Provincial Council there has decreed that a child must go to the school in which teaching takes place in the language of the home, and the sinister part of it is that the decision on this matter is not left to the parents. An inspector decides, and he is likely to be influenced by the parents' name; however much they may want their child to learn a world language like English to perfection, Afrikaans must be protected and its influence extended. This arbitrary selection, I should add, applies only to junior schools. Even so, it is increasingly resented by those Afrikaners who want their children to learn English. Many of these children are now sent to convents, and this may soon lead to friction between the Roman Catholics and the Dutch Reformed Church.

One would have expected a government that supported "apartheid" to encourage European immigration to strengthen the white community. Smuts, before Malan, rejected many opportunities of admitting highly skilled Displaced Persons from the European continent at the end of the war, but the Nationalists have gone much further. The South African Citizenship Bill allows no immigrant to vote until he has been five years in the country, instead of two years, as formerly. But even at the end of the five years the Minister will decide whether he should be granted a Certificate of Registration as a South African citizen. The immigrant must show that he has "an adequate knowledge of the responsibilities and privileges of South African citizenship," and the Minister may refuse him a certificate without giving any reason for so doing. In introducing this bill, Dr. Dönges, the Minister of the Interior, explained that even greater powers were given to the Home Secretary in the United Kingdom, but it has never been suggested or suspected —as it has been in South Africa—that his powers would be used for party political motives.

Lest those who have acquired citizenship should act in a way displeasing to the government of the day, the Nationalists, as far back as 1948, reduced the validity of passports from five years to one, and have now brought out new passports altogether which bear the statement that the Government has the right to withdraw them at any moment. Nor is this ban on travel confined to those who might be accused of conspiring against the State, since it has already operated against such people as Senator Ballinger and his wife, members of the Upper and Lower House respectively. And the campaign to prove that Senator Ballinger was not a South African citizen and could therefore be expelled from the country has dragged on for years. Mrs. Ballinger has South African nationality in her own right, since her father was a Free State Burgher who fought in a Boer Commando.

But it is by the Suppression of Communism Act that the Government can hit hardest at those fellow-Europeans whose political opinions it dislikes. As in most countries of rapid development and unusual opportunity, there are very few Communists among the Europeans—even among the Non-Europeans there are far fewer, as yet, than the circumstances in which they live would lead one to expect. Sam Kahn is the only Communist ever to sit in either House in Cape Town. This scarcity of Communists did not prevent the Government from forcing through its Suppression of Communism Bill, which, I imagine, gives the widest interpretation of that doctrine ever to

be put on any statute book. One clause, for example, decrees
that Communism includes any organization "which aims at
bringing about any political, industrial, social or economic
change within the Union by the promotion of disturbance or
disorder, by unlawful acts or omissions or by the threat of such
acts or omissions or by means which include the promotion of
disturbances or disorder or such acts or omissions or threats."

In ordinary English this means, or is generally taken to mean,
that the Government can now treat as a Communist anybody
who encourages any change the Nationalists do not like. The
two most notable and obvious victims of this legislation up to
date are Sam Kahn and Solly Sachs, founder of the Garment
Workers' Union. Both these men are, or have been, Communists, but the Government has already "listed" other citizens
who, in other countries, would be classed as upright but rather
old-fashioned Liberals. Sam Kahn has been deprived of his seat
in Parliament and of his other offices. Solly Sachs's arrest in
June 1952 because he defied the order not to make public
speeches was accompanied by some of the nastiest behavior by
the police yet known in Johannesburg. Even more drastic is the
Criminal Law Amendment Bill of 1953, which appears to give
the government the power to punish anybody who expresses
sympathy with African Colored or Indian protests against dis-
criminatory legislation.

Apart from these and other measures to weaken the British
South Africans, the Nationalists took effective measures to assure their victory at the 1953 general election and on all subsequent occasions. As in Britain before the Reform Bill, the
system of constituencies is in any case heavily weighted in favor of the *platteland* farmers—fewer of their votes than of
those of city dwellers are needed to elect a Member of Parliament. In the case of the former German colony of South-West
Africa, which the Nationalists included in the Union despite
the protests of the United Nations, this discrepancy between
rural and urban voters has been carried to an astonishing ex-

treme, since nearly three times as many votes are needed to produce an M.P. in the Union proper than in this territory, so many of the German inhabitants of which were passionate Nazis. Thus Dr. Malan was able to add six supporters to his rather small parliamentary majority.

Next came the case of the Cape Coloreds, who were given the vote almost exactly a century ago, the threat of whose removal from the common roll in 1952 caused the worst crisis since the Act of Union in 1910. At the time of the Union, both Coloreds and Natives in Cape Province were allowed to vote, but not in the other three provinces. The maintenance of this right in Cape Province was guaranteed in the new constitution by one of the "entrenched clauses," which could not be changed without the consent of a two-thirds majority of a joint session of both Houses of Parliament. In 1936 this majority was forthcoming in the case of the Natives, and they were removed from the Common Roll. The value of the Colored vote had also been reduced by the extension in 1930 of the suffrage to European women, but not to women members of the Colored community.

The Natives were said to be compensated by the right of the Cape Natives to elect three Europeans in the House of Assembly, and by that of the Natives in each of the four provinces to elect one white Senator. Thus Mrs. Ballinger is one of three representatives of the Cape Natives in the lower House and her husband is one of the four Senators representing the Natives of the four provinces. A further consolation for the Natives was to be an advisory Native Representative Council to study all legislation affecting the black race; it has been given so little power and influence that, even while General Smuts was still in office, it decided to adjourn indefinitely. In any case, it was greatly under European influence—four of its sixteen Africans were nominated, and there were six Europeans, being the six principal Native Affairs Commissioners. The Malan Government has since passed the Bantu Authorities Act, which abolishes it and claims to replace it by a new system based upon the fast-disappearing authority of the tribes.

In the case of the Colored voters in the Cape Province, the Government could not be sure of the two-thirds majority necessary to override one of the "entrenched clauses." But it would be a mistake to believe that the refusal of the United Party to play was due solely to the desire to defend the democratic rights of the Colored community. Their indignation has two other causes. One is that, *faute de mieux*, the Coloreds are more likely to vote for them than for the Nationalists, and have been instrumental in winning for them a few marginal seats. The other reason is that another "entrenched clause" in the constitution guarantees the maintenance of English as one of the official languages, and if one clause can be torn up, the same fate might befall the other. That, at least, is what English-speaking South Africans fear.

But this United Party opposition to a change did not prevent the Nationalists, with a very small majority in Parliament and an actual minority of votes in the country—442,338 for the "Nats" and Dr. Havenga's Afrikaner Party, as against 623,-716 votes for the opposition United Party—from introducing a Bill which would fit in with "apartheid" and reduce the strength of the Opposition in the House. Nationalist spokesmen in Cape Town assured me that the Coloreds would actually gain from the change since they would now have four European members specifically representing them, instead of being the junior section of an electorate voting for candidates who paid no attention to them except at election time. Under the old system, these spokesmen added, the Coloreds were becoming so numerous that, although their women-folk had no right of suffrage, there would soon have been one Colored voter to every two Europeans. In Cape Province as a whole they formed less than ten per cent of the common roll, but in six constituencies they formed over twenty per cent. And that sort of thing must not be allowed to continue.

Hence the attempt to abolish the direct Colored vote by a simple Parliamentary majority and to appoint a High Court of Parliament to overrule the Appeal Court, despite the latter's verdict that the proposed legislation would be a breach of the constitution and although that verdict represented the unanimous opinion of the four judges, three of whom had been appointed by the Malan Government.

In the spring of 1952 I followed this debate from the Press Gallery of the House of Assembly in Cape Town. With Order Papers very similar to those in Britain, with members addressing themselves to "Mr. Speaker," and with Government supporters and Opposition facing each other across the floor, I found it difficult to avoid the illusion that I was back again in the House of Commons—until I listened to the speeches, some in English, some in Afrikaans, and all in a tone of bitterness such as one very seldom hears in the Palace of Westminster. In any other country one would have decided that civil war was a certainty.

But probably not in the Union. The whole atmosphere in this beautiful country is poisoned by hatred, and it is as tragic as it is dangerous that the bitterest of the hatred is for the moment between two sections of white men whose apparent reconciliation forty years or so ago was looked upon as such a triumph for tolerance and good sense. And yet one senses something artificial about it all since neither side dare provoke the other beyond a certain point; there is always in the background the thought of that overwhelming majority of black men. And since the Nationalists at any rate knew what they wanted—a Republic in which they might still have the economic advantages of belonging to the British Commonwealth while becoming indisputably the senior partner in the Union—it was not surprising that they won the election.

For the United Party was as handicapped as are the Social Democratic parties in face of the Communists, as are moderates all the world over in face of extremists. Many of its members, especially those outside Cape Province, would have been distressed if they had been the victors and had then been expected to restore the Colored vote, in defense of which they had made such vigorous speeches. That dilemma, however, was spared them since the election of April 1953 returned the Nationalists to parliament with 94 seats out of a total of 159 (al-

though their poll was more than 140,000 lower than that of
their opponents). One effect of that election has been to hasten
the formation of two new parties, the Liberals and the Union
Federalists, who have broken through the Iron Curtain by demanding that color should no longer be the test of civilization.
The Liberals receive most of their support—qualitative rather
than quantitative—in Cape Province. The Union Federal Party,
with a good many members of the Torch Commando in its
ranks, has some strength in Natal, for reasons outlined later
in this chapter. The Nationalists may go to such extremes that
these new parties, now cursed and condemned, may soon develop an influence out of all proportion to the numbers of
their adherents.

In the great square in front of Cape Town's City Hall, an
excessively English voice over the loud-speaker ordered torches
to be lit. Down the long corridor they made through the crowd
marched "Sailor" Malan, and a group of military-looking men.
I had seen all this before, I told myself, in Nazi Germany. But
that is where I was wrong.

Any organization of ex-Servicemen who combine for political
reasons must cause anxiety; it is so likely to turn Fascist. But
one does not, on closer inquiry, get that impression about the
Torch Commando, for it differs from most other movements of
the kind in that it exists not to overthrow a democratic form
of government, but to defend one. Group-Captain Malan, Battle of Britain fighter pilot, is a quiet and modest man who
shows no sign of personal ambition—some of the officers
whom he commanded in Normandy remember little about him
except his habit of queueing up with them, tin mug in hand,
as though he were the most insignificant Pilot Officer. He is no
great orator, although a better one than I had expected, and he
is encouragingly frank in answering questions to which the
many lawyers in his movement are inclined to give discreet and
evasive replies.

One evening in Cape Town I had the opportunity of meeting the members of the National Executive of the Torch Commando. A more sensible and serious, less dogmatic and dictatorial bunch of men I could not wish to meet. Major Kane Berman, the National Chairman, is a successful Johannesburg lawyer of Jewish extraction. The National Organizer used to be a newspaper man. Several other members of the Executive are prosperous and well-established professional men, men anxious to defend rather than to destroy.

But why an organization of war veterans? Various members of the Executive gave me various answers; "Sailor" Malan came straight to the point. "Apartheid" and republicanism, he said, had a tremendous emotional appeal; the only equivalent appeal for the opponents of these doctrines was the appeal to men and women who had served in the war. In any case, since its formation, it has become widely representative, with British and Afrikaner generals, ex-judges who are alarmed by the Government's open contempt for the constitution, and some two hundred thousand ordinary folk, predominantly of British stock, who have been aroused by the threats to their ordinary individual liberties and by the strong suspicion that Mr. Erasmus, as Minister of Defense, is packing the higher ranks of the Army with his own political nominees. The Torch Commando, in fact, is one of the most spontaneous mass movements in history. It is helped by wealthy men in Johannesburg—indeed, "Sailor" Malan is actually employed to run a farm near Kimberley by Mr. Harry Oppenheimer, the most famous of them all. But no number of plutocrats could have created these little groups of uneasy but determined men in almost every town in the Union.

The Torch Commando has one great strength and one great weakness. Its strength lies in its appeal to those Afrikaners who served in the war and are now scoffed at as "Hans Khakis" by their fellow-Afrikaners in the Nationalist Party. These Afrikaners have gone back, many of them, to their farms on the *platteland,* and they find that El Alamein and all that have widened their interests and altered their opinions about the misdeeds of the British and the Blacks. And the Torch Commando, in a

way the United Party could never do, goes out to the remotest
villages to talk about the necessity and possibility of reconciliation between all white South Africans, about the consequences
of the Second World War rather than of the Anglo-Boer War.
One line of South Africa's defense is the "Skietkommando," a
militia comparable with the marksmen's clubs that have played
so important a part in the defense of Switzerland, and
composed mainly of young farmers (and, consequently, of
young Afrikaners). There are at least 100,000 of them, and
there is very little doubt that their organizers are politically
"safe"; they might be used against the Torch Commando in a
crisis. But they might possibly refuse so to be used if the
Torch Commando has meanwhile convinced them of the dis-
ruptive nature of the Nationalist policy.

The great weakness of the Torch Commando is also that of
the United Party. Where does it stand on the color issue? At
its first great Cape Town meeting in May 1951, held to protest against the Government's plan to abolish the Cape Colored vote, thousands of these Coloreds listened to the
speeches with fresh hopes in their hearts. They, too, had played
their part in the war, and had held a proud annual parade until the Malan Government had dealt a gratuitous and cruel
blow at their patriotism by disbanding their own Cape Colored Corps. It seemed so logical that an ex-Servicemen's organization, marching in protest against official discrimination
against the Coloreds, would welcome Colored ex-Servicemen!

But deep-rooted prejudice has been too strong. The Government at once accused the Torch Commando of bringing in the
Non-Europeans to fight the Europeans. Despite the almost ex-
aggeratedly non-Communist composition of its membership, it
was accused of Communism; it was, Dr. Malan declared, merely
a variant of the Springbok Legion, a war veterans' organization
without a color bar, which was accused of having Commu-
nistic affiliations, although I have come across no evidence at all
that it owed its existence to the Communists. The Torch National Executive found it advisable to have no Non-Europeans
in the next celebration of El Alamein Day.

The excuse it gave was plausible, but not very convincing. "Our chief weapon is the vote," the National Executive declared, and "at present no useful purpose could be served by the admission of Non-Europeans as members, or the formation of Non-European branches in those areas where Non-Europeans cannot exercise the franchise." For its part, the Colored Ex-Servicemen's League stated that "the Commando's fight is the white man's fight to re-establish the integrity of his word, and in this work the Coloreds obviously can have no part."

This evasion of a difficult problem had a mixed reception—even so respectably stolid a paper as the Cape Times wrote that "although the technical position may fully justify the exclusion of a Cape Colored contingent, the danger of a slight to a most patriotic section of the South African people should be avoided." In a subsequent statement the Torch Commando[1] promised that there would be no color bar to membership. The first task, members of the Executive reminded me, was to get the Nationalists out of power. This has not been done, and the Torch Commando has therefore provided most of the members of the new Federal Union Party, one aim of which is to give every Non-European rights "commensurate with his degree of civilization."

General Smuts suffered from a defect common to most great men—he disliked having outstanding men around him. The present leader of the United Party, Mr. J. G. N. Strauss, who was formerly Smuts's private secretary, is hard-working and conscientious, but reluctant to learn that orthodox and constitutional methods are ineffective in checking unconstitutional tendencies and ambitions. The election was no accurate guide to public opinion since 8,000 rural voters, predominantly Afrikaners, elect an M.P. as against 12,000 voters in the urban areas. Thus South West Africa, all Nationalist, returned 6 members with 23,326 votes whereas Natal, predominantly United Front, returned only 15 with more than six times as many votes. But what lost the United Front the election, despite good organization, hard work, and an unexpectedly high

[1] Cf. "Torch Commando," by Colin Legum. New Era, February 1952.

proportion of Afrikaner supporters, was above all the fact that its solution of the racial problem was only a weaker version of the solution offered by the Nationalists. "Apartheid and water."

In 1952 the Europeans of South Africa held great celebrations of the tercentenary of van Riebeeck's landing at the Cape. The English-speaking South Africans joined in loyally, as they had joined in the celebrations of the great Voortrekker Monument built (at a cost of $1,000,000) outside Pretoria in 1949. Cecil Rhodes was born in 1853, and he saw a vision of a great and united South Africa such as van Riebeeck never saw. "We human atoms may divide this country," he said once, "but Nature does not and the Almighty does not." And as he lay dying, while the Anglo-Boer War was still being fought, he said of the Boers: "They are a fine people and you must work with them; we have to work together." As Sarah Gertrude Millin has pointed out, these two peoples were still fighting when he decided that his Cape Town home, Groote Schuur, should be the home of future Prime Ministers of a United South Africa. "And there, whatever he might think of Rhodes, every Union Prime Minister has lived, and every Union Prime Minister has been a Boer." But Dr. Malan has not seen fit to organize national celebrations of the centenary of this outstanding South African.

Yet even Cecil Rhodes, with all his great visions for the future of Southern Africa, was not sure where he stood on the color issue. Sarah Gertrude Millin reports that he used to speak of "equal rights for every white man south of the Zambesi," but that, after he had lost the Boer vote as the result of the disastrous Jameson Raid he changed this to "equal rights for every civilized man south of the Zambesi. What is a civilized man? A man, whether white or black, who has sufficient education to write his name, has some property, or works; in short, is not a loafer."

These Coloreds, the unwilling cause of all this political uproar, are remarkable people, for the strangest mixture of blood runs in their veins. In the first place, there was the mixing of van Riebeeck's Hollanders with the Hottentots and the Bushmen, small yellow men who were probably the earliest inhabitants of Africa, driven down to the south-west corner of the continent by the advancing Bantu. The Cape Town Museum has life-casts of these Hottentots and Bushmen, and the latter, with their grotesquely large hindquarters (the fat of which is alleged to have given them staying power as its hump gives staying power to the camel) must certainly have been among the most primitive of all human beings. But some of them not only cohabited with, but even married, the early Dutch arrivals —after all, there were nearly one hundred men and only five women and a baby girl in van Riebeeck's ship.

Then came the decision—so unfortunate for the whole development of the European in South Africa—to import slaves. Some were Bantu from the East coast of Africa, some were brought from India, some were West African Negroes, some were Chinese, many were Malays from the Dutch colonies in South-East Asia. And for many generations these races were mixed up together, in or near Cape Town and along the coast of Cape Colony, before the Boers, taking some of these slaves with them, climbed the steep passes to the high plateau of the Karoo and spread out over South Africa.

As color prejudice developed, the characteristics of the dominant race—the European—of course became the most prized. The colored women to-day probably spend a far larger proportion of their incomes on having their hair straightened than European women spend on having theirs curled. I once visited a Negro music-hall in New York's Harlem and found that the beauty chorus consisted entirely of girls who could easily have passed as white in Europe or any other areas where there was no need or excuse for acute color consciousness; in the same way, thousands of the Cape Coloreds to-day are more Nordic in appearance than are, for example, most Sicilians, or Greeks, or other Southern Europeans whose ancestors gave us our Western civilization.

But they are not always pale enough to step from the under-

privileged category of Coloreds to the privileged category of
Whites. And those who fail in this cruel and chancy selection
—which, for those who succeed, must involve a complete break
with their families—have hitherto consoled themselves with the
thought that even they were privileged in comparison with the
two other Non-European communities of South Africa, the Natives and the Indians. They had *some* of this strangely valuable
"white" blood in their veins, and this fact was recognized by
their privileged position. The vote might not have much political importance to most of them; its social importance, however, was immense. It gave them a certain self-respect, pathetic
rather than ridiculous. And it is this self-respect which Dr.
Malan's Government has set out deliberately to destroy.

In effect, it is rather the self-respect of the European which
has suffered, for in many cases these Coloreds have achieved
positions which suggest that this attempt to limit the Colored
vote is rather an act of fear—fear of competition—than a le-
gitimate desire to maintain certain high standards. In their
desire to proclaim their superiority, the Europeans are driven
to gratuitous acts of bad manners and to illogical behavior
which hurts them at least as much as those against whom it is
directed.

In Capetown station, for example, two notices caught my eye
—"Europeans: Gentlemen," "Non-Europeans: Men." In the
neighboring post office I found a long queue of Europeans
waiting to buy stamps at one pigeon-hole, with nobody at all
at the Non-European pigeon-hole next door. After buying their
stamps without risk of contamination, many of these Europeans
probably went home in a public bus and found themselves sitting with Non-Europeans (although, when I was in Cape
Town last year, there was much discussion of a plan to institute "apartheid" into the bus service at an increase of at least
fifty per cent in the fares. The local Nationalist Party was also
appealing for separate ambulance services so that nobody
should have his life saved by being brought to hospital in the
wrong ambulance). The Europeans had, of course, left their
children in Non-European care.

On Sundays, the Coloreds come out in all their finery—with just that slight exaggeration so common among people with an inferiority complex. Everywhere they go, they are faced with the notice "Slegs vir Blankes: Europeans Only." But some of them, especially the young Malay girls, walk with so proud and graceful a beauty that one wonders who suffers most from "apartheid."

During the debates that preceded the Act of Union more than forty years ago, the belief of the Cape members was that the voting concessions they had made to the Coloreds and the Natives would, sooner or later, be extended to the other provinces of the Union; they never imagined that these concessions would be withdrawn even in their own province. Far more recently, in November 1935, so convinced an Afrikaner as General Hertzog said of the Colored man: "his way of life is fundamentally that of the European and not that of the Native, and he uses the language of the white man as his mother tongue. In his case there can be no question of segregation. . . . The time has come when the northern provinces also should recognize his right to be represented in Parliament through his vote. To deny him this would be in the highest degree unjust and unwise."

"The man of color," wrote André Siegfried,[2] "is not most feared when he is inferior in civilization, but when he raises his level of civilization, for then he is feared as a virtual competitor who might soon declare: 'After all, I am your equal.' "

Something should be added about the special position of Natal, the only province of the four which never came under Boer rule. The early Trekboers, it is true, had some of their most bitter fights against the Zulus in its north-western area, and the little town of Weenen—Weeping, in English—commemorates the scene of the worst of the Zulu massacres, when their leader, Piet Retief, was treacherously murdered by Dingaan, the Zulu leader. Also they spread down to the coast, and

[2] *African Journey* (Jonathan Cape).

the capital of the province, Pietermaritzburg, is named after
Pieter Retief and another of the Voortrekkers, Gerrit Maritz.
"The struggle of these pastoral and inland people for a window on the sea," writes Professor de Kiewiet[3] of the Boers' advance to Port Natal, "is a fascinating episode in the nineteenth
century. But a Power that had captured the Cape because it
commanded the vital route to India could not complacently
watch the establishment in Natal of a body of men who denied
their British allegiance." A party of Englishmen had come
round the coast by sea from Cape Colony some years before
the arrival of the Boers, and had established themselves on
ground that later became known as Durban, after Sir Benjamin
D'Urban, Governor of Cape Colony. Natal was therefore
claimed by the British and the Boers were driven back from
the coast. The Colony was annexed a century ago, and has
since been the greatest stronghold of British sentiment in South
Africa. The uproar in 1952 over the Nationalist proposal for
a High Court of Parliament was not the first occasion when
many British in Natal have talked of seceding from the Union.

But Durban is, I imagine, the only city in the British Commonwealth where the European, African and Asian populations are almost equal, and the British in Natal cannot show
much righteous anger over the Nationalist treatment of Coloreds since they desire to treat the Indians in Natal in very
much the same way. This Indian question must be dealt with
in a separate chapter, for it is one affecting not South Africa
alone, but the eastern half of the continent. All that need
be said here is that there is not a great difference between the
color prejudice of the British South African in Durban and
that of the Afrikaner in Stellenbosch or Pretoria.

In the Durban Municipal Native Compound, for example, I
found some 10,000 Africans crowded into a place that was built
for half that number, and was nothing to be proud of even
then. The Natives paid 5s. (70 cents) a month, but got very
little for that sum except freedom from the fear of arrest. If they

[3] *A History of South Africa* (Oxford University Press).

could not get into this compound, where they might have to sleep in the open, they had to doss down where they could in the city and risk being picked up by the police as vagrants. The few Native housing estates were terribly inadequate, and no facilities at all existed for those Native teachers and so on who, by exceptional gifts or industry, had managed to lift themselves out of the rut. For such people there is no chance of moving to a finer house. One of my guides in Durban was a teacher and economist called Selby N'Cobo, graduate of one of the American universities, who sits on every conceivable committee. A man with both brains and ideals. But he has to go on living in a miserable little Native house where noise and overcrowding must make reading almost impossible. I should add that the Housing Committee has recently developed three excellent Native townships near Durban, but there is still appalling overcrowding, especially among the Indians.

Thus it seems improbable that Natal will break away from the Union, for the breach would presumably bring it into closer touch with London, and London upholds a Native policy which few Europeans in Natal would wish to adopt. Were such a development to take place, however, it would entirely change one of the most difficult problems between Great Britain and the Union, namely the problem of the three British Protectorates of Swaziland, Basutoland and Bechuanaland, to which I have referred in an earlier chapter.

The unhappy and mismanaged affair of Seretse Khama in Bechuanaland has shown how the Colonial Office and the Commonwealth Relations Office can get themselves all confused by the desire to remain on the best of terms both with the Europeans in South Africa and with the Natives in the African colonies. But if Natal were to walk out of the Union, Basutoland—at present an island Protectorate in a Nationalist sea—would have a common frontier with another territory anxious to escape from the effects of Afrikanerdom. So would Swaziland, farther away to the north. And Bechuanaland already has its common frontier with the proposed Central African Federation. These three Protectorates would still be economically dependent upon the goodwill of the Union, but politically and geographically they would cease to be isolated. Should the other three provinces of the existing Dominion of South Africa decide to become a Republic and adopt policies which could not be accepted by the rest of the British Commonwealth, Basutoland and Swaziland, would have as their hinterland a new Dominion of Natal.

But must we seriously consider such a possibility? I have suggested that the thought of the Natives, the Coloreds and the Indians watching from the sidelines is likely to prevent the dispute between English-speaking South Africans and Afrikaners from developing into that civil war which, from their parliamentary speeches in the High Court of Parliament debate, sounded almost inevitable. On the other hand, the Afrikaners are the grandsons of the Voortrekkers, than whom no more stubborn men have ever appeared on the political scene. It is both tragic and frightening to read the expressions of unswerving loyalty to the British Crown that were uttered by the Afrikaners during the debate on the Draft Act of Union; there is not now much attempt to conceal the intention to end that loyalty and to set up a Republic.

There would seem to be only two possible ways out of a dilemma which must otherwise end in disruption. At one I have already hinted—the economic need for skilled Native labor might break down the color barrier, as it is rapidly doing in the United States of America, and it will be helped to do so by those Europeans who are working either privately or publicly for the return to the Cape Liberal tradition of sixty years ago that there must be "equal rights for all civilized men." The alternative seems to be the replacement of the present Union by a Federation. This final section on South Africa will consist almost entirely of extracts, taken with gratitude but without apologies, from a book by Dr. Arthur Keppel-Jones,[4] of

⁴ *Friends or Foes* (Shooter and Shuter, Pietermaritzburg).

Witwatersrand University, the principal exponent of Federation.

"Consider the matter first on the low plane of European self-interest, safety and survival," he writes. "Educated and civilized Natives, of whom there will be an increasing number whatever policy governments may adopt, are as susceptible to the promptings of self-respect and ambition as the peoples of any other race. They want careers, wealth, respect, influence and above all the feeling that they count for something and are accorded a place in society and the State in keeping with their talents and characters. . . . If our white regime is challenged by an angry black population, we shall look round the world in vain for sympathy in our distress. . . . If, after fastening our white supremacy upon South Africa, we came into conflict with any other country, four-fifths of our population would be a natural ally and fifth column for our enemy. . . . Thus, while prating of 'saving white civilization' we are in fact destroying it. We betray every principle in it that deserves to be defended." On the other hand, he points out, "a black majority would never preserve the security measures which the white people regard as necessary. That being so, the white race in self-defense refuses justice to the black."

It is now very unlikely that the Nationalists will ever be satisfied unless they are the complete and absolute masters. It is equally unlikely that the English-speaking South Africans would be satisfied to live in a country in which any show of loyalty to the Crown would be treated as "a treasonable activity" (to quote Dr. Malan, speaking on this subject, and reported in "Die Burger" of March 5th, 1951). And it is equally unlikely that the Coloreds, the Natives and the Indians, for all of whom South Africa is "home," will be satisfied to have so little part in running it and so few of the advantages it provides.

That being so, the only way to avoid an angry and forcible bursting of links that have become bonds would seem to be by replacing Union by Federation. It would be silly to think that such a change could take place easily or quickly—for example,

European farmers who for three hundred years have depended upon a fairly plentiful supply of black serfs would find it very difficult to replace it by white labor.

Keppel-Jones envisages that, for generations to come, white men would be needed in the Native States and Natives in the white man's towns, but he proposes that in such cases the strangers should be allowed to own the land in their locations and should not be moved from them without full compensation. Nor would these strangers, these members of the non-paramount race, have voting rights; instead, they would have much the same sort of indirect representation in the State Legislature as the Natives have in the existing House of Assembly in Cape Town. There are ingenious arrangements for the Coloreds and the Indians, and the members of all these non-paramount groups would be guaranteed the same full civil liberties as were enjoyed by the other citizens of the State in which they lived.

It would, of course, be very difficult to establish States for the four language groups of the Union without leaving a lot of people on the wrong side of the frontier and in the Transvaal, the most populous of them all, no such division could be made; with the modifications to its present frontiers suggested by Keppel-Jones, there would be fifty-one per cent of the people speaking Afrikaans and forty-three per cent speaking English. But, of the European population outside the Transvaal, "seventy-six per cent of the English-speaking, eighty-three per cent of the Afrikaans-speaking, and eighty per cent of the total would be living in states in which their own language-group was dominant."

There would be, in this Federation, four Native States— roughly the present Native Reserves; one small Indian State, immediately to the north of Durban; three small States in which English would be the predominant language; two large Afrikaans-speaking States; and the Transvaal, the testing-ground for collaboration in which "each section, having a secure foothold in other parts of the country, would be less influenced than at present by the fears which are the source of hatred and friction."

It will be seen that Arthur Keppel-Jones, starting from a liberal thesis, comes to the conclusion that some form of "apartheid" is essential. But not the selfish "apartheid" that refuses the black man any genuine chance of developing his talents and fulfilling his ambitions. For reasons which he explains in detail, the present Union places an increasing strain on each of the main communities it was designed to unite. Even should his scheme be dismissed as unpracticable—and on that the visiting journalist has little right or qualification to express an opinion—it has one very great merit, which is to remind sober-minded people in the Union that it is their duty to seek out some way of checking the present drift to disaster.

6

BROWN MEN IN A BLACK LAND

"Over there," said somebody on deck, waving his arm toward the west, "is Kilwa Kisiwani." We were steaming northward along the Tanganyika coast towards Dar-es-Salaam. Behind us lay Mikindani, which I knew was to be developed as part of the groundnuts scheme; ahead lay Mafia Island, behind which, as I also knew, the Germans had so successfully hidden the *Koenigsberg*, their successful raider in the First World War. But Kilwa Kisiwani? I confessed my ignorance. This little port, I was told, dated back to King Solomon and had for centuries carried on trade with Arabia, the Indies and China. Through it, perhaps, had passed the treasures of King Solomon's mines.

Farther north, in Dar-es-Salaam and Mombasa, I spent hours watching the Arab dhows arriving from the Persian Gulf. They are shaped like small galleons, with a high poop deck on which the owner and his family recline on Persian rugs and cushions, and offer you bitter coffee and sticky sweetmeats. The north-

74

east monsoon brings them down the coast of Africa and the south-west monsoon takes them back again, and the chants that float across the water as they sail proudly into port can hardly have changed since the times of the Pharaohs.

One day we anchored half a mile off Zanzibar, and the air was scented with the smell of cloves, for most of the world's supplies come from this one small island, or did until the clove trees there were smitten with disease and Madagascar took first place. The ancestors of the men who sailed their canoes and catamarans out to our ship were Arabs, for Zanzibar was formerly a famous Arab city, and wealthy slave-traders used to live in the palaces with heavy doors studded with huge brass nails. There are still 45,000 Arabs in the Protectorate of Zanzibar and Pemba, as well as 15,000 Indians, 200,000 Africans and under 300 Europeans.

In Mombasa the clerk who cashed my check was an Indian. So was the man who sold me my railway ticket. So was the man who made my tropical suit. So were the telegraph clerk, the shop assistants and the engine driver. For all down the East coast of Africa are Asian settlers, and the Indians create a special problem: whereas the Arabs came of their own free will, the Indians were for the most part brought in at the request and for the convenience of the Europeans.

The problem they create has been, of course, simplified or postponed by the fact that they are not all Indians any more —by dividing themselves into Indians and Pakistanis they have made themselves easier to rule. But if one groups them all together, as brown men in a continent of black men ruled by white men, they become numerically very significant.

In the Union of South Africa there is only one Indian to eight Europeans and to twenty-three Natives. But these Indians were brought in the first place to Natal, and the other three provinces have always refused to admit their share of them—indeed, an Indian traveling through the Orange Free State is not allowed even to step outside the railway station. And the result is that in Natal the Indians are almost as numerous as the Europeans, and their population increases almost twice as fast. In Kenya they outnumber the Europeans by three to one. In Uganda they outnumber them by more than ten to one. In Tanganyika, they outnumber them by four to one.

There are now 365,000 Asians, including Arabs and Chinese, in the Union, and at least four out of five of them were born there. Although the Indian Government has brought their plight on several occasions to the attention of the United Nations, very few of them could in any circumstances be induced to return to India. A lot of them are children or grandchildren of workers who were encouraged to come, from 1860 onwards, to help in the sugar plantations in the hot swampy country near the Natal coast. The Indian Government of the day was opposed to their employment overseas, but the Europeans in South Africa were very persistent. The African workers were too undependable; without these Indians there could be no prosperity in the South African sugar industry. For a time the Natal Government even paid £10,000 a year toward the cost of their transport, and promised them that after they had worked for ten years in Natal they should have the option of settling there.

But that was in the nineteenth century, and this is the twentieth. Too many of them took advantage of this promise; too many Indian merchants followed them, established themselves in Natal, and under-cut and out-worked the Europeans. For more than half a century the Natal Government has been trying to rid itself of these immigrants whom it invited so cordially. In 1891 it passed a law providing the Indians with free passages back to their country; they ignored it. In 1893 it passed a law refusing the vote to settlers who came from countries which did not enjoy parliamentary franchise. In 1896 it imposed a tax on those Indians who did not choose to return home, and placed them under lifelong indenture to some European if they could not pay the tax. It also deprived them of their parliamentary franchise—and completed the process in 1924 by taking away their municipal franchise as well. In 1897 it became a crime for an Indian to marry a white woman, and it is only fair to the Nationalists to point out that the government which promoted this law—unlike the government which promoted the recent Mixed Marriages Act—was neither Nationalist nor Boer, but British.

In 1927 the South African and Indian Governments made a fairly genuine effort to end this dispute. They signed a Cape Town Agreement—of which Dr. Malan was the principal author on the side of the Union—containing an "uplift clause" in which the Union Government "accepts the view that, in the provision of education and other facilities, the considerable number of Indians who will remain part of the permanent population shall not be allowed to lag behind other sections of the people." In return, the Indian Government pledged itself to encourage the return of as many Indians as possible to the country of their origin and to find them work when they got there. But the Agreement came to nothing, each Government accusing the other of failing to do its part. Politically, the Indians in Natal are now worse off than they would have been if the Indian Government had never intervened on their behalf—new legislation has made it still more difficult for them to acquire land, and the fact that they have a foreign government to take up their case makes the loyalty to South Africa of even those who were born in the country and have never set foot in India more easily open to question. The attitude of the Union Government, in fact, is driving the Indians to develop that double loyalty which it most wants to avoid.

The campaign of attrition goes on. In 1924 there were nearly three times as many Indians working in the coal mines as in 1933. They find more and more jobs on the railways and in the civil service barred to them. They are constantly reproached for their failure to adapt themselves to Western standards, but no attention is paid to their reply that they cannot do so unless they are allowed to buy more land. According to the Department of Economics of Natal University, seventy per cent of the Indians in Durban live below a very modest poverty-datum line, and there are roughly five times as many deaths from tuberculosis among them as among the Europeans.

There are, of course, valid arguments on the other side,

as there always must be where there are two communities accustomed to very different standards of living. The immense
industry which has led the European to claim contemptuously
that the Indian "can live on the smell of an oil rag" should not
make one forget how often the product of that Indian industry
is shoddy and bad. The rich Indians in Durban, with very few
exceptions, show far more interest in maintaining their right
to acquire property along the Berea, the ridge whereon the
wealthier Europeans build their homes, than in the abolition
of the Indian slums. There is very little evidence that the Natives anywhere in the eastern half of the continent receive
treatment from the Indians as good as they receive from the
Europeans, although many of them very readily work as domestic servants in Indian homes. And only those who have
never been east or south of Suez would deny that overcrowding and other abuses cause property to lose real as well as sentimental value when it changes from white to colored ownership.

For these reasons, many Europeans in South Africa claim
that, whatever the personal hardships and international bad
feeling involved, these Indians must all be sent back to Asia.
But when you ask them if they really mean what they say,
most of them begin to hedge. These noisy and clamant South
Africans overlook the fact that they would be in the greatest
distress if they had themselves to undertake all the menial jobs
now done for them by the Indians. One notices that it is always the other fellow's Indians who are a danger to the country.

The Indians, in fact, have made themselves indispensable in
all the countries of Eastern Africa, but they constitute an awk-
ward element. It would in any circumstances be difficult to as-
similate people, some of whom worship cows that the rest of
the population wants to eat, or whose views on purdah make
it so difficult for their girls to receive such higher education
as the South African authorities can be persuaded to offer.
Patient propaganda by a few Europeans has in fact overcome
Indian opposition to the opening of a girls' secondary school

in Durban, and has made the place so successful that these girls were the first really happy-looking Indians I saw in Africa or elsewhere.

The difficulty of assimilation is increased by two other facts—one, that most of the original Indian immigrants were "coolies," very different in their behavior from the highly-civilized Indians some of us admit rather hesitatingly to our clubs in England or the United States; two, that these "coolies" and, still more, the merchants who have followed them from India, do nevertheless belong to an old and proud civilization. They, much more than the Coloreds, who have nobody to whom they can turn, are likely to react against constant affronts.

Hitherto this pride of race has kept them away from close association with other disgruntled members of the community, and the Natives in South Africa, on their side, hesitate to ally themselves with the Moslems whose exploitation they resent. In Kenya the situation seems to be different, in that African resentment is directed rather against the Hindu, his competitor for a job. In Kenya, an African engine driver, for example, receives about half the wages paid to an Indian and one-third the wages paid to a European. Ever since the white man began to open up Africa there has been this, or an even larger gap, between white and black wages, but the Indian, as distant from the Arab, is more or less a newcomer, and his presence is resented by the Native as much as by the European. For he occupies the intermediate job to which the more ambitious African is beginning to aspire. And in South Africa itself the serious Durban riots of December 1948 showed how deep is the distrust between brown men and black.

But in 1952 the African National Congress and the Indian National Congress began to co-operate in a campaign of civil disobedience—the only form of resistance open to people who have no possibility of obtaining arms and no knowledge of their use. There could be no more significant condemnation of the policy of "apartheid." And a recent development which should interest Europeans throughout Eastern Africa is the Indian Government's offer to African students of a certain number of scholarships at Indian universities. These students are flattered and fussed over almost as much as are those who find their way to Prague or some other of the universities east of the Iron Curtain, and it is not surprising if they return home filled with ideas of a brown-black coalition against the white man.

Durban has a magnificent, modern sea front which has about it something of Miami and something of Blackpool. Its hotels are crowded with European holiday-makers, and short strips of its sea are crowded with European bathers—there are not enough lifesavers available to protect bathers in a wider area from the strong currents and the improbable sharks, and the sea here is so fierce and so filled with pain-giving creatures such as Portuguese men-of-war that one feels the same kind of reluctance to be the outside bather as to be in the front row of a rioting mob. There's safety in numbers.

The Native rickshaw runners on the sea front are world-famous, and they know it. Each man wears an immense headdress of bull's horns, dyed ostrich feathers and painted electric light bulbs, and socks of a most intricate pattern are stencilled in white paint on his legs. These men have been photographed by cameras from every corner of the world, but they are not Durban. This city, with its equal numbers of Europeans, Indians and Africans, gives one the impression of belonging rather to Asia than to Africa, and this impression of Asian influence is, of course, intensified in Mombasa and Dar-es-Salaam, where the proportion of Indians is much greater. The older hotels in these places are built round courtyards that remind one of Calcutta or Karachi. The arcaded streets are like those of Singapore or Hongkong. And, until the dispute between the governments of South Africa (then led by General Smuts) and India induced the latter to institute a boycott of South African goods, the warehouses of these African ports were stacked with Asian produce.

But it is a mistake to think of the Indians only as people who crowd the cities and live by taking in each other's washing and tricking the innocent European. They are, of course, the middlemen, the shopkeepers of Eastern Africa, as the Syrians are the middlemen and shopkeepers of the Western half. Even in Nairobi, so desperately conscious of its Britishness, there are nearly four times as many Asians as Europeans and more and more of its property, even along the select Delamere Avenue, comes into Indian possession. The Indian in Africa, I would point out in parenthesis, is accused of selling out the continent if he sends his savings back to India, and of buying it up if he invests his savings in real estate.

It is also true that, from the European point of view, the Indian does not play the game, in that he works, and makes the members of his family work, for disgracefully long hours. In Nairobi the shops are shut on Saturday afternoons, but one is barely aware of the fact in the Indian section of the city; it is extraordinary how many of the shop doors are left ajar for the benefit of the window cleaner or somebody of that kind, and how warmly a customer is welcomed if he happens to drop in.

Nevertheless, the real Indian contribution to the development of Africa is less in the cities—where it is frequently a damaging one—than in the remote rural areas. The loneliest place I know is the Ngorongoro Crater, in the north of Tanganyika. Although it is one of the greatest centers in the world for big game, a thick mist concealed everything during the two days I spent in camp there, and I was reduced to walking along the rough track, wondering what I ought to do if I met an elephant or a rhinoceros, and trying to identify the animals that had been there by their droppings. With an increasing sense of adventure I followed a little side-track through high elephant grass, and soon arrived at an African village. In the middle of it stood one hut that obviously did not belong to an African—one square home in a group of round ones—and outside it sat an Indian with a turban and a fine, curly beard.

The Europeans complain that few of the Natives work for

more than five or six hours a day; the Indian storekeeper in the remote Native areas, with his brightly-colored cottons and fancy goods, does more than anybody else to arouse an incentive to work. The Indian—and throughout this chapter the word "Indian" covers also the Pakistani—will go to live in places rejected as too lonely by all Europeans, except, possibly, the Greeks, who have also played a great part in opening up the African continent. And in this respect the Indian deserves fewer kicks from the Europeans than normally come his way; the halfpence he will manage to acquire from the Africans.

7

PORTUGUESE BLACK CITIZENS

This is not intended to be a political guide-book to the whole of Africa. But to write of the Black-White struggle only as it affects South Africa seems to me absurd and unfair. The actions of the police in Johannesburg may influence the prospects of Central African Federation or the policy of Dr. Nkrumah in the Gold Coast. Our own African slums on the outskirts of Nairobi should moderate our criticisms of African townships in the Union. On the behavior of the Abyssinians may depend the future of Egypt.

I have therefore written mainly of those countries which are likely to have some influence on the future of the continent. On the basis of the achievements of its explorers, Spain should be playing an important part in Africa. She gets some soldiers and supplies from her African territories, but is herself far too poor to contribute much in return. Spanish Morocco is, of course, a country untouched by the problems of a black

population. Even the few inhabitants of the colony of Rio de
Oro, stretching along the coast south-west of Morocco for some
900 miles, are mainly nomadic Arabs and Berbers. Despite its
name, the colony is impoverished, and seems likely to remain
so. Spanish Guinea may have other resources besides its timber,
but little has yet been done about them. Spanish influence on
Africa's development could scarcely be smaller.

The Portuguese colonies cannot be dismissed so easily, since
Angola and Mozambique, or Portuguese East Africa, are together more than twenty times the size of Portugal itself, and
two railways, the one from the Transvaal and the other from
the Rhodesias, reach the sea in Mozambique. Angola has a
coastline of 1,000 miles on the Atlantic; Mozambique has a
coastline of 1,500 miles on the Indian Ocean. Both colonies are
of increasing economic and strategic importance, and they
supply a very large proportion of the Johannesburg miners. Yet
so little is known about them and so few people visit them that
one of the best newspaper cutting libraries in London has
added only one clipping about Portuguese Africa since 1923!
There is a great deal of land suitable for white settlement in
Angola but very little encouragement to white men to take
advantage of it. In territories which would cover well over half
of Western Europe there are fewer than eighty thousand
Europeans and ten million Africans.

The Portuguese of the fifteenth and sixteenth centuries must
have been the greatest explorers in history. With a hostile Spain
behind them, their trade had of necessity to be carried by sea,
and even the voyages of the British in the first Elizabethan age
were much less remarkable than those of the Portuguese. The
population of Portugal at that time was probably about one
million, but their courage, their seamanship and their insatiable
curiosity took the Portuguese to so many parts of the world
that Pope Alexander VI found it necessary to define the spheres
of Portuguese and Spanish exploration by drawing a line from
the North to the South Pole, at a distance of 370 leagues west
of Cape Verde, and to give to Portugal all lands that might be
discovered to the east of that line. The Portuguese have left

more early traces of their occupation round the coasts of Africa and Asia than have any other Europeans.

But they had not the manpower to make the occupation of their newly-discovered territories effective. During their period of forced union with Spain, Philip II lost the Spanish Armada, which included many Portuguese ships, and other disasters to Spain equally affected Portugal. By a very elastic interpretation of the 370 leagues to the west of Cape Verde, the Portuguese had occupied Brazil, which absorbed all the manpower and money they could spare. The Portuguese colonies in Africa, although so vast, have therefore been less developed than any other territories with similar potential riches. Mozambique contains, in its Zambesia Province, some of the richest undeveloped soil in tropical Africa. Angola has diamonds, asphalt, bitumen, copper and gold, but a thorough study of its mineral resources has still to be made. It is less pestered by tsetse fly than most other African tropical countries and its cattle alone are valued at over $20,000,000. In 1940 its exports to South Africa were worth only $16,520; by 1944 their value had risen to nearly $2,800,000.

Nevertheless, these colonies are, at present, more interesting politically than economically. The Portuguese do not talk of colonies—they refer to them as "overseas provinces"—and there is less sense of a color bar than in any other European colonial territories in Africa. Those few Africans who can pass a test of means, education and a European way of life—only about one-tenth of one per cent in Mozambique—are classed as "citizens" and, except perhaps in Mozambique near the borders of Southern Rhodesia and the Union, are treated on much the same footing as other citizens; there is relatively little interference with the way of life of the other Africans, either to their detriment or to their advantage, beyond the fact that, as in the Belgian Congo, they run some danger of being impressed to work for nothing on such jobs as roadmaking. Also the rights of "citizens," white or black, are not very extensive. Apart from voting for three members of the National Assembly in Lisbon, they may vote for five unofficial members

of a ten-member Government Council which has no powers
except to advise the Governor.

From the early days of exploration the Church has played a
great part in the Portuguese colonies. In their work of convert-
ing pagans to Christianity, the Catholics have shown very little
tolerance toward missions of other denominations, with one
advantageous result, namely, that the Africans have escaped
that deep and disastrous confusion into which they are plunged
in British colonies by the many rival versions of Christianity.
In the case of Portugal, the co-operation between religion and
imperialism has been so close that, in earlier days, the Catholic
missionaries were able to convince themselves that the slave
trade deserved encouragement. They found that the natives in
Brazil were soft and gentle people whose souls could be much
more easily saved than those of the Africans. Slaves were
needed in Brazil, and it therefore seemed right to protect
the natives of Brazil by importing the necessary labor from
Africa. Besides, these African slaves were themselves much
more susceptible to Christianity when they had the Atlantic
between them and their witch doctors. The great Portuguese
forts one finds dotted along the coast of Africa were centers
from which, under the dubious protection of the small local
garrison, missionaries and "factors"—the former to collect souls
and the latter to collect trade—went on explorations of almost
fabulous danger and hardship.

Since the overseas territories are "united" with the mother
country and are represented in its National Assembly, there is
still virtually no African nationalism. The mass has no political
aspirations; more educated Africans have no serious complaint
since they are on the same footing as the white citizens. Almost
all the builders, artisans and mechanics are natives. The Portuguese colonies are among the least progressive in Africa, but
it is quite probable that, for this very reason, the majority of
Africans would rather live in them than in one of the territories
of rapid political and economic development. The white man
saves them from the tyranny of the more brutal chiefs, gives
them priests who are gentler than their witch doctors, and

provides advancement for those among them who have the ambition to become citizens. Also, the black "citizen" has far less fear than in any other African country ruled by Europeans of being snubbed on account of the color of his skin. The Portuguese are obviously and naturally determined to maintain these conditions as long as they can; the question that may worry them is whether the rest of the world, anxious to take part in the development of the great black continent, will be willing that so large a part of it should advance so slowly.

8

THE CONGO

The Belgian Congo is probably the richest territory in Africa, and its exports are second in value only to those of the Union of South Africa. In 1951 its exports showed an excess over imports of $71,200,000; Kenya showed a deficit of about $39,200,000. And yet, in common with most other parts of that continent, the home government accepted responsibility for it only with the greatest reluctance. For more than ten years it was the cause of political crisis and controversy in Brussels. What should a small country like Belgium do with a colony seventy-seven times its size?

Two men, a King and a workhouse boy, share the greatest credit for the development of the Congo; the workhouse boy was British. Sir Henry Morton Stanley, whose real name was Rowlands, was brought up in a Welsh workhouse under a brutal schoolmaster who died a lunatic. His father was a farm laborer and his mother was no better than she ought to be.

He was bullied and knocked about, and, after working for some time as a butcher's errand boy in Liverpool, he ran away to sea. In New Orleans his luck turned for a short time—a merchant there named Stanley befriended him and gave him his own name.

But the merchant died, and young Stanley was taken prisoner while fighting with the Confederate forces. He managed to return to England, but in bad health and in rags, and his mother turned him away from her door. Stanley went to sea again and enlisted in the United States Navy, where he began to write down his adventures. He had already had an unusually exciting career as a foreign correspondent when *The New York Herald* sent him on his historic and successful search for Dr. Livingstone. The little workhouse brat had become famous, and Queen Victoria presented him with a gold snuff-box set with brilliants.

Stanley was not contented to settle down, and all the less so because, like Speke and other great explorers, he found that his account of his journey was greeted with widespread and impolite disbelief. Financed by the owners of the *Daily Telegraph* and *The New York Herald,* he set out on another journey from Bagamoyo, on the coast of Tanganyika. He crossed the African continent from east to west, and arrived at Boma, near the mouth of the Congo River, in August 1877, nine hundred and ninety-nine days later. Of the 350 bearers and other members of his expedition only 115 finished the journey with him, but he had discovered the secret to the development of the Congo. Although ships are held up by rapids less than a hundred miles from the river mouth, he discovered that navigation became possible again some 250 miles further upstream. If a railway could be built to this navigable stretch, the great resources of the country could be brought down to the Atlantic, and thus spared the far longer and more difficult journey to the east coast.

Excited by this discovery, Stanley tried to arouse the enthusiasm of his compatriots. But for them the Congo had a bad name. Some sixty years earlier the British Admiralty had organized an expedition under a Captain Tuckey to explore this river. Tuckey and seventeen of his colleagues died of fever, and no member of the expedition penetrated more than 200 miles into the interior. The British wanted to hear nothing more about the Congo.

But not so King Leopold II of Belgium. This extraordinary man, who never himself visited Central Africa, had a passion for exploration. He had already founded an "International Association for the Exploration and Civilization of Africa" which had organized two rather unsuccessful expeditions from the east coast. Leopold at once realized the importance of Stanley's arrival on the west coast, and he sent two of his agents to meet him at Marseilles on his way home, with a pressing invitation to visit Brussels. Disappointed by the scepticism of his compatriots, Stanley joined forces with the King, who hastened to form another association, the "International Association of the Congo." Stanley became the Association's principal agent in the field. He opened trading stations along the river, negotiated treaties with the chiefs, and supervised the portage through two hundred miles of jungle of the component parts of the first steamer to operate on the Congo. In this way he opened up some 6,000 miles of navigable rivers. Then he retired to England where he became a knight and a Member of Parliament.

The work was carried on by another remarkable man, this time a Belgian named Captain Thys, who had been an aide-de-camp to the King. Twenty-one years after Stanley had reached Boma, Thys finished the railway from Matadi, near the coast, to Stanley Pool, where are now the two flourishing towns of Leopoldville, capital of the Belgian Congo, and Brazzaville, capital of French Equatorial Africa. King Leopold, like Cecil Rhodes, saw Africa as a whole. He planned a railway from Stanley Falls to the Nile. But meanwhile a German, Paul Reichard—after a journey lasting five and a half years, in the course of which both his German companions died—discovered the copper of the Katanga, upon which so much of the wealth of the Congo depends, and attention turned southward toward the Rhodesias. The deposits are so immensely rich that they are believed to contain more than one-third of all the copper in the world. Reichard returned to Germany to persuade his Government to claim the territory; while it was hesitating to do so, the Belgians took possession of most of the copper country and the British took the rest.

Thus the International Association found itself governing an immense territory, but with no properly established legal status for doing so. King Leopold set about turning the territory into a Free State, which soon lapsed in the same kind of difficulties as the British South Africa Company in the Rhodesias and the British East Africa Company in Kenya—too much money had to be spent on suppressing revolts by Natives who found, on closer acquaintance, that they objected to European "protection." Whether Roger Casement, then British Consul at Boma, exaggerated the degree of harsh forced labor need not now be discussed. Perhaps one heard more about it in the case of the Congo than elsewhere in Africa, because, being a Free State, the way in which it was governed aroused a wider interest. The Congo was, in a very moderate degree, the precursor of the United Nations Trust Territories of to-day.

The King's next step was to try to turn the Free State into a Belgian colony, but the first government in Brussels to accept responsibility for this African giant was overthrown for doing so. Criticism dealt not only with the treatment of the Africans, but also with the way in which so much of the country was reserved as crown lands. Between 1901 and 1908 the completely autocratic powers the King had proposed to reserve for himself were whittled away until the Belgian Parliament was assured complete control over Belgium's one colony. But the system of monopolies established under the Free State led toward the immense industrial companies which, with a large measure of government participation, run the Congo to-day.

For the Congo differs radically from all other African territories. Its 76,000 Europeans (of whom three-quarters are Belgians) and its 12,000,000 Africans probably live in greater material comfort than the Europeans and Africans of any other

tropical African country. But none of them has a vote. There
are few white settlers, and they receive very little official
encouragement. The Governor-General is advised by a Government Council in which their members have a majority, but he
nominates them, and is under no obligation to accept their
advice. In any case, the Council meets for only a few days each
year. Most of the Europeans are civil servants or are employed
by one or other of the five great development companies, half
the shares of which belong to the Belgian Government. These
companies have control over nearly nine-tenths of all the capital
investment in the Congo, and most of the white and black
workers depend upon them for their comforts, their consumer
goods, their fertilizers. In 1950, the most important of them
declared a gross profit of about £20,000,000; they can afford
to attract African workers by offers of very favorable conditions.

Sixty per cent of the African miners in the Johannesburg
goldfields come from outside the Union, and live as bachelors
in mine compounds. But well over eighty per cent of the
African miners in the Congo have their families living with
them and they are encouraged to look upon themselves as
permanent urban dwellers, whereas in most other parts of
Africa it is made shockingly plain that they are allowed near
the European's towns only because the European cannot do
without them. Indeed, one of the difficulties of the Congo is to
attract enough workers for the mines and the industries, for the
slave-raiders of an earlier generation left the country very
under-populated. Pleasant villages are built for them and there
are even special farms to provide them with fresh foods. They
come to know such luxuries as electricity and running water. In
the Belgian Government's ten-year plan for the Congo, approved in 1950, the development of medical services comes
second only to the development of communications.

The mine-owners in Johannesburg are proud of the fact
that most of their miners go home at the end of their year
much healthier than when they reached the Rand. But their
care applies to the men only. Not so in the Congo. My distin-

guished colleague, Charles d'Ydewalle, found nothing more astonishing, on his recent long journey in Africa, than a Belgian maternity center where the young African mothers had sheets on their beds. The African port of Leopoldville now has 220,-000 inhabitants, and the Government is putting up a stadium to accommodate over 60,000 African spectators.

The Congo is the African's Brave New World, and it has about it certain features of control and compulsion which he probably dislikes nearly as much as we should dislike them if, or when, Aldous Huxley's fiction becomes fact. Nowhere else in Africa is so much care taken to preserve a healthy and contented labor force. Nowhere else are there such opportunities for the African to develop his skill as a mechanic and to get a well-paid job that would be done elsewhere by a European or an Indian. But discipline is strict. Political agitators are removed without hesitation or delay to some remote area where they can do no harm. There were more than 3,000 such deportations in 1951. The African peasant-farmer who does not work hard to grow some cash crop as well as his own food is likely to find that he cannot pay his taxes; if he cannot pay his taxes he is likely to find himself in a prison gang, building new roads. He will receive orders to do work on behalf of the community, as his father and his grandfather received them before him—for that was a tribal custom common throughout Africa. But the chief who now gives him the orders will, in turn, have received his orders from a Belgian administrator, and will be sacked if he does his job badly. The chief must keep as up-to-date as the young men of his tribe who bring back new ideas after working for a year or so in the mines. This is an impressive contrast to the British version of "indirect rule" which, by supporting an ultra-conservative chief, has so often turned the younger generation against the British administration as well as against the chief himself.

There is about the Congo a sense of urgency and self-confidence such as one does not find even in the Rhodesias. People are in such a hurry that they do not call their towns by their full names—there is no time for anything more than "Leo," "Stan" and so on. In the European part of Leopoldville they are building the first skyscrapers in tropical Africa, and immense blocks of flats are replacing the typical bungalow in its pleasant garden. A helicopter circles the town every day, spraying insecticide so effectively that one can sleep without a mosquito net. The percentage of Europeans with large cars is far higher than in any other country in Africa, and people are in as great a danger as in the United States of losing the use of their legs. In order to brighten the streets of Elisabethville, the center of the copper mines, thousands of jacaranda trees were brought all the way from Brazil. Even Johannesburg cannot show more luxurious villas and better restaurants.

Thus the Congo is ruled, openly, unashamedly and very successfully, from Belgium by the Minister of the Colonies, advised by a Colonial Council. In the British African colonies too much attention has been paid to the political advancement of the Native, and too little to the economic demands to which such advancement must inevitably give rise. In the Union of South Africa, European fear has delayed both political and economic progress. The authorities in the Congo treat both methods with a certain contempt. Malan's clock, they say, is fifty years slow; that of the Colonial Office is twenty-five years fast.

For in the Congo there are no "poor Whites," and therefore no frightened people to hinder and cramp the development of the Blacks. "The 'poor White' is absolutely unknown . . . because the day when the white man is without resources, without the 50,000 francs he must possess when he enters the country, the government (of the Congo) informs him without delay that he must return to Belgium. I believe this to be one of the wisest measures I have come across on a journey from one end of Africa to the other." [1]

The result of this measure is that the Belgian supervises and controls. The more skilful the African becomes under his

[1] Charles d'Ydewalle, *Nation Belge.* August 25th, 1952.

orders, the higher his own earnings will be. For there is no
danger, at least for decades ahead, that the economic expansion
of the Congo will cease or that the demand for labor will
lessen.

In the first place, water power is almost unlimited. "The
Congo alone could supply 134 million horse-power, at least
20 million more than all the American rivers put together,"
writes Anton Zischka,[2] and he foresees the time when power
from this river will be brought by cable all the way to South-
Western Europe. Such forecasts probably glide much too easily
over the great difficulties of tapping these water supplies in a
continent so immense and so lacking in communications. But
the Belgians have already made great use of their rivers to
supply power to their Congo mines. They have the largest
known reserves of uranium (and in 1951 they were responsible
for ninety-six per cent of the world's total production), to say
nothing of copper, gold, platinum, industrial diamonds, rubber,
cadmium, manganese, palm oil and a whole list of other mineral
and vegetable supplies. Copper is exported to the value of
$84,000,000 a year. Ten per cent of the world's output of tin,
eighty per cent of its industrial diamonds, seven per cent of its
gold, and important supplies of at least half a dozen other
valuable metals, come from the Congo.

In operating its ten-year plan, the Belgian Government will
spend roughly twice as much as was invested in the Congo
between 1870 and 1936, and most of this money will be spent
on communications, power supplies and other facilities for the
development of industry through private investment. But the
total annual exports are worth about $280,000,000, as com-
pared, for example, with about $56,000,000 from Kenya.
Probably nowhere else in the world is there such profitable
co-operation between industry and the State, and such material
progress for its backward workers.

But for how long? The settlers, outside these great industrial
concerns (but, of course, getting indirect benefits from them by
way of better communications, a good market for their surplus

[2] *Afrika* (Stalling Verlag, Oldenburg).

food production, and so on) are not content. They begin to be
haunted by the same fears as the settlers in the British colonies.
The African is rising too quickly and too far, and he will soon
be demanding political control. Therefore one must assure
the continued predominance of the European by an immense
program of white immigration. Their federation has recently
launched a nation-wide slogan: "A hundred thousand Belgian
settlers in ten years, or the Congo will no longer be Belgian."
To the objection that these colonists would provide a new chan-
nel to drain away a supply, already short, of African labor in
industry, it suggests that an area of the high land should
be set aside exclusively for Europeans. Large areas of the
Congo, it claims, are empty, and the Europeans who settled
there would be able to provide a useful quantity of food for
the natives.

This experiment in "apartheid" might be much easier to
organize than in the case of a British colony, for the Belgians
have a great pride in their Congo. The Englishman slinks away
to Kenya or the Rhodesias in a slightly shamefaced way—for
there is still a hangover from the days when the ne'er-do-well
was packed off to the colonies to make good—and he will look
upon the African as a possible competitor who must be kept
out of such skilled or semi-skilled jobs as he himself could do;
the Belgian goes off with a certain *panache* to this wealthy
African territory where such fabulous developments are taking
place, and he will do his best to encourage the skill of
the African, so that the developments may be even faster and
more fabulous. One Belgian newspaper, *La Nation Belge*, de-
votes an entire page to Africa every week.

So the settlers might find a number of willing immigrants, if
they were allowed to immigrate. But this is just what the
Government will not allow them to do. While some Southern
Rhodesians are hoping to make themselves independent of
African labor by the mass importation of Italian and other
Mediterranean unskilled workers, in order to establish their
own system of "apartheid," the Belgian Government is hoping
to keep out of the Congo all Europeans who are not highly

skilled. It wants no "poor White" problem on its hands, and its resistance becomes all the more remarkable if one realizes that the area lying at over three thousand feet, and thus able to carry a white population, is somewhere about twenty-five times the area of Belgium itself.

Sooner or later, of course, there must also be demands from the Africans. In most colonies, too many of their *élite* become lawyers, some become doctors, too few become engineers, agriculturists or veterinary surgeons; in the Belgian Congo they are all excluded from the liberal professions. Nor are they given the opportunity to study in European or American universities, in which their most probable intellectual acquisition would be very bitter, but very understandable, resentment against the color bar. Although in many cases their housing conditions are already far better in the Congo than elsewhere in Africa, and 40,000 more Native houses are to be built under the ten-year plan, they live in strictly segregated areas. Segregation, indeed, works both ways, and the European must have a special pass before he can visit Black Leopoldville at night. Industry has developed at such a pace that nearly 2,000,000 Africans now live in Native cities or "noncustomary centers"—places in which tribal discipline no longer operates.

Although the wages of the African in the Congo compare favorably with those of the Africans in neighboring countries, they are still only about one-tenth of the wages received by the European; this fact must create an increasingly vehement demand for political and trade union rights. Hitherto this demand has been met in part by a system of promotion to the category of "evolved" African, which assures better treatment in all sorts of ways than that which is accorded to the mass. But the Belgian Government is experiencing the same difficulty as that of other governments with colonial responsibilities—it is precisely among the *evolués* that the sense of frustration is the greatest. Also, there is the danger that, without the encouragement of promotion for the Blacks, the Whites will in time become the "dominant," rather than the "creative," minority.

One can find much to criticize about this Brave New World, and the power it leaves in the hands of the big concessionary companies to crowd the African off his land and into the companies' service. The African settler, indeed, is not much more welcome in his own country than is the settler who comes out from Europe. But in one respect the Belgian administration seems to be doing something which has not been done elsewhere in Africa, except, perhaps, in the Portuguese colonies and others where there is practically no color bar. It is creating an African middle and lower-middle class. The greatest danger of friction between Whites and Blacks arises in those parts of Africa where the Europeans, or the Europeans and Indians, dare not allow the Africans to become skilled. In those countries, the very few Africans who nevertheless manage to enter a profession or to make a lot of money lose touch with their own people or use them for their own ends. Those ends are not necessarily discreditable, but they are almost inevitably anti-European.

But the encouragement given in the Congo to African skilled workers is turning an African proletariat into a lower middle-class. And it is not so long ago that, even in Great Britain, there was a wide gulf between "trade" and the "professions." That gulf will inevitably narrow; meanwhile, given the opportunity to develop their skill and intelligence, the Africans of the Congo show none of that surly discontent that is becoming so marked a feature of cities such as Johannesburg and Nairobi. The African in the Congo may not become a doctor or a lawyer, but he may become the captain of a steamboat or the driver of an engine (until he reaches the frontier of Northern Rhodesia, when a European takes over—or so I am assured—in order that the European on the other side of the frontier may not be humiliated). The Belgian Government is now beginning to build up, from the smallest communities, a simple system of elections which will gradually teach the Africans to accept responsibility. Political development is beginning later in the Congo than elsewhere; that fact certainly need not make it any the less successful.

9

THE NEW NIGERIA

The best approach to West Africa is from South Africa, and preferably by air, so that the impressions of one area are still vivid when one reaches the other. I arrived at Kano early one afternoon in the month of May, the hottest month of the year. And the heat that met me in the doorway of our pressurized aircraft made me stagger back. "You are the tenth man out of that machine," a B.O.A.C. official on the tarmac said to me, "and all but two of you have called upon the Almighty in amazement or reproach."

But it was not only the heat that took me by surprise. I had not expected the customs and other officials to be Africans. I had almost forgotten that black men are called Africans in most places outside South Africa, where they are called Natives lest they should be confused with white Afrikaners. I was not prepared to be taken to see the Emir in his palace, and to find myself in the presence of a most dignified old man, in front of whom other men prostrated themselves in the dust. These other men, it is true, were Africans, but to prostrate themselves in front of a black man! South Africa had led me to anticipate that such respect would be reserved for the Whites! On the corner of almost every building sat a vulture, with its revolting, scraggy neck sunk between its wings; I had not expected my companion to tell me, with respect in his voice, that these birds were "protected." One would no more think of killing one of these invaluable and evil-looking scavengers than of killing one of the famous scavenging crows in Colombo. Or, indeed, an albatross.

The first thing one learns about West Africa is that the frontiers of the countries composing it are cruelly artificial. Europeans who occupied and annexed part of the coastline took it for granted that the hinterland also belonged to them. Nobody, of course, dreamed of consulting the local inhabitants. And the result is that the tribes along the coast who had a good deal in common with each other have found themselves placed under different European administrations with entirely different methods and different ambitions. And also they have found that they are expected to treat as their compatriots and allies northern tribesmen against whom their ancestors had always been at war.

These ancestors are believed to have migrated along the southern edge of the Sahara from Egypt and the Nile valley, perhaps three thousand years ago. The southerners are Negroes, and are closely related to the Bantu who pushed southward instead of westward. The Fulani, among the northerners, have much lighter skins, and many of them have thin lips and finely-chiselled noses. They are devout Moslems, and they tend to find ideological links with the Moslems of Egypt and the Sudan rather than with their fellow-Nigerians in the south. The Emir's palace in Kano had baked-mud walls that reminded me of the Mahdi's palace in Omdurman, and high domed ceilings which might have been very unsophisticated copies of the Moorish magnificence of Granada.

Kano, indeed, is much more Arab than Negro, more Mediterranean than African. Its mud-brick buildings are rectangular, instead of circular, in the normal African fashion (although you can go to the market there and buy a ready-made framework for the roof of a standard circular hut, an unexpected example of pre-fabricated building). Its position on the southern edge of the Sahara has made it important throughout the centuries. It has twelve miles of city walls, and a separate city of some 60,000 traders and other pagans from the south, who now have their own municipal council. In the middle of some of its great, sandy market places there are pits filled with indigo dye, for its blue cotton cloths are famous throughout West Africa. Its importance changes with the centuries—when a British expeditionary force occupied it only fifty years ago slaves were still bought and sold in these markets; now it is a great airport, half-way between Europe and the Union of South Africa, with the very uncommon advantage in this part of the world of a railway linking it to the sea.

Near this railway I found immense pyramids covered with tarpaulin—piles of groundnuts awaiting transport to the coast. And these groundnuts are important politically as well as economically, for they represent a good proportion of Nigeria's wealth, and are therefore a strong argument in favor of continued national union. The tin mines of Jos are also in the north, and no government in Lagos could light-heartedly lose these two great sources of revenue. On the other hand, the southerners are impatient for self-government. Nigeria is the largest territory in the British Colonial Empire and has the largest population of any State in Africa. Its politicians are intensely jealous of the fact that the nearby Gold Coast is one step nearer independence than their own country, and intensely alive to the fact that a noisy and extremist policy made the extra step possible. But their own extremism leads to very strained relations with the more conservative Moslems in the north.

Nigeria, like Gaul, is divided into three parts. "Whatever you do," they said to me in the Northern Region, "don't be misled by those people in the south. Lagos doesn't in the least represent the opinions of Nigeria." In the Western Region they criticized the East; had I managed also to visit the Eastern Region, I should doubtless have heard similar criticisms of the West. I had expected some rivalry between the larger tribes— the Hausa and the Fulani in the North, the Ibo in the East and the Yoruba in the West. I had not expected the British officials also to feel such strong regional loyalty.

Among the Africans themselves this rivalry is understandable enough, for a good many of them can still remember inter-tribal warfare, even within the Regions. Some of them, indeed, might still remember the attack on the headquarters of the Royal Niger Company when forty-three of the employees were taken off by cannibals. The northerners, as Moslems, have been slow to develop schools, and the southerners are therefore inclined to treat them with contempt. But the Mohammedan religion has given them a respect for good manners and a standard of conduct which are often lacking in the south. Many of the southerners have swallowed Western civilization hook, line and sinker; not all of them have managed properly to digest it.

For this, missionaries as well as business men are to blame. The missionaries have for years patiently and valiantly carried most of the burden of education, and, as you drive through the jungle, you pass notices directing you off the main road to the most astonishing variety of mission stations. But their Christian message has too often shown signs of rivalry between them, and the unfortunate Africans have become confused. In many cases, by way of precaution, they have retained their own tribal superstitions and have thus given themselves a double set of taboos. Their motor lorries go rattling along the laterite roads of West Africa with all manner of slogans painted above the windscreen, such as: "Trust in God," or "Man proposes, God disposes," and in Takoradi I rode in a taxi which had this sad admission painted on its back window: "It's so hard to be a gentleman."

But even the best efforts of the best missionaries have been handicapped by the other Europeans who introduced various habits that are not easily reconciled with Christian purity, tolerance and brotherly love. Here and there, dotted along the coast, are the ruins of the old forts—Danish, Dutch, British, or Portuguese—which were built, from the fifteenth century onwards, for the protection of European trade in West Africa. And the fact that strongholds of this kind were necessary to defend so peaceful an activity as the exchange of goods is a useful reminder both of the manner in which the white man forced his way into Africa and of the nature of the goods thus exchanged. For generations the most valuable traffic was in slaves and gin. In the fishermen's quarter of Accra you can still see a shabby archway which, a hundred and fifty years ago, led into the slave market. The Africans of to-day do not like this reminder of their past. Actually, they should be proud of it, for it indicates the progress they have made. It is the Europeans whom it should fill with shame. They have no right to forget their share of the responsibility for the more disquieting characteristics of the African.

These characteristics are most blatantly obvious in a place like Lagos, and they help to explain the anxiety of the British officials in the other regions that the visitor should not take the people in that city as typical of the country as a whole. They leave one worried by the question, how ready is the African for power?

One of the commonest words in West Africa is "dash," which is West African for "backsheesh." A patient in hospital has much more hope of getting the medicine or the treatment the doctor ordered if he "dashes" the African nurse or orderly. Too many African civil servants are ready to accept bribes, although the service they render has already been paid for by the State. It is perhaps not so much that the man who does something for an African expects a bribe; it is rather that the African expects to show his appreciation for services rendered. It is the outcome of a personal relationship which does not fit in with the idea of impersonal service to the community. But this tradition of courtesy is all too likely to lead to corruption.

Not even among the Japanese has one so strongly the feeling
of undiscriminating enthusiasms as along the coastal belt of
West Africa. The European is violently criticized but he is
slavishly imitated—in his bad behavior as well as his good. In
the Island Club in Lagos—the only club I have found in Africa
where Europeans and Africans manage to forget the color of
each other's skins—most of the Africans, who include many of
the Ministers and higher civil servants, drink imported Dutch
beer at two and threepence a bottle; the Europeans generally
drink the local product, at ninepence. Prices of Nigerian exports have risen so steeply, and the African change of status
has been so sensational, that a certain *nouveau riche* ostenta-
tion is easy to understand. The disquieting side of it is, however, that the wealth will, for many years to come, be dependent on European advice, technical help and capital, and
the tendency is to dismiss them as unnecessary.

What the white man can do, one is assured, the black man
can do. Hence the enthusiasm throughout black Africa for the
advantages of education. This enthusiasm is pathetic, inspiring, depressing, according to your way of looking at things.
Pathetic, because the people are prepared to make such sacrifices to attain it and have such exaggerated ideas of the happiness and contentment it will bring them. Inspiring, because
the changes being wrought by it, for good or ill, are so tremendous even in the remoter hamlets. Depressing, because
there is still so little understanding of its aims and objects,
there are still so few Africans who understand that an ability
to quote slabs from Shakespeare or to solve some fairly simple
mathematical problem does not carry with it automatically the
ability to rule other men wisely.

Nationalism is another of the enthusiasms of the African,
and it is one with which most of us have a good deal of
sympathy, even though it has seemed to involve a depressing
lack of gratitude toward governments or officials with a genuine sense of trusteeship. The desire to run one's own country,
even if one runs it badly, is a natural desire, especially if the

existing overlords are men not only of another race but even of another color. But the nationalism that finds expression in the Lagos newspapers is such a virulent form of the disease that it lessens one's optimism about the country's future.

These depressing sentences are possibly unfair, for the fear of demagogy has always been widely expressed with each development of democracy. They are based partly on one so-called press conference which I had to face in Lagos. There were, as far as I can remember, only two questions, which were both in the do-you-still-beat-your-wife category. The intention of one was to suggest that there was no Nigerian nation because the British had deliberately united north and south on the old principle of dividing in order to rule. The intention of the other was to suggest that there must be a lot more, and a lot more aggressive, Nigerian nationalism, since nationalism was the only weapon by which the British could be driven out of the country. A third suggestion which came vaguely through the din was that the British investor ought to be producing a lot more capital which the Nigerians could "nationalize" when they became independent.

Despite the uneasiness with which Lagos filled me, I have no doubt that wisdom demands concessions to nationalism once it has become sufficiently strong to prosper on opposition. And this is the case in West Africa. It might have been much better for the masses if their advance toward independence could have been a little slower, a little easier for them to comprehend and appreciate. But the brake, to be effective and useful, can now be applied only by Africans themselves.

Hence the importance of the Northern Region. One has only to drive from Kano to Kaduna, the capital of this region, to realize that the people at present feel no urgent desire to rid themselves of British rule, at any rate until they have had time to train their own fair share of officials and administrators. If the British were to go to-morrow their places would be taken by southerners, and this prospect causes such distress that the Northern Region refused to join the new Federation unless it was allowed to send as many members to the Central Legislature as the two Regions of Southern Nigeria put together.

Each of the three Regions has its own Lieutenant-Governor and its own Parliament. The Clerk of the House in Kaduna welcomed me in a red fez, a blue cloak, pale green trousers and a white flowing shirt. But he spoke the language of the House of Commons, he obeyed much the same rules of procedure, and the Speaker was trying to develop, in the space of a few months, the same kind of authority over the Assembly as the Speaker in Westminister has acquired with the help of centuries of tradition. A parliamentary delegation from the United Kingdom attended the first meeting of the Central House of Representatives and presented its Speaker with a special copy of Erskine May's standard work on Parliamentary procedure; there could be no tougher test of the African's intelligence.

Under the present constitution, which came into full operation in 1951, the three regional legislatures choose from among their own members the members of the House of Representatives—sixty-eight from the North and thirty-four each from the East and West. At present, the Ministers, both in the Council of Ministers and the Regional Executive Councils, are chosen by the Governor or the Lieutenant-Governors, subject to agreement by the particular parliament concerned. The Nigerian newspapers can therefore complain that they are still some way from self-government, but at present no other method would produce men selected mainly for their competence and ability to work well together. It is quite a strain for so new a country to produce all these legislators, and Nigeria now has to find civil servants as well, for Europeans are being replaced as quickly as possible by Africans. These newcomers are adapting themselves to the new conditions far more readily than many Europeans had anticipated. But the riots in Kano in May of 1953 have made it necessary to re-examine a constitution introduced with such optimism a bare two years earlier.

In the Northern Region the two main tribes are the Hausa and the Fulani, the latter being a tribe of cattlemen, fine, tall, and great fighters in the old days. Men to be compared with the Masai in Kenya and Tanganyika and the Zulus in South Africa. Their cattle have the longest and widest horns of any I have ever seen, and there is apparently quite an export of these horns to the United States, where they can be sold as belonging to Texas Longhorns. But these animals are driven on the hoof for anything up to a thousand miles, and they arrive in the most lamentable state at the slaughter-houses in Lagos. Taking account of the beasts that die on the way, each animal loses an average of 100 lb. on the journey.

The Hausa are agriculturists, and less belligerent. They, too, depend for their prosperity on trade with the south. The groundnuts, their cash crop, were selling in 1951 for $100 a ton, whereas the average price between the wars was about $14, and it once went as low as $4.20. The result is that too much of this desert-like country is given up to cash crops, and too little to food, so that there is too much to spend and too little to eat. A man who is suffering from malnutrition may have a smart new bicycle, the African's equivalent of a motor car.

As you go southward from Kano, the desert gives way to the kind of thorn scrub that covers so great a part of Africa. The only tall trees are obscene-looking baobabs, with their disproportionately inadequate foliage, their grossly-swollen, purple, shiny trunks and, in almost every case, a small parasite tree which, in due course, will uproot its protector. And, here and there in this otherwise endless bush, you come across a town. An over-crowded and lively African quarter, with scores of laughing and chattering market women squatting on the ground. Two or three stone-built offices and banks. The official quarter, with "boys" busy all day bringing water for the cream or pink flowers of the frangipani, the scarlet flame trees, the pale blue jacaranda.

By constant effort and at great expense of labor, Western civilization just manages to hold its own. The small group of European officials, grossly overworked and underpaid—overworked, since they have to train inexperienced Africans, and underpaid, since African ministers could not at this stage ask their Central House of Assembly to increase European salaries without also increasing the salaries of African civil servants who, in the eyes of the ministers, are already too important. The small group of officials' wives with too little to do beyond worrying whether the children can stand the climate and whether they will be posted to another station and another house on their next "tour." The small group of business men with more money but less prestige, and little of the official's paternal sense of responsibility for the African's development toward independence.

Down the road are the African quarters and the market. Nests of half a dozen cola nuts—the astringent bitterness of which will keep a man going without food for very many hours—spread out on large leaves on the ground; the "World Press," the "Cosmic Press and Printing Works" and "The London and African Bookshop"; the medicine shop, with its dried chameleons, its bundles of dried herbs, its snake skins, its dried mice on little skewers, the "Easy Life Barber," the "Hosanna Patent Medicine Store," the "Good Will Photo Works," the "All Well Patent Medicine Store"; and, lastly, the innumerable wine and beer shops, with such names as "Universal Restaurant," "Lord Will Provide Bar," and "Piccadilly Bar." In appearances these places have probably not greatly changed with the generations, and none of them covers more than some twelve square feet; it is by their names that they show the march of civilization.

Of the market stalls, those which sell cottons are the most attractive. Bales and bales of brightly-colored materials which the women buy in ten-foot lengths in Nigeria and twelve-foot in the Gold Coast (since the manner of wrapping them round oneself varies in each country). The most sought-after cloths are those that come from Holland; the wax which is put on the parts that are to remain white cracks slightly, so that thin streaks of the dye come through. Also the pattern is stamped on by hand, and varies slightly from piece to piece, and the

African women are at least as anxious as the white women who look to Paris for their clothes to get something that is slightly different from anything owned by their rivals.

Some of these women will wear three lengths of cotton of entirely different patterns and colors; these colors ought to clash, and they would clash against a white skin; somehow, against a black skin, they do not. But these lengths of cotton are also bought as an investment, and one hears of people with a hundred or more of them. The women of West Africa have done several things the women of East and Central Africa have not yet managed to do. They have emancipated themselves sufficiently to persuade their menfolk to carry some of the burdens and to do some of the agricultural work—near Lagos I almost ran over a cyclist with a pickaxe, a hoe and a spade balanced on his head. Also their liking for finery has provided their menfolk with an incentive to work which is still lacking in many other parts of the continent. Elsewhere in Africa, the men have the wealth, in the form of cows; in West Africa, the women have it, in the form of bales of cotton.

I went from Kaduna, the capital of the Northern Region, to Ibadan, the Western capital, by air, which is, of course, the poorest way of travelling if you want to see the world. We were flown in an alarmingly small machine by a pilot who sported an enormous red beard. The only event occurred when he handed back a slip of paper which I thought would give us the usual details of height, speed, and estimated time of arrival. Instead, it had only the words: "Arsenal nil. Newcastle United one," The result of the greatest soccer match of the year.

In this instance the flight had one advantage—it enhanced the contrast between north and south. Kaduna had been hot and parched; Ibadan was hot and humid. Both heats were excessive, and helped me to realize the importance of the "wash boy" in every comfortable household. In Ibadan the mere effort of typing an article sent rivers of sweat trickling through my hair and down the small of my back. But at least

Ibadan was green—deep, tropical green, with flowers of every kind in the garden and young teak trees everywhere with immense rich leaves. Outside the town, creepers the thickness of one's arm reached down to the ground again in traditional jungle fashion from the topmost branches of the mahogany trees. The wealth of the district comes not from groundnuts, but from cocoa trees, which are much more pleasant to look at. One could tell who was making money out of cocoa, a friend said to me, not by the taxes that were paid but by the new roofs of corrugated iron one could see if one looked down on Ibadan from one of the surrounding hills. And there were certainly a lot of new corrugated iron roofs.

Ibadan, as capital of the Western Region, has its Parliament building, but Lagos, the most important town in Nigeria, comes within this Region. There are therefore inhabitants of Lagos who spend part of the year in the Regional Assembly in Ibadan, and inhabitants of Ibadan who spend part of the year in the Central House of Representatives in Lagos. And this resulted in a singular conflict between the two outstanding political figures in Nigeria, between Azikiwe, leader of the National Convention of Nigeria and the Cameroons, and Obafemi Awolowo, leader of the Action Group. Dr. Azikiwe—universally known as "Zik"—built up the strength of his party in the Eastern Region among the Ibo tribesmen, while Awolowo depends upon the Yoruba in the Western Region. The Action Group won a majority in the Western House, and the N.C.N.C. in the East. But Zik's spiritual home is in Lagos and at the elections he chose to stand as a Lagos candidate for the Western Regional Assembly, and not for some constituency in the Eastern Region. All five successful Lagos candidates for the Western House were N.C.N.C. men, and in the normal way one might have expected that Zik would have been among the members of that House chosen to go on to the Central House of Representatives. But there was some slightly disloyal activity among members of his own party, and he was omitted from the list.

Thus the man who, more than anybody else, has used the

arguments of democracy to further his nationalist campaign, found that the machinery of democracy had pushed him out into the wilderness. And Awolowo, whose Action Group was looked upon as the more moderate of the two parties, has become an even severer critic of British administration than Zik had been. Although these two men are bitter rivals for power, they are momentarily united in the demand for self-government by 1956. The ministers of the Northern Region refused to support this demand; they want first to be sure that they would not come under southern domination. And the resulting strain between the Northern Region and the other two Regions may destroy national unity. With the removal of this system of checks and balances, each Region will be economically the poorer, extremists in the Western and Eastern Regions will outbid each other in their hostility to Britain, and the chances of agreement between these two Regions when the British have granted their demands for self-government will be tragically diminished.

It is probable, and natural, that part of the enthusiasm of British officials for Northern Nigeria is due to the fact that there they can still carry on a benevolent kind of patriarchal administration through the Emirs. Some of the Emirates are almost independent. The Sultanate of Sokoto, for example, is twice as large as Holland, and it has less than thirty white officials, of whom only seven take part in its administration. Its one and a half million inhabitants are kept in order by 300 unarmed Native police.

But the difficulty is that such peaceful autocracies cannot continue. Contact with Southern Nigeria is too disturbing. The demand for education, for political responsibility, is becoming too insistent. With nearly half the total population, the Northern Region has only about one-eighth of the secondary and one-fifth of the primary schools of the country. In the first general elections the northern cities produced some very lively and radical young politicians in a party called the Northern Elements Progressive Union, linked closely with the N.C.N.C. Party, but they were eliminated between the "primaries" and the final election to the Northern House of Assembly by methods that were questionable.

The advantages and handicaps of "indirect rule" are discussed elsewhere in this book; the cordiality with which one is greeted in the north is pleasant and heart-warming, but that should be no argument in favor of encouraging the emirs to deny the inevitability of change. For the Nigerian experiment is as important to the African continent in one way as Malan's experiment with "apartheid" is important in another.

In South Africa, the Europeans and the Natives pass each other in the street with just the same kind of pretense that the other does not exist as one found in Germany immediately after the war and at the height of the non-fraternization period. No downright rudeness on either side—merely the absence of any sign of interest, the ability to look through a person, that one might, and possibly, does, display in the presence of ghosts. In West Africa, outside Lagos and Accra, and especially in the Moslem regions of the north, there is a spontaneity of welcome which is extremely cheering after the dourness of racial contacts in Johannesburg.

The welcome takes various forms. In Northern Nigeria, near the attractive Arab town of Zaria, two African men were so busy curtseying to each other, or rather, going down on one knee in the dust and then shaking hands, that we had to jam on the brakes of the car to avoid knocking them both over. They were as intent on this greeting as two courting pigeons. In Ibadan, the capital of the Western Region, we were greeted with raised, clenched fists, which did not mean that the Communists had been making converts. Presumably the Yoruba, the principal tribesmen in this part of the world, were far in advance of the Marxists in selecting this form of greeting. And the cheerful friendliness, the readiness to laugh, of these Africans is one of the principal reasons why the British show such an affection for a part of the world that used to be known as the White Man's Grave.

The greatest surprise of all in Nigeria and in West Africa as a whole is the attitude of the Europeans—"expatriates" is the ugly official word by which they are now known. My arrival in Kaduna coincided with a plague of flying ants. My host's little daughter was delighted—they were all on their honeymoon, she explained, and she wanted to know why her parents had not been able to fly on a similar occasion. With ants crawling over me, I felt less romantic. After dinner ladies removed insects from their bare shoulders as calmly as they might remove a crumb from their laps, while I manoeuvered my way toward the chair farthest from the light. Harmless but revolting sausage-flies with squelchy bodies blundered against the lampshades, and from time to time immense beetles shot into the room, banged themselves against the wall, and fell stunned to the floor. I was consoled by the assurance that I was lucky to escape the earwig season. White ants under the floor of the Lieutenant-Governor's drawing-room, had eaten pathways through his nice new carpets.

In Ibadan the Public Relations Officer proudly showed me a large black scorpion he had just killed under his wife's bed. In Lagos, huge toads encumbered the steps of the first house in which I stayed. Outside the second, as the night went on, fruit bats worked themselves up into an unbelievable frenzy of whines, squeaks, yappings and monotonous metallic clangings. No other creature, I imagine, makes such a variety of noises. When it rained, the heat became even more nearly intolerable, for the humidity was intensified. The men wore knee-high mosquito boots with their evening clothes, and one would as soon forget to wash one's teeth as to take one's daily dose against malaria. If a dog which develops rabies has licked one's hand, the precaution consists of a score of extremely painful injections in the stomach.

These are, of course, only the minor discomforts of this West Coast, but they would suffice to make most of us want to pack up and go home. I had expected to find my compatriots there looking forward to retirement as I used to look forward to the end of term during my schooldays. Instead, although a few

senior officials may have decided that the changes were greater
than they could stand, and were therefore retiring on pension,
the majority from the Governor, Sir John Macpherson, downwards, were genuinely interested in making a success of the
political experiment.

This applies even to social relationships as well as official
ones. I shall doubtless get myself into trouble for saying so, but
in colonial territories the female of the white species is generally so much less tolerant, so much more class and color conscious, than the male. But I found far fewer evidences of that
attitude in West Africa than I had expected, and far more
cases of genuine and friendly interest in the efforts of the
African wives to adapt themselves to a new kind of life.

Science has, of course, done much to remove the terrors and
discomforts of the White Man's Grave. The refrigerator, the
airplane, and radio and preventive medicine. Troops going
round bareheaded during the war have put an end to the spine
pad and the topee, now reserved almost exclusively for non-
Europeans. Before the war, only a few missionaries brought
their children out from Britain, and they were strongly criticized for doing so; now the nursery is one of the principal features in the ships that serve the Coast. Even District Officers
in the bush can now lead ordinary home lives, with no more absence from their families than commercial travellers in England, and leave is so frequent that officials in West Africa are
the only ones in the Colonial Service who, on retirement, do not
find that they are strangers in their own land.

But these improved facilities would not explain why so many
government officials in West Africa are working harder than
any other civil servants I have met in peace-time to help their
respective Regions through the bewildering political changes of
the moment. They may regret the good old days of paternal
control, they may be sceptical about the ability of some of the
African civil servants who will succeed them. But for most of
them there is no selfish significance behind the phrase with
which they finish almost every discussion about the future:
"If only we could be sure of another ten years!"

This chapter must end with a few words about the economic importance of Nigeria, for this country not only has a population more than double that of the Union of South Africa and nearly five times that of Kenya; it also has great wealth, actual and potential. The value of its exports cannot compete with those of the Union of South Africa, whose exports (thanks mainly to gold) are almost equal to those of the Rhodesias, the Congo and Nigeria lumped together. Nevertheless, Nigeria's export of palm oil and palm kernels far surpasses that of any other African territory, and, with that of the Belgian Congo and French West Africa, amounts to about half the world's supply. With the Gold Coast and French West Africa, its exports of cocoa amount to more than half the world's exports. In Africa, Nigeria is second only to French West Africa in the export of groundnuts and to the Belgian Congo in the export of tin. Nigeria's timber resources are far greater than those of any other African territory.

But in most cases the resources of Nigeria and other countries of Western Africa are as useless to the world as the gold reserves buried at Fort Knox unless they can be associated with capital from the United Kingdom or other overseas countries. "It is clear . . . that the economic development of the African territories has proceeded furthest in those areas which possess readily exploitable mineral wealth and other resources which have a world demand. Indeed, it is the possession of these mineral and other resources which has led to the substantial inflow of capital to the Union of South Africa, the Rhodesias, Belgian Congo and Nigeria and to their relatively rapid development. Capital from abroad moved precisely to those areas which offered substantial returns, or at any rate the prospect of such returns. . . .

"The distribution of the capital invested from abroad is illuminating. Some $1,465,000,000 was invested in the Union of South Africa, or about forty-three per cent of the investment in all territories. The most important fields of investment have been: the Rhodesias, which absorbed about $285,000,000; Nigeria, $210,000,000; Tanganyika, $145,600,000; Kenya and

Uganda, $128,800,000; the Gold Coast, $98,000,000; and South West Africa, $89,600,000. The total investment in the Union of South Africa and all British territories at the end of 1936 is estimated to have amounted to $2,660,000,000, or about four-fifths of the total capital investment in Africa south of the Sahara. In non-British territories, the greatest investment has been in the Belgian Congo, which is estimated to have absorbed some $390,000,000 before the war. The territories, in which the smallest amount of capital investment has taken place and which are among the most backward, are the possessions of France. Capital investment in French West Africa and French Equatorial Africa is estimated to have amounted to $84,000,000 and $58,800,000 respectively."[1]

These facts may vitally affect West Africa. It is right and reasonable to blame the capitalist when he uses his investments for selfish political ends—as he has too often done in Africa. But it is wrong and unreasonable to blame him when he is reluctant to use them for the selfish political ends of other people. African nationalists can hardly grumble if the white man takes seriously some of the attacks made upon him in their newspapers, and decides not to risk further capital in countries with so uncertain a future. And in some circumstances this hesitation might apply to governments as well as to ordinary business concerns.

Under the Colonial Development and Welfare Act, each colony has prepared its ten-year program. Nigeria is to receive $154,000,000 as against, for example, $43,680,000 for Kenya, $49,280,000 for Tanganyika, and $14,560,000 for the Gold Coast. And even allocations for development rather than for welfare help to raise the African standard of living. In Lagos harbor, for example, there is always a long file of ships riding at anchor off the Marina, and often a similar line anchored in the open roadstead. Either they are waiting for a berth at which they can unload their cargoes, or their cargoes must go through the slow and costly process of being unloaded into lighters. Lagos is an island, and is so overcrowded that there

[1] *Africa South of the Sahara* (Oxford University Press).

are some of the worst slums in the world in the very center of the city. The main wharves are on the mainland at Apapa, a few miles away, and I spent one of the hottest mornings of my life being shown round the new harbor scheme there, which will not only add half a mile of deep-water berths, but will also house some 19,000 workers from the Lagos slums. Three square miles of derelict land are being drained, and then filled with sand. The enthusiastic engineers who took me round pointed out the empty spaces where they could see great new warehouses, and railway tracks and housing estates, and I could see nothing but sand. But already all the future warehouses had been let. . . .

For decades, the British public has shown a shocking lack of interest in the welfare and development of its vast colonial territories. The war and the fear of Communism have broken down that indifference, and the British taxpayer is handing out many millions to help the backward areas in the Commonwealth. The alternatives to this official action are either a continuation of neglect or an excessive intervention by "big business." The problem for the West Africans will be to reconcile their intense and very natural ambition for independence with the maintenance of sufficient British goodwill and material gain to continue the supply of capital and technical help.

10

THE GOLD COAST

No people in the world, I imagine, has such a passion and such a need to educate itself in a very short time as the people of the Gold Coast, and its expenditure on education has, in fact, risen from $2,083,200 in 1948 to $7,025,200 in 1952. By accident rather than by design, the Gold Coast is likely to become the first Black Dominion in the British Commonwealth, even earlier than near-by Nigeria with about seven times the population and about four times the area. It broke one record in 1946, when it became the first tropical African colony in which the majority of members of the Legislative Assembly was elected, and not nominated. Five years later it broke another record when it was granted an Executive Council—in other words, a government—in which eight ministers out of eleven are Africans, and a Legislative Assembly in which seventy-five out of eighty-four members are elected. Three of the remaining nine—

118

all of whom are Europeans—are members by reason of their office, and six are chosen to represent special interests in commerce and mining.

In the last eighteen months the number of Africans among the senior officials has been nearly doubled. Already almost a quarter of these senior officials are Africans. The Gold Coast is now establishing its own civil service, which comes under the authority not of Whitehall, but of the Governor. This local service includes all new African recruits, and also such Europeans and previously-recruited Africans as choose to join it.

These changes are due to the fact that a period of remarkable prosperity has coincided with the emergence of a remarkable African leader. This has permitted a lot of political experiments which would probably have been resisted in other and less favorable financial circumstances, and Dr. Nkrumah might not now be Prime Minister in Accra if the world demand for cocoa were not so phenomenally high. In British African territories, wherever there are crops grown on a large scale by African peasant farmers primarily for export, marketing boards buy the crop at less than the world market price and put the surplus into reserve funds, partly for purposes of research but mainly to cushion the producers against a sudden fall in world prices. Cocoa is so valuable that the reserves of the Gold Coast Cocoa Marketing Board are now roughly equal to five years of national revenue. The equivalent Board in Nigeria recently gave the University College of Ibadan $2,800,000 to endow the faculty of agriculture.

And coincident with this unexpected prosperity in the Gold Coast has been the rise of a determined and extremist political party whose slogans demanding "self-government now" may still be seen here and there on the buildings of Accra. Dr. Kwame Nkrumah, its leader, has been accused of Communism. A Commission of Inquiry into the colony's constitutional development, the Watson Commission, reported in June 1948 that his evidence before it showed that he "has not really departed one jot from his avowed aims for a Union of West African Soviet Socialist Republics." On the other hand, he declared emphatically during the election campaign that he had never been a Communist, but a Marxian Socialist.

All such terms acquire a new significance in an African colony where fewer than half the children can attend even a primary school. What does matter is that Mr. Nkrumah's party won a smashing victory in the elections of 1950, while he himself was in prison serving a sentence for sedition and incitement to an illegal strike. And also that, in view of this vote of the people, the Governor of the Gold Coast at once released him from prison and called on him to lead the new government.

Nkrumah had broken away in June 1949 from the United Gold Coast Convention Party, whose leader, Dr. Danquah, was already considered extreme in his demands for self-government. Nkrumah won support by concentrating his campaign for his own Convention People's Party on the villages. His red, white and green flags flew everywhere. He made still more extravagant demands and promises than his rival and former leader. People, for example, would travel free in the buses when he came into power. And his trouble is that his past tends to make him more extreme than his present will permit.

No country which depends for its prosperity upon exports can afford consistently to neglect or offend its markets, and well over one-third of the exports from the Gold Coast go to Great Britain. It is also from Great Britain that nearly all the capital for the development of the Gold Coast, as of Nigeria, must come. The Prime Minister has learned this lesson, but some of his followers have not yet done so. This frank and jovial young man talked to me in Accra with a moderation that he would himself have denounced most bitterly less than a year earlier. He would need the help and advice of the "expatriates" for years to come. He realized that his sudden transfer from prison to the Prime Minister's office must have caused alarm abroad, and he must allay that alarm, since the Gold Coast must have capital. . . . Nothing that he said to me could have caused offense to the most diehard imperialist—except that the things he was saying were said by a black Prime Minister!

He was merely saying the things he thought I would like him to say. Possibly, and yet I doubt it, for even while I was in the Colony he had a secret meeting with his leading officials —which, like all such functions in West Africa, at once became known in all its details—and told them very bluntly indeed that there must be more efficiency and less corruption. The truth seems to be that Dr. Nkrumah is learning very fast that power also involves responsibility.

He may be punished for his willingness to learn. The Convention People's Party is a mass movement, and masses seldom understand moderation. People find they must still pay to travel by bus, and his other wilder promises are coming home to roost; at the same time, the more conservative politicians whom he routed so thoroughly in the elections of 1951 have now got their second wind. In 1952 they formed the Ghana Congress Party—Ghana being claimed as the historic name for the Gold Coast. One great handicap to democracy in both the Gold Coast and Nigeria is that virtual self-government has come in advance of the formation of genuine political parties to provide alternative administrations. There is therefore the temptation for the Government to believe itself irreplaceable and to take dictatorial measures in order to become so, and for the opposition to try to oust it by extreme and discreditable methods.

I visited Accra very shortly after a visit to Southern Africa, and the Prime Minister questioned me very closely about "apartheid" in the Union, and federation between the Rhodesias and Nyasaland. It might be wise, he suggested, for him to organize an African campaign of protest against such developments. A man who has had such a spectacular success in his own country may be forgiven if he sometimes thinks of himself as a black Napoleon, destined to drive the white man out of Africa. But he would be well-advised, however, to concentrate his attention on the immensely difficult job of deciding how much nationalism he can afford without damaging the prospects of his nation. Both his party and the opposition, however, ended 1952 with demands that "Ghana" should be proclaimed a sovereign and independent state, with Queen Elizabeth II as its head, in the course of 1953. And one doubts whether such a demand, however understandable, will encourage the steady flow of foreign capital.

Cocoa, gold and manganese, mahogany, diamonds and bauxite—these are the principal exports upon which the Gold Coast must depend to pay for the rapid social progress to which Nkrumah and his colleagues aspire. And these exports must all pass through the one bottleneck of Takoradi harbor, or be taken out by Africans in surf boats through the great breakers that pound incessantly the coast of West Africa.

But one of the most ambitious schemes in the whole continent is being planned for the Gold Coast—always providing the capitalists whom Nkrumah's followers so berate can be persuaded to put up at least $112,000,000 toward the cost. The colony's reserves of bauxite, the ore of aluminum, are estimated at the fantastic figure of two hundred and twenty million tons. Much of it is in deep layers on the tops of hills, and is therefore easy to work. But there are difficulties of water, transport and power. The scheme, therefore, provides for a dam across the Volta River which would provide all three and, at the same time, would form probably the largest artificial lake in the world—some 240 miles in length. This lake, in turn, would solve part of the country's problem of communications with the Northern Territories, since it would make the river navigable over a great distance where there is now no railway and very little in the way of roads. The water power would be used mainly for an aluminum-smelting industry but also for irrigating a large area near Accra. Even should the Volta River scheme come to nothing, a new port will anyhow be built at Tema, nineteen miles from Accra, partly for the shipment of the ore, but also for the benefit of the Gold Coast as a whole.

This country, about the size of Great Britain with one-tenth of its population, is able to embark on the most ambitious development plan of any colony in the British Commonwealth —costing more than twice as much as the plan approved for Kenya and nearly one-third more than that approved for Nigeria. And, unlike Nigeria, which is to get $66,469,200 from the Colonial Development and Welfare Fund out of a total of $146,286,000, the Gold Coast expects to supply most of the money out of local resources—$136,614,800 out of a total of $209,574,800. Only $8,400,000 will come from C. D. and W. These sums do not include the cost of the Volta scheme, although the rest of the plan will have to be modified if the Volta scheme materializes. And how is the cost to be met? Partly from loans, but mainly from an additional export duty on cocoa. There could be no more impressive example of the dependence of the Colony upon exports and of the benefits that may come from them.

This is, perhaps, the best moment to explain that the use of the word "Colony" is strictly inaccurate, since each of these West African countries is divided into a coastal strip, which is the Colony, and the hinterland, which is a Protectorate. In the case of the Gold Coast there is the Gold Coast Colony, the Colony of Ashanti, the Northern Territories Protectorate and the Trusteeship Territory of British Togoland, now administered as though it were part of the Gold Coast, except that reports on its development are submitted to the Trusteeship Council of the United Nations.

Togoland is a geographical absurdity, for it is some 500 miles in length and only some sixty miles wide. All its tribes spread across into neighboring territory, and signposts to mark the border have little effect beyond causing the Africans some disquiet lest they should be handed over to some fresh group of white men with a fresh bunch of queer ideas. The other half of the former German colony of Togoland is under French administration, and a similar anomaly occurs in the case of the Cameroons, also divided after the first world war into mandates, the one administered from Nigeria and the other from French Equatorial Africa.

This is also, perhaps, the moment to make a comment which, as a former official of the League of Nations and a strong supporter of the United Nations, I make with the greatest reluctance, and it is that I have met no official in Africa who has had dealings with the Trusteeship Council of the United Nations and has retained the slightest respect for that body. Under the Mandates system of the League of Nations most of the members of the Mandates Commission were people who had had long experience of administering backward territories— Lord Lugard was for many years one of the members—and all of them were appointed as individuals with exceptional knowledge of the problem. They dealt conscientiously with petitions sent in from the Mandated territories, and the representative of the Mandatory Power had to face a very thorough cross-examination on the points raised by the petitioners.

Under the Trusteeship system of the United Nations, the members are representatives of governments, some of which have scarcely raised their own people above the colonial level and others of which have the clearest possible political motives for creating difficulties. More serious still, the procedure of discussing petitions in the relatively calm atmosphere of Geneva has largely been replaced by the dispatch of commissions of inquiry to the Trust Territories. Some of the members of some of these commissions have been quite shockingly inexperienced and morally inadequate. Their visit inevitably lessens the authority of the Trusteeship government; their behavior, or the behavior of some of them, equally inevitably lessens the respect of the Africans for the United Nations. Expert international advice and criticism should be very valuable in the administration of these territories, and might lead to closer co-ordination between the governments which, for one reason and another,

will have the great responsibility of guiding the Africans for
some years, decades or even generations; international political
interference of the kind allowed by the Trusteeship Council
seems to me mischievous as well as useless. The Council consists of members administering Trust Territories and of an
equal number of non-administering members. The Soviet Union, as a Permanent Member of the Security Council, is also a
Permanent Member of the Trusteeship Council. In 1952,
other members included Siam, Irak, El Salvador and the Do-
minican Republic.

It would be silly to pretend that the aluminium companies
which have been considering the possibility of the Volta River
scheme have been solely interested in the welfare of the Africans, or even that the British Government would have considered the possibility of finding a large contribution to it for
this consideration alone. That contribution could much more
usefully be spent on the technical and administrative training
of Africans, or on half a dozen other ways of raising the
standards of the people. But it has been one of my purposes in
this book to emphasize that there must be a two-way traffic if
Africa is to catch up in a reasonably short period with continents that have had a start of several centuries. Unless there is
to be a period of revolutions, followed by a climb toward
prosperity which would be appallingly slow in countries with
so little in the way of industry and technical know-how, there
must be co-operation with the outside world.

Although great concerns such as the United Africa Company,
which has interests of every kind along the West Coast, have
developed good social services for their African workers, the
international conscience will no longer leave so much responsibility in private hands, and the problem is to work out the
best co-operation through governmental agencies. And one reason why British taxpayers' money is likely to be available for
the Gold Coast in such quantities is that this colony is one of
the greatest dollar-earners. Cocoa, manganese, diamonds and

gold can all be sold in America, and the Volta River scheme may mean that in six or seven years aluminium will also be earning dollars in a big way.

At present cocoa accounts for more than seventy per cent of the country's exports, and it is cocoa that has provided the greatest test of Dr. Nkrumah's statesmanship. The trees have been attacked by a disease called swollen shoot, for which, until recently, the only cure has been the drastic one of cutting down infected trees. But the cocoa is grown by hundreds of thousands of small peasant farmers—the very men who put Nkrumah's party into power—and one can imagine their bitter dislike of the compulsory cutting-out policy when one remembers the unpopularity in Great Britain of the policy of slaughtering cattle to check foot-and-mouth disease. In August 1951, against the advice of British experts, the Government withdrew its compulsory order; perhaps some less drastic policy would do the job instead.

But more and more trees dried up and died. The disease has gained ground in an alarming way. The great cocoa buyers began to wonder whether and where they could find alternative producers, and the end of the foreign demand for cocoa would be the end of the prosperity of the Gold Coast, which, in turn, would be the end of the social developments that have brought so much popularity to the country's first African Government.

In October 1952, the Prime Minister announced that compulsory cutting-out was to be resumed. This, he claimed, was in response to the requests of the great majority of farmers. "The minority," he had previously declared, "will not be allowed to persist in opposition to control measures which are the will of the majority." One may wonder when and how this majority has expressed its will. But the important fact is that this first African Government in any British territory has found the courage to choose a definitely unpopular policy in the long-term interests of the country.

11

HOME FROM THE COAST

For the last time I drove along the Marina and through the slums of Lagos. Past the one-roomed beer and wine stores made of old petrol tins, stray bits of wood, palm leaves and rusty corrugated iron. Past the "Easy Life Barber" and the "All Well Medicine Store." Across the congested bridge to the mainland and past the slaughter-house, with the skinny cattle awaiting the grim termination of their thousand-mile trek from the north. Out to Apapa, and the white ship, the one trim and tidy object in a chaos of cranes and bare-footed porters and piles of luggage and great blocks of concrete waiting to be placed under the water where the new wharf is to be built.

We steamed slowly past the Marina, past Government House with people on its balconies waving farewell to the retiring Lieutenant-Governor of the Eastern Region, past the jetty from which I had set out on my one essay in tarpon fishing, past the Yacht Club . . .

And there, in the gardens of the Yacht Club, was a military band of the Royal West African Frontier Force, lined up to play a Hausa farewell to the Lieutenant-Governor. I wondered how the participants in this moving little ceremony felt—the British civil servant going home to comparative obscurity, rationing and washing-up, at the end of a distinguished career of instruction to the Blacks how to get rid of the Whites; the African soldiers, so proud of their uniforms and their service, saying good-bye to one more of these white masters. And I recalled an article written by J. H. Huizinga, the Dutch journalist, in an admirable series published by the *Manchester Guardian* some years ago. I had put it aside at the time, and later discovered it among the thousands of cuttings I don't want to lose but never know what to do with.

He deplored—as to Elspeth Huxley and other writers who know Africa well and love it—the haste with which we are ridding ourselves of responsibilities which we created, by opening up the continent in the first place, and he questioned the fine, democratic arguments with which we justify our action. "There is," he wrote, "an extraordinary lack of correspondence between the measure of self-government accorded to the different subject peoples and their apparent qualifications for it." The French Moroccans, for example, have had centuries of contact with Western civilization, and the British may proudly point out to the French that people in British African territories, with scarcely more than two generations of that contact, are now accorded far more control over their own affairs than are the Moroccans. But the British cannot afford to feel self-righteous unless they are absolutely convinced that their policy of "emancipation through disintegration" of the British Empire is going to lead to greater prosperity and contentment among its peoples than the French policy of "emancipation through integration," of raising up an African *élite* which helps to run not only its own country, but also the government of Metropolitan France."

"We have had rule by quality in Europe," wrote Huizinga, "however roughly the quality was determined, for two thou-

sand years. We have it no longer. We have forsworn the aristocratic principle in favor of counting noses. It seems to me that,
in the moment of doing so, we put 'paid' to our imperial mission. I cannot help thinking that the democratic colonial rule
is faced with an insoluble dilemma. It seems to me . . . that
the advance of a 'primitive' people toward fitness for self-
government, depending as it does on the gradual spread of
education and prosperity, proceeds in something like arith-
metic progression, whereas the pressures for self-government
seem bound to increase in a geometric progression."

Even those of us who do not share Huizinga's regrets that a
democratic principle should be replacing the aristocratic one
must, if we are honest about it, feel a little humiliated when we
reflect how much we are being influenced in Africa not by high-
minded respect for the human personality, but by the ability
of a few politically-minded Africans to make life uncomfortable
for us. I am convinced that many of the British civil servants
who resist the rapid emancipation of the Africans are far more
genuinely interested in the welfare of the individual African
than are many of the British politicians who are determined to
push ahead with emancipation, however unready the individual
African may be for it.

The Hausa soldiers, now far behind us, marched away, and
the officers, who had stood so rigidly at attention, became human again, and waved their farewells. We steamed out past the
evil-looking mangrove swamp to the open sea.

The Nigerians have a reputation along the "Coast" for snob-
bishness. This is due in part to the ease with which one can
make bad rhymes with the use of "Nigeria" and "superior,"
but more to the fact that they supervise and serve so large and
populous a country. But I am inclined to think that this
reputation is also linked with the fact that Nigeria is at the end
of the Elder Dempster run. We, the passengers from Lagos, had
barely had time to choose our favorite table in the smoking-
room, our favorite corner on deck, when a horde of strangers

arrived on board at the Gold Coast port of Takoradi. They invaded the swimming pool and gossiped in the lounge about an entirely new set of people. They were at least as busy, they let us understand, in extending the wharves at Takoradi as we were in extending the wharves at Apapa. And we rather obviously took a poor view of them.

One sensed something of the rivalry which turns everybody into an Oxford or a Cambridge fan on boat race day, however exiguous their links with either University. (I once, in my League of Nations days, accompanied to Chiswick the members of an international conference of experts on double income tax, and before the race was over they were strongly, almost bitterly, divided.) On the least excuse, the Gold Coasters would tell you how greatly superior their Achimota University College (which is not Achimota any more, since it has been removed to Legon Hill a few miles away) was to Ibadan University College, in Nigeria. Their exports earned proportionately far more dollars than those of the other West African Colonies. A few African passengers moved to and fro—oblivious of the way in which the Europeans were boasting about their countries, smiling, very humble now that they were so far away from the vehemence of the newspapers of Lagos and Accra.

But the Nigerians and the Gold Coasters united when we anchored off Freetown. Its very name reminded one of its origin—it was founded, like Monrovia, the capital of Liberia, the one independent African republic, by liberated slaves. In the case of Freetown, these ex-slaves were sent out from Britain, America and Jamaica a century and a half ago, and the authorities of the day obligingly added a few white prostitutes. Later a naval squadron had been stationed at Freetown to intercept slave ships, and thousands of liberated slaves from various parts of Africa had also settled here. It really wasn't the sort of place I should want to visit, my fellow-passengers told me, and in any case it had one of the heaviest rainfalls of any place in the world.

The inhabitants of Sierra Leone do not at all feel that way about their capital. Immediately behind Freetown there are

great hills covered with vegetation as rich and varied as that
of Hong Kong, and they have one of the finest bathing beaches
of the Coast. Their Fourah Bay College, affiliated to Durham
University since 1876, attracts many students from other West
African territories. In common with Lagos and Takoradi, they
are building new deep water wharves. At Marampa they have
at least twelve million tons of high-grade iron ore which can be
mined by open-cast methods and shipped quite easily overseas,
and large supplies of diamonds. And, they tell you proudly,
they frequently need blankets on their beds at night. Yes, it
does rain a lot, but you get used to it, and people go round
the town carrying those multi-colored umbrellas that one sometimes sees on golf courses in Britain. Drake and Hawkins both
called here and, during the last war, some of the largest convoys ever seen assembled at Freetown. The *Queen Mary* has
anchored within earshot of the shore.

The divergencies between people who live along the coast
and those of the interior are far greater in Sierra Leone and
the neighboring Republic of Liberia than in the Gold Coast and
Nigeria. Nobody thought much of the desires of the established
inhabitants when plans were drawn up to send the liberated
African slaves back to Africa, and the gap between them, between the Protectorate and the Colony, has never been entirely
bridged. However, the People's Party, which stands for the integration of Colony and Protectorate, easily defeated the more
exclusive National Council at the elections in 1951. The Creoles of the Coast, with their fine features and golden-brown
skins, are extremely beautiful, and they have retained some
of the leisurely courtesy of the nineteenth century. This means
that they are less urgent and less extreme in their political demands than are the coast dwellers of Nigeria and the Gold
Coast, for any kind of system based on the counting of noses
would place them in a minority. Even the Krus, the tribesmen
who lived along the coast before the arrival of the liberated
slaves, have little understanding of the tribesmen of the interior; they live on and by the sea, and must be among the finest seamen in the world—the Commodore of the Elder Demp-

ster line tells me that he has seen their little dugout canoes up
to ninety miles from the shore, and the agility with which the
men who dive for money circled our ship in their bark canoes,
with the help of a kind of scoop that can also be used for baling,
has to be seen to be believed.

But it was in Bathurst, the capital of the Gambia, that I
wondered most about the call of the West Coast. It is built on
what is little more than a sandbank, selected in 1816 as a
military control post for the suppression of the slave trade. Indeed, it lies so low that it has suffered from frequent flooding,
despite an ambitious scheme now being carried out to drain
away the water. Its best road is separated from a fine beach
by an immense cemetery. On the other side of the road is a
mangrove swamp. Compared with Nigeria, the Gold Coast
and even Sierra Leone, the Gambia, with no considerable export except groundnuts, is poor and primitive, and the Old
Coasters lined the ship's rail and looked pityingly—almost contemptuously—at its palm trees and slightly decaying early
Victorian architecture.

And yet I wonder. There is great dignity about these early
Victorian colonial-style buildings, appropriately sited round
the cricket field. There is a mixed club—white and black—
which I am assured is still more successful than the Island
Club in Lagos. There are no political demands—the Government is granting them before they can be formulated. And for
nine months in the year the weather is like that of an English
summer at its best. I asked a senior official where he would
live at home when the time came for him to retire, and he
looked at me almost with surprise. "Nowhere. The Gambia is
my home," he told me, as though no alternative was even
worthy of consideration.

The Colony of the Gambia consists of Bathurst and its very
short strip of coast. The Protectorate stretches three hundred
miles inland for about ten miles on either side of the river that
gives the country its name. In the Colony, as in the Colony of
Sierra Leone, there is a strong element of Creoles, proud,
touchy, and extremely beautiful. Many of them are descended

from Negroes of the West Indian Regiment who were given land a century ago on condition that they remained on the reserve in case of emergency. The women of the Wollof tribe parade the streets of Bathurst wearing immense and fantastic head-dresses of dyed lambs' wool crowned by a strip of some very bright material. They cannot, therefore, carry burdens on their heads, as do almost all the women of Africa. They carry them by hand, but they do so with their arms bent almost double and their open palms facing upward on a level with their shoulders, like waiters carrying trays in a restaurant. They probably looked just as majestic in the days when the first Queen Elizabeth of England granted the merchants of London and Devon the sole right to trade with the Gambia, or when James, Duke of York, formed, in 1660, the company of "Royal Adventurers Trading to Africa."

Up the river the population is almost entirely Moslem, with the tribes related to those other Moslems in Northern Nigeria, the Northern Territories of the Gold Coast, and the vast Moslem areas of French Sudan and Senegal. Ornaments found in the Gambia and Senegal show that migrants from Egypt must have reached the Atlantic Coast here during the eleventh and twelfth centuries. It is doubtless absurd that there should be this thin strip of British territory in the middle of French African territory, but its Governor is one of the happiest men in the Colonial Service—his territory is small enough for him to maintain contact with its people and there is still a warm friendship between European and African.

Too many officials in the ship were going home for good. Too many of the Europeans now coming out to West Africa are men on contract to do one particular job and then to go home again. Too few young men are coming into a service where politics make the prospect so uncertain. Too few of the Africans who come over to study in Great Britain will become administrators when they return home—indeed, one of the serious complaints of the Gold Coast is that quite a lot of these students, especially those who become doctors, fail to return at all; they stay on in Britain.

And there are so many projects to be carried through if the real earnings of the Africans are to keep pace with their ambitions or even their most urgent needs. I found overworked white officials who talked with enthusiasm about their schemes —the Gonja project in the Gold Coast, where Africans are being brought to almost uninhabited areas, are each given two or three acres of their own, and have to look after another twenty-seven acres, half of the produce of which becomes their property. There is a similar project at Mokwa, in Nigeria. But always one hears the same complaints—shortage of trained and trustworthy personnel, reluctance of the African to learn new methods of cultivation, more and more land losing its fertility.

In one of his despatches to the Secretary of State for the Colonies in 1947, Sir Philip Mitchell, then Governor of Kenya, wrote this: "The major problem can be stated simply and plainly by saying that an ignorant man and his wife with a hoe are a totally inadequate foundation for an enlightened society, a high standard of living and elaborate social services, and that unless an alternative foundation, capable of bearing these things, can be devised, or, when it exists, can be expanded, a great deal of modern talking and writing about colonial development and welfare is moonshine."

Or, to quote Elspeth Huxley: "Certainly most Africans (though not all) want the outward benefits of civilization; better houses, finer clothes, literacy, European food, the status of an 'educated man': but as yet many have not counted the cost, and we cannot be sure that they will be willing to pay when it is brought home to them in full. For he who would be civilized, even outwardly, must give as well as receive. If Africans are to be freed from hook-worm, illiteracy and black magic, they must give up also the dance after harvest, the bride-price bargaining, the day-long beer-drink under the tree."

One would feel so much more optimistic about the future of West Africa if these benefits of civilization were dependent not upon the high world price of cocoa and other exports, but upon African experience, enterprise and hard work. "So much to do," said Cecil Rhodes on his deathbed, "so little done."

The white ship slid out of the muddy waters of the Gambia River into the blue-black Atlantic, and steamed northward for home. In the saloon the "Old Coasters" drank cheerfully to their three months of leave in Britain. But, their leave over, many of them will have been up on deck, anxious to see again the palm trees and the mangrove of the Coast.

12

LAND OF THE FREE

The one Black Republic in Africa is nearly as depressing and significant a warning as is the move toward a White Republic in the Union of South Africa. This State, founded in 1821 with so proud a name and with a capital named after President Monroe, has so definitely failed to fulfil the hopes expressed for it. It seemed right and romantic that the liberated American slaves should return to the continent where their ancestors had been marched along jungle tracks in chains, to be herded into the dark and stinking holds of ships and sent across an immense ocean. Working on the cotton plantations in a strange country, they had sung sad little songs which passed on from one generation to another the embellished memory of their homeland.

During the American Civil War so many slaves fled to the north from the southern States that they began to create a serious social and political problem. They could not be sent back against their will, and they were certainly not wanted in the north. Sailors from Dieppe and, later, from Portugal had visited the Pepper Coast between what is now Sierra Leone and Cape Palmas, but nobody had found it worth while to lay serious claim to this land. The surf, the rocks, the sandbanks, the unfriendly Natives and the feverish climate had combined to give the place a very well-deserved reputation for inhospitality. It was not an ideal home for the liberated slaves, but it was better than nothing. Or at least it was thought to be so. And the American Colonization Society even sent a dozen white technicians with the first party of black ex-slaves to help them build their houses and start their plantations. It was a small but sincere attempt to make amends for the crime of enslavement.

Land for the first settlement of eighty-eight liberated slaves, whose *Mayflower* in reverse reached Africa in 1822, was bought with an odd variety of goods—beads, rum, hats, muskets, knives, iron bars, shoes and so on—to the value of some $40. Other settlements were established, but they were separated from each other by hostile tribes. Fevers caused heavy casualties, and the grant of civil rights to Negroes at the end of the American Civil War soon dried up the trickle of Africans who might otherwise have been anxious to return to the continent of their origin. Even to-day, after more than 130 years, Liberia has only some 22,000 Americanized Africans and 40,000 indigenous Africans who, having been converted to Christianity and classified as "civilized," are on the side of the ex-slaves against the tribes of the hinterland.

The first African president of this new State declared its independence in 1847. A proud year. But the tragic fact about Liberia is that these descendants of slaves have themselves carried on with slave-trading. In 1930, the Liberian Government appealed to the League of Nations to inquire into allegations of slavery in its country, but even its request for the inquiry contained these rather startling admissions: "It will be easily understood that an inveterate scourge cannot be extirpated root and branch in the space of a few years. However, owing to the energetic measures taken by my Government during the last twenty-five years, the practice of slavery and forced labor has, little by little, been considerably diminished, and it can be asserted to-day that slavery and forced labor are no longer practiced in principle as a normal social system in Liberia."

This request was followed by one for financial help, without which the Government could not enforce the ban on slavery, and conditions had become so bad that the Scottish doctor who was sent out by the League in advance of the Commission of Inquiry found that the first task put upon him was to stop a war, in the course of which the people from nearly all the Kru villages along the coast had fled into the bush. By imposing taxes the backwoods Natives could not pay, the Liberian Government was providing itself with an immense supply of forced labor. When the financial situation made it advisable, slaves were exported to the Spanish colony of Fernando Po, a thousand miles down the coast.

The League Commission of Inquiry made some strange discoveries. For example, that the interest on foreign loans absorbed sixty-seven per cent of the national revenue and that in 1929 the appropriation for military bands had been greater than the expenditure on the people's health. Its report on conditions was so unfavorable that the British and American Governments ceased to have any diplomatic relations with the Republic. And the scheme of financial reconstruction which the League prepared called for such drastic reforms that the Liberians turned it down.

There has been a very considerable improvement in the last fifteen years or so. It seems that there is now virtually no slavery. The dignified colonial-style houses built in Monrovia in the early days of the Republic are now less dilapidated and fewer of their roofs are made of rusty corrugated iron. There are forty-five miles of railway and a dial telephone service. But wages are far lower than in any British West African colony. The demands for labor from the Firestone Company, formerly very excessive, are far more moderate, and the company's rubber accounts for about ninety per cent of all Liberia's exports and for twenty per cent of its national revenue. During the war the Americans built an enormous airport which now belongs to the Liberian government, and they gave Monrovia one of the finest harbors on the west coast, so that people and goods no longer have to come ashore in open boats through the surf.

This harbor is under the control of an American development company. A third company, which may in time rival the Firestone in importance, is the Liberia Mining Company, which built the country's one railway to the Bomi Hills. The company is now exporting the richest iron ore in the world. Tin, lead, copper and gold are also reported. So Liberia, under American guidance but without loss of independence, seems to be on the road to prosperity.

Even politically there has been some improvement, for there were more than 300,000 voters in the elections held in May 1951. The provinces of the interior may now each elect one of the twenty-five members of the House of Representatives. According to *Africa South of the Sahara*, "The President and all members of the Executive and Legislature are members of the True Whig Party." The True Whigs, in fact, have been in power for more than sixty years and are likely to remain there for some time to come. Each civil servant "voluntarily" subscribes one month's salary to the party funds, and this subscription is generally deducted at source—it's easier and surer that way. Bearing in mind the measures to limit the non-European voters in South Africa, one reads with a certain wry amusement that the constitution insists that "Electors must be of Negro blood."

It is understandable, but grossly unfair, that Liberia should be compared with those other countries in Africa where black men are taking over control. The white South African talks disparagingly of the Gold Coast, but the African in the Gold Coast talks disparagingly of Liberia. Nor were the Liberians

much helped in their early years by their British and French
neighbors, who were not very pleased to see part of Africa
governed by Africans. And one does need to remember that
the Americo-Liberians were slaves who had never had the
slightest experience of responsibility. Advice would have been
perhaps even more valuable to them than money; they received
very little of either. The American Colonization Society doubtless had the finest motives in repatriating these slaves and
they must of course be excused for their ignorance of the conditions which the slaves would have to face. But it was, in
effect, a cruel act.

There may be some cruelty in the decision of the British
Government to hand over so much power to the Africans in
the Gold Coast and Nigeria while the overwhelming majority
can neither read nor write. There are some who would argue
that the cruelty lies in postponing the transfer of power, since
they are black men's countries, and should therefore be ruled
by black men. History will decide. But meanwhile, as I have
explained elsewhere in this book, British officials with long experience are still there in the background, ready to advise and
help. There are enough differences between one white man's
government and another to show the injustice of predicting for
the Gold Coast a future similar to that of Liberia, merely because both governments are run by black men. And the tragedy for Liberia is that it has hitherto been too poor to give its
people those chances of education toward democracy which
the Gold Coast, with five times the national revenue, is doing
for its children.

Nor should one underestimate the changes in Liberia itself.
The present President, Mr. William Tubman, used strangely
undemocratic methods to assure his re-election at the end of
1950, and he is surrounded with a pomp which his country
cannot afford. But he is genuinely popular, and lets himself be
carried in a hammock to parts of the interior which few senior
officials have ever visited. It is greatly to his credit that the
national revenue was more than quadrupled from 1950 to 1951.

Liberia proposes to spend well over $28,000,000 on economic and social development within the next decade, and twenty per cent of the budget will be used for this purpose. What the Liberians cannot pay will come from the United States under ex-President Truman's "Fourth Point." Perhaps, led by Mr. Tubman, the Land of the Free will now become worthy of the men, black and white, who faced such hardships and dangers to establish it a hundred and thirty-four years ago.

13

FRENCH AFRICA

In the interval between the grapefruit and the breakfast egg I peered out of the window. Twenty thousand feet below us lay Africa. French Equatorial Africa. We were passing over dense forest, but from our height the trees were a uniform, dull gray. Beneath the very thin veil of cloud they looked like small pebbles at the bottom of a clear stream.

For most of the night we had been flying over French Africa—first, the Sahara and now the tropical forest. The first white man to cross that desert to Timbuktu had needed 1,400 camels and 75 days for the journey. That was in 1822. The country below us had been almost as difficult to penetrate, so that the immense French territory is very sparsely populated. Leaving out of account North Africa, where the non-Europeans are much more closely related to Asia than to the rest of the continent on which they live, one finds that French West Africa covers very nearly 1,800,000 square miles and has
142

about 16,000,000 inhabitants, while French Equatorial Africa, which lay below us, covers nearly a million square miles, with about four and a half million people. The largest British Colony, Nigeria, has only 225,000 square miles and some 25,-000,000 inhabitants. The French rule over an area of Black Africa considerably larger than ten times that of Metropolitan France.

"In thirty seconds," said the captain over the inter-com., "we shall cross the equator. You will clearly see its white line crossing the jungle from West to East." The Greek family crowded to the windows. The Belgian woman who was going out with her small son to join her husband in Leopoldville was most indignant when I suggested that the captain might be having his little joke. It must be there, she argued, because it was marked on the little map of Africa she had torn out of some school atlas.

I wondered about the people who lived on the equator below us. They belonged to an unbelievable mixture of tribes who had drifted in at different times from Egypt and beyond, and had all but eliminated the pygmies who were apparently the original inhabitants of this huge area of Africa. Their country is so thinly inhabited not only because the forest is so dense, but because, until so recently, slave-raiders had made their way even through this forest and had taken the young people away. Some had been marched down to the coast to be shipped to North or South America, since the slave trade had been quite respectable until the end of the eighteenth century. But others had been taken—and much more recently—to the Moslem kingdoms that had formed a wide barrier, from the Atlantic coast to the Nile, between the Sahara and Black Africa.

Not very far to the north of us was Lake Chad, forty-two times as large as the Lake of Geneva. And it was from Lake Chad that General Leclerc's army had set out to help in the struggle in North Africa against the Nazis and the Fascists. Natives from these areas had fought on all the fronts in Western Europe. Probably the few tribesmen living in the jungle below us had long since ceased to wonder at our shining forty-five tons creeping across the vault of the sky. They had seen more fantastic things than that.

The aircraft lost height and we tightened our safety belts. Ahead of us was a zig-zagging, shining streak. The River Congo, wide and placid. For this was Stanley Pool, above the rapids and more than a thousand miles below Stanley Falls. And, facing each other across the river are two towns, Brazzaville, capital of French Equatorial Africa, and Leopoldville, capital of the Belgian Congo, as unlike as two neighboring towns whose people speak the same language could possibly be.

French Equatorial Africa is five times the size of Metropolitan France, with little more than double the population of Paris. It is in many ways shockingly backward, for, until fairly recently, a few private companies had the sole rights to exploit its resources, and the exploitation that took place fully merited the derogatory sense which is attached to the English use of the word. The State took fifteen per cent of the companies' profits, obtained by paying the lowest possible prices for native produce and charging the highest prices for goods the Natives had to buy. In 1927 André Gide wrote of it that it was destined to be one of the richest and most profitable colonies, but was in fact the worst and most neglected.

This system was as uneconomic as it was cruel. Under the French variant of the British Colonial Development and Welfare Corporation, considerable sums are now being spent in Equatorial Africa, mostly on communications. Even so, its people include some of the most backward in all the continent and expenditure on native education is less than one per cent of the total expenditure of the State; it is only natural that most help should go to those territories that will most profit from it. Apart from timber and cotton, the cultivation of which has enormously developed in the last decade, Equatorial Africa still has little to export that the world greatly needs. One should, perhaps, make an exception in the case of Gabon, one of the colonies that makes up Equatorial Africa, for it shares with

Spanish Guinea, its neighbor to the north, the monopoly of a special kind of ebony. With its cocoa and its gold, it has a shortage of man-power, and it imports whole families of workers from Eastern Nigeria, with a British Vice-Consul to see that they are well-treated.

Roads are being built to the colonies of the interior, and sooner or later immense quantities of timber will find their way down to the coast for export; before the war, Africa, despite her huge forests, used to import five times as much as it exported! But Equatorial Africa is still looked upon by the French as a very grim place to which to be posted, and, since French civil servants are never well paid, the best Frenchmen are unlikely to be found there, except around Lake Chad and in the Trust Territory of the French Cameroons, where the administration appears to be admirable.

Negley Farson, who drove through this country just before the war, has some very harsh things to say about the officials in Equatorial Africa. But these men, whose ambition was to retire to some small villa in France where they could live humbly on their small pensions, nevertheless rejected Pétain's surrender to the Germans. "I think these men," he writes, "who have willingly accepted exile from France, temporary or final, are possibly the most gallant Frenchmen I have ever seen. For their bravery is not the act of a moment, or of things done in company; it is just the bitter resolution to stay out of France until they and the British can take it back from the Germans. And that's long-distance courage." [1]

The long-distance courage has since been rewarded, and the four colonies which constitute French Equatorial Africa each elect five members to the Governor-General's Grand Council in Brazzaville, and deputies to both houses of the French Parliament in Paris. The would-be political leader Khus has outlets for his ambitions which make his demands for complete independence very much less strident than in the British colonies in West Africa.

Until 1946 the twenty million Africans in French Equatorial

[1] *Behind God's Back* (Victor Gollancz).

and West Africa were "subjects"; since that year France has
followed the example of the Emperor Caracalla, in the third
century, who gave the rights of "citizen" to all inhabitants of
the Roman Empire. This change is not likely to make much
difference to the African in the bush, but there is an African
majority in the Brazzaville Grand Council. In Dakar, the capital city of French West Africa, the whole staff of the Grand
Council and also of the Dakar municipality is black. Only three
out of the thirty-six members of the City Council are Europeans, and the Lord Mayor is not one of them.

French West Africa—the western bulge of Africa—has been
much more favored than Equatorial Africa both by Nature
and by successive French Governments. Not only must Dakar
become an increasingly valuable airport for transatlantic traffic,
but the seven colonies of which it is the capital are rapidly
growing in economic value. It now has one of the finest universities in Africa, and its Institut de l'Afrique Noire (I.F.A.N.)
is making an admirable effort to interest the Africans in their
own history, and therefore less anxious to copy blindly and in-
effectually everything that is European. Many of the men who
are running West Africa were in the Resistance Movement during the war and they have visions of a greater France in the
future.

And they have great resources awaiting development. Immense supplies of bauxite and iron ore are within easy reach
of Dakar or Conakry, in French Guinea, a few hundred miles
farther south. At Abidjan, on the Ivory Coast, they have just
opened a new port, as artificial but as valuable as the port
of Takoradi, on the neighboring Gold Coast. It lies in a
lagoon which has been opened to the sea by a canal cut through
the great bar of sand which stretches for hundreds of miles,
roughly from Cape Verde to the Gold Coast. The first canal was
cut in 1906, but, in common with several subsequent attempts,
it was soon silted up by the great breakers that beat along

this coast. The present canal was made after more than a year of experiments with a model.

The ease with which aircraft cross the Sahara has for the moment made talk of a railroad seem old-fashioned. But a railway to Timbuktu has been under discussion and investigation for the last ninety years or so, and in the course of studying the various projects various mineral deposits of great value have been discovered. During the German occupation of Metropolitan France the French pushed the railway southward from Oran to Colomb Bechar, which opens up new coalfields. One reads of the largest deposits of phosphates in the world, of zinc and copper. The French territory to the north of the Gold Coast—French Sudan and Upper Volta—might produce rice and cotton in great quantities if it were properly irrigated, and if the railway were there to take it down to the coast at Dakar, Conakry or Abidjan. It is claimed that a Trans-Sahara railway would no longer be alarmingly costly to build since there would be few bridges and it would run mainly over flat ground. It seems quite probable that the great waste known as the Sahara —roughly the size of Europe without Scandinavia—will turn out to be one of the most valuable reservoirs of those minerals that our civilization requires in ever-increasing quantities.

The ordinary little Frenchman sitting outside his café on the Grande Place of his home town is, of course, still more interested in North Africa than in these huge territories south of the Sahara for which he is responsible. North Africa barely comes within the scope of a book mainly about white-black relationships. The struggle there between Europeans and Africans bears astonishing resemblance to the struggle between Europeans and Africans at the southern end of the continent. But in this case the Africans are not black. Indeed, most of them are not even Africans, except that the arrival of their ancestors from Asia or other Mediterranean countries took place a long time ago.

In French North Africa there is a settled white population
—over a million and a half—as against an African population of nearly twenty millions. The proportion of European to
African is thus much smaller than in the Union, but the French
are geographically so close to their own motherland that they
not unnaturally look upon North Africa almost as an extension
of France. This is particularly the case in Algeria. When the
French landed there in 1830—partly in the hope of putting an
end to the Barbary pirates and partly because the Dey of Algiers had slapped the French Consul's face with his fly-swatter
—they found a chaotic country in which the authority of the
Turks had almost entirely disappeared and that of local chiefs
was uncertain and ephemeral. Their campaign lasted some
seventeen years, but since 1881 the country has been treated
more and more as a part of Metropolitan France; it now sends
fourteen Senators and thirty Deputies to Paris. Nowhere else
in Africa has the French technique of "assimilation"—in contrast to the British technique of education for autonomy—been
carried so far.

Tunisia and Morocco, on the other hand, are Protectorates,
governed—at least in name—by a Bey and a Sultan belonging
to ancient dynasties. In both of them the demand for a
greater degree of democratic government has coincided with
the growth of nationalism, and has turned against the French
—to such an extent, in the case of Morocco, that the Sultan
himself periodically expresses his support for it. Whether, in
fact, he would prefer to deal with the Istiqlal than with the
French Resident-General is very doubtful. But his policy is a
fairly obvious one—to demand concessions of the French
which he knows will not be granted.

His resentment is explained by the fact that, until 1912, his
country had been unconquered for over a thousand years, and
the French Protectorate has, in effect, involved a conquest of
the whole country. Nine out of ten senior officials nominally in
his service are Frenchmen.

On the other hand, in the early years of this century, the
power of the Sultan had dwindled to a small area around Fez,

and an international conference was held at Algeciras in 1906 in order to seek agreement on ways of putting an end to the dangerous chaos. And the French can claim that, without them, the whole economic apparatus would collapse. The example of that great man, Marshal Lyautey, has continued to inspire the officials, and they have, quite literally, made the desert blossom, as nobody has done in South Africa. The Moroccans—and also the Tunisians—give the reply which the Indians were wont to give the British, namely that, if they are so unready to take over the administration the fault must be that of their rulers. Besides, it seems to them absurd—as indeed it is—that Libya, whose 1,200,000 people are so much more backward, should have been given their independence, and they take it far too much for granted that the United Nations or the United States would see them through the difficult period after the departure of the French, as they are seeing the Libyans through their teething troubles.

Immense investments have been made in these countries, particularly in Morocco, and immense supplies are coming out of them. The output of Moroccan phosphates is now nearly five hundred times what it was thirty years ago. Coal, manganese, iron, lead, zinc and other minerals are being exported in rapidly increasing quantities, and, as I have already tried to show, the economic development of the Sahara is still in its early stages. Casablanca, which the experts told Marshal Lyautey could never be given a properly protected harbor, is now the fourth largest port in the French Union and, even so, is too small for its trade. Its population has grown from 82,500 in 1912 to 600,000, and there must be very few cities in the world where huge office buildings are being erected at greater speed or in greater numbers. Hydro-electric and irrigation schemes in the Atlas mountains are adding greatly to the country's wealth. The national revenue to-day is more than four times what it was at the end of the war. And the population has risen from three and a half millions in 1912 to more than nine millions at the present time.

In view of this spectacular progress, it is not astonishing that the French should be both alarmed by the extreme nationalism of the Istiqlal party in Morocco and the Neo-Destour movement in Tunisia, and depressed by a sense of Arab ingratitude. But in 1916, Lyautey wrote of Morocco: "We are in the presence of a political, religious and economic élite which it would be foolish to ignore, to misunderstand and not to use." Since Tunis and Morocco have been dragged into French party politics even more than Kenya has been made a political issue in the House of Commons, one fears that the time to use this élite has passed. Until recently the censorship in Morocco was so severe that the Istiqlal has sometimes called "le Parti Blanc," so great were the spaces left blank by the censor.

Possibly the sensible long-term policy would still be one of concessions to a nationalism that must grow stronger under suppression. The kind of policy the British carried out in India, Pakistan and Ceylon. But, as in the case of Southern Rhodesia, the white settlers are too numerous and too powerful to be overridden in any matter of Native political progress. Indeed, in Morocco and Tunisia there are more than five times as many Europeans as in Southern Rhodesia.

Nevertheless, two factors give North Africa a far better chance than South Africa of coming peacefully through this crisis of growth. One is that, despite the backwardness of the masses, they are far more "Europeanized" than the Natives in South Africa have been allowed to become. Neither the Istiqlal in Morocco nor the Neo-Destour in Tunisia is really a Pan-Arab movement, although the Arab and Moslem members of the United Nations have brought the attitude of the French Government to the attention of that organization. In Tunisia, most of the Neo-Destour propaganda emphasizes the Western cultural traditions of the Tunisians which, it claims, existed long before the arrival of the French on the scene. The Moroccans, of course, have been linked far more closely with Spain, for example, than with Arabia. Most of the Istiqlal leaders have been educated in France, and many of them have French wives.

The French settlers have doubtless hindered the grant of

reasonable concessions which might possibly have checked the Nationalist campaigns. But they are entitled to claim that at least the Istiqlal movement is almost entirely urban, and that they themselves produce most of the food that keeps the growing North African population alive or is exported to pay for necessary imports. And the French administration has organized several admirable schemes to show, by example, how modern methods of cultivation can increase the output of the land. Istiqlal, by associating itself so closely with a feudal-minded Sultan, has weakened itself in the rural areas.

Tunisia, on the other hand, is a more united country than Morocco, and Neo-Destour has much wider support. Most civil service posts are now being filled by Tunisians, despite the tough and bitter resistance of the minor white officials, who are not members of the regular French colonial civil service and who therefore have a strong vested interest in maintaining white domination. In any case, Neo-Destour wants an entirely Tunisian Legislative Assembly to which the Government would be answerable. The French settlers have some reason to object to this, since, even after two or three generations, they are treated as "foreigners" in these Protectorates, and would therefore have no part in the Legislative Assembly. Nor would the Bey of Tunis be likely to show much enthusiasm for democratic government—over two hundred members of his or of other princely families are paid out of the Tunisian exchequer.

Although the three territories have produced rather similar Nationalist movements, so closely linked that the murder of a Nationalist leader in Tunisia in December 1952 led to very serious disturbances in Casablanca, the differences between them are profound. For a thousand years before Christ the whole of North Africa was occupied by the Berbers, who are said to be of the same origin as the European races. Their own name for themselves is "Imazighen," or "Free Men," but in Tunisia and Algeria they have lost their racial identity, having been over-run by the Arabs and ruled by the Turks. In Morocco, however, they still form a distinct section of the population—more than one-third of the total. Although they, too,

are Moslems, they are very different from the Arabs in character. They are agriculturists rather than cattle-men. They are
less feudal in their outlook.

They are descended from the people who made the Barbary
Coast a place of terror. For some three centuries pirates from
these three territories and from what is now Spanish Morocco
attacked traffic through the Mediterranean and raided the
towns along its northern shore. Their sailing ships ranged
even to Iceland. At one time in the seventeenth century more
than 20,000 captives were imprisoned in Algiers alone and
thousands of Christian slaves ended their lives at the great
oars of their galleys. They profited magnificently from the dis-
unity of Europe, whose governments paid handsome bribes
to buy safety from these gangsters and to encourage them to
harry their commercial rivals.

The Turks ruled over both Tunisia and Algeria until the
nineteenth century. The French claimed Algeria by right of
conquest, and therefore had no obligations toward the local
rulers. Hence its union with France after 1830. In the case of
Tunisia, they occupied the country in 1881, and "persuaded"
the Bey (for there were both Beys and Deys) to accept a
French protectorate.

Thus each territory is on a different level in its relations to
France. Nationalism has temporarily united them, but there is
naturally much less racial or color feeling in French North Africa than in the Union of South Africa. Even the backward
masses are far closer to the Europeans than are the Africans
in the Union. Differences of religion discourage much inter-
marriage—although many of the Arab political leaders have
European wives—but both races are Mediterranean, and represent great and old civilizations. Agreement between them does
not yet approach the impossible.

14

THE EMERALD SNAKE

Between French North Africa and Egypt is the large area of
Africa's latest independent state—a country one-quarter the
size of the United States, with less than one-hundredth of its
population. "The United Kingdom of Libya" was proclaimed
an independent and sovereign state on Christmas Eve, 1951,
to the considerable astonishment of many British soldiers who
had fought the Germans and the Italians in the desert between its two capitals, Tripoli and Benghazi.

This premature independence was forced upon its people
rather than achieved by them. The British had given pledges
to the Emir Idris of the Senussi—now the country's first king—
which would anyhow have made it impossible for the Italians
to continue their quite remarkable job as colonists, and the
brutal treatment of the Senussi by their own Fascist rulers had
made such pledges inevitable. Strategic requirements, and a
certain distrust between the major members of the United Na-

153

tions, produced a deadlock which could be solved only by
granting independence to a country in which the average income is little more than $28 a year, only sixteen people have
university degrees, and its three component areas are separated by hundreds of miles of desert.

In these circumstances the United Nations has done a remarkable job. The British and French who had governed the
country since they liberated it from the Italians—the British
in Cyrenaica and Tripolitania, the French in the Fezzan—
are temporarily underwriting its budget deficits and, with the
United States and some other countries, are supplying money
to its Public Development Agency. The Technical Assistance
Board, with a Resident Representative and with generous help
from the American Mutual Security Agency, has planned an
ambitious program of education, agricultural development
and scientific research. It is also supplying the necessary technical experts. This abysmally poor country has become Exhibit
A for United Nations aid to the "under-privileged." Homer
wrote of it as an area of great fertility; irrigation and good hus-
bandry may put much of its desert under cultivation again.

Much farther east, in Egypt, a vivid emerald snake winds
across a desert that varies from light fawn to deep chocolate.
Seen from a height of twenty thousand feet, one appreciates
the importance of the Nile; the green strip on either side of
it is so pathetically small and ends so abruptly where irrigation
ceases to carry its waters. Sometimes the strip may be twelve
miles wide, sometimes only two or three. And beyond it on
either side there is no sign of human activity or life.

For the first time one realizes why wave after wave of immigrants have swept downwards across Africa from the north-east.
Many, it is true, came across the Red Sea or from Southern
Arabia to Somaliland. Others spread along the southern coast of
the Mediterranean. But the Nile, the second longest river in the
world, has been for thousands of years the main pathway into
the interior of Africa.

Thousands of years before Christ, ships sailed up it, bringing treasures and tribute of every kind to decorate the tombs of the kings in a wild valley near Luxor—for probably no other people ever showed a greater preoccupation with death than the Egyptians. At high water, it is navigable for 2,900 miles, and immense blocks of stone, each weighing two tons or more, were brought down it to build the pyramids and the temples. From the time of Alexander the Great onwards, countless explorers have tried to reach the sources of this great river.

The explorers, and the waves of immigrants that followed them, found that there were two Niles—the Blue Nile, which is as yellow as the Blue Danube, and which rises in Abyssinia, and the White Nile which comes from hundreds of miles beyond Lake Victoria. The mountains of Abyssinia, and the tribesmen who live among them, have not welcomed newcomers in large quantities; on the White Nile, long before the immigrants could reach Lake Victoria, they were checked by the immense marshes of the Sudd, in Southern Sudan, where the ground is so nearly level that the river falls less than 200 feet in 475 miles. This swamp is the southern frontier of Islam. Some of the immigrants turned westwards along the strip of fertile land between the southern edge of the Sahara and the northern edge of the tropical forest, while others worked their way round the swamp until they reached Lake Victoria, and then spread southward. Somehow the superintendent of the library in Alexandria was able to state, in about 250 B.C., that the Nile had its source in lakes on the Equator.

In the days when the greatest artists of the time were carving on the walls of the deep, limestone tombs in the Valley of the Kings, Luxor (Thebes), a few miles away on the farther bank of the river, was the capital of Upper and Lower Egypt, with a hundred gates and twenty thousand war chariots. Today it is a town of some 30,000 inhabitants, many of whom live by the tourist industry.

They guide you round the tombs and temples; they ferry you across the river to the Valleys of the Kings and Queens;

they drive you to the fabulous temple of Karnak; they sell you postcards and antiques and vulgar little reproductions of the masterpieces of their ancestors. And the superficial contact between past and present is one which helps to explain the exaggerated sensitiveness and natural pride which you find in Egypt to-day. National pride leads rather to denials of an obvious and terrible poverty than to its recognition and explanation.

In the tomb of a land overseer who lived three thousand five hundred years ago, sculptures show you the daily life of the peasant; they might almost have been carved to-day, so little change has there been in the methods of ploughing, reaping and threshing. Then, and throughout the intervening centuries, the peasant has had to pay to overseers and absentee landlords so large a proportion of his produce that he has been kept in the direst poverty and limited to the most primitive farm implements. The great irrigation schemes have enabled the population almost to triple itself in the last fifty years but not to raise its standard of living. And even now only about one acre in four hundred is habitable. The rest is desert.

There is no reason, people tell you, why any of the Nile water should be allowed to reach the sea—no reason except the appalling cost of adequate schemes for further irrigation and for the drainage necessary to prevent the land from becoming sour. Thus all of Egypt that matters—unless and until the schemes for reclaiming the desert can be put into operation—is a very narrow emerald strip running across the desert from tropical Africa to the temperate climate of the Mediterranean.

One result of this is an astonishing range of color and type—some people as dark as Seretse Khama and some as fair as Snow White, but all equally Egyptians. There is virtually no color prejudice, and Egypt may find it a great advantage to have overcome—possibly without being aware of its existence —an obstacle which so alarms most countries with mixed populations. But the Egyptians have other obstacles ahead of them. They have almost the highest birth-rate and densest population of any country in the world, and, although the death-rate is also almost without parallel, the increase of population is greater than the land can carry. The land hunger is such that in every village all the pots, pans, tools and utensils that would elsewhere be left out in the yard are piled upon the flat roofs of the mud-walled houses.

This overcrowding has had two evil consequences. One was that it has been easier to make more money by buying more land, which inevitably and automatically increased in value, than to invest in new industries or in long-term schemes to bring more desert into cultivation. The other consequence has been that while the streets of Cairo were crowded with American cars and its shops with luxury goods, the appallingly low standard of living of the peasants had sunk even lower in the last two or three decades. Few revolutions in history have been more justified than was the revolution begun by General Naguib.

The flooding of the Nile is as regular as clockwork. "For two or three weeks before the high water in summer the Nile, otherwise clear, begins to turn green. It brings down immense quantities of small algæ from the swamps of the Sudan. Then it is turned dark red-brown by the volcanic sediment from Abyssinia. Every year 110 million tons of extraordinarily rich silt pass Wadi Halfa, roughly a thousand miles from the Mediterranean."[1] And, by flooding and irrigation, this water enables each fertile acre to produce three, or sometimes four, crops in a year.

It is not therefore surprising that even in Old Testament days the Pharaohs and their people were preoccupied by what people higher up the Nile might do to its waters. There has been a perennial struggle between the Sudanese, pushing northward down the river, and the Egyptians pushing upstream. Mohammed Ali, in 1821, conquered nearly all the Sudan and he and his successors ruled it for sixty years. Or rather, they ruled over what later became the Anglo-Egyptian Sudan, for "Sudan" means "the country of the Blacks," and it stretches

[1] *Afrika*, by Anton Zischka (Stalling Verlag, Oldenburg).

right across the continent, between the Sahara and the tropical forest, from the Red Sea to the Atlantic. He was a man of remarkable ability, but he organized the slave trade there, and is remembered with less than no affection.

It was against Mohammed Ali and other "Turks" that the Mahdi began his religious war, in the course of which General Gordon, charged with evacuating the Egyptian garrisons, was stabbed on the steps that lead down from the Governor's palace in Khartoum to the Blue Nile. Both he, and Kitchener, who undertook the reconquest of the Sudan with a combined Anglo-Egyptian force, were serving the Egyptian Government, and, in the early years of the Condominium which was established after Kitchener's victory (with the help of the Maxim gun, which was used for the first time at Omdurman) the Egyptians took an active part in governing the Sudan. They supplied most of the money and the junior civil servants; the British supplied the senior staff. In fact, however, the Condominium failed; even before the murder of Sir Lee Stack, the Egyptians played very little part in governing the country. When posts were vacant, there was very little competition among the Egyptians to go so far south. It had become almost a disgrace for a Cairene to be posted even to Upper Egypt, and, *a fortiori*, to the Sudan. And the Wafd Government first denounced the Condominium, leaving the British in complete control, and then claimed that Farouk was nevertheless the King of the Sudan as well as of Egypt.

As between the British and the Egyptians, there can be no doubt that the latter had a good claim, based on history and on law, to a much larger share in the government of the Sudan. But the Sudanese had taken to self-government far better than the inhabitants of any other African territory—partly because the British civil officials there had done all their service in the country, and were not moved from territory to territory, and even from continent to continent, as normally happens in the Colonial Service. Nowhere else—not even in West Africa— have I found British officials who so associated their own interests with those of the people they govern.

From the terrace of the Grand Hotel in Khartoum one looks across the Blue Nile to a sandy plain, beyond which rise the mosques of Omdurman. The avenue flanking the river outside the hotel is called after Kitchener. Rather unsuitably, one of the local cabarets is called after General Gordon, and the port of call on the White Nile for B.O.A.C. flying boats is called "Gordon's Tree" although there is now no tree to be seen and it is doubtful whether he ever sat under one when it was there. Even the names of the streets remind one of the romantic days when the soldiers of Queen Victoria marched about in their scarlet tunics to secure order and obedience throughout her Empire.

Things have changed. The son of the Mahdi has been so closely linked with the British that Egyptians used to suspect a British plot to make him King of the Sudan. The boy who sells stamps at the post office must be descended from the Fuzzie-Wuzzies who harassed Kitchener in the Red Sea Hills. Many of the servants in the hotel have negroid features which suggest that their parents or grandparents were brought from the Southern Sudan as slaves. At all hours of the day and night, airways buses bring to the hotel passengers who have just flown over desert too harsh even for bedouins, or jungle still crowded with wild game, or the great marshes of the Sudd, where the White Nile is so clogged up that—until it can be by-passed by the proposed new canal—evaporation will continue to rob this thirsty land of half its flow. What will then happen to the areas which now benefit from the water that evaporates, nobody seems to know.

In these fantastic changes the Sudan has been spared most of the major difficulties. Unlike the other countries in the eastern half of the continent, it has no large infiltration of Indians to form a layer of tradesmen and minor civil servants which hinders the emergence of the Africans themselves. But its present prosperity still depends upon the Nile. The Sennar Dam, built in 1925 across the Blue Nile, permitted the development of a cotton industry which assures great prosperity as long as the price of long-staple cotton remains high, and has also made possible a development scheme which should be carefully studied in every other part of Africa. The Kilimanjaro Native Co-operative Union has been a remarkable example of African development; the Gezira Scheme in the Sudan is a remarkable example of European-African partnership.

The Gezira—island, in Arabic—is a five-million acre plain between the Blue Nile and the White Nile, and the Sennar Dam has made it possible, with the help of five thousand miles of irrigation channels, already to bring about one million acres of this plain under cultivation. 100,000 acres of this irrigated land are producing as much food as formerly came from the five million acres of the plain; cotton is the crop grown on the rest of it, and in 1951 the 25,000 tenant farmers, who had formerly lived barely above subsistence level, each had an average revenue of $2100 from cotton alone. The Sudan Government's share of the crop in 1951 was worth about fifty million dollars, plus another twenty-eight million received from export duty.

But the value of the Gezira scheme lies less in the money it earns than in the way its capital has been supplied and used. It gives no possible excuse for the normal accusations against the capitalist or for the violent nationalism that is so likely to alarm the potential investor. A commercial firm, the Sudan Plantations Syndicate, was granted a concession for twenty-five years, during which its shareholders averaged twelve per cent on their money and at the end of which they got their capital back, as well as the official thanks of the Sudanese Parliament. The advantages to the peasant farmer have already been mentioned. The third partner in the concern was the Sudan Government which made the scheme possible by expropriating the original landlords—who each received decent compensation and a forty-acre tenancy. The Government's share of the profits has been sufficient to enable it to take over the company's assets at the end of the twenty-five years.

"In most of these (backward) lands," writes Mr. Arthur Gaitskell,[2] the former manager of the Syndicate, "the vocal

[2] See *English-Speaking World*, October 1952.

people are strongly nationalistic. They want to stand on their own feet and not to be treated either as suckers or as poor relations. They tend to suspect that a foreign capitalist is getting far too big a share of the products of their land or they fear his economic interests are going to lead him to dominate them. Further they resent the idea that some major asset in their country is owned by foreign capital instead of by themselves. This kind of attitude naturally kills investment. No one wants to put his savings, or his nation's taxes, into countries where they risk confiscation, arbitrary taxation and so on."

And the advantage of the Gezira scheme is that it avoids all these dangers. As much administration as possible has been put in the hands of village and estate councils, in which the humblest peasants have a chance of taking part in the management of their own affairs. Part of the profits of the scheme— far more than could be made available by a government dealing with a similar population—comes back to the area to supplement the normal government contribution for social development. Probably nowhere in Africa is the ordinary peasant receiving so thorough a grounding in the practical side of democracy.

Mr. Arthur Gaitskell can rightly claim for the scheme that "it has brought scientific development. It has encouraged and made possible democratic political independence. And it has seen that the wealth created has gone, not to a few landlords, but to the local peasant farmers and to the Government of the Sudan, without having to shoot all the landlords or to impose a State tyranny."

The Sudanese might be even more prosperous if they were allowed to use more of the Nile water that flows through their immense territory (one quarter of the area of Europe). And yet it cannot be denied that Egypt needs the Nile even more than does the Sudan, the southern half of which can depend upon rainfall. The merest suggestion of Sudanese independence has therefore caused deep alarm to the Egyptians in the past. And as Anglo-Egyptian relations deteriorated, owing to the conflict over the maintenance of British troops in the Canal Zone, Egyptian suspicions of British intentions in the Sudan deepened.

General Naguib's reversal of the policy of the Wafdist leaders—due, in part, to the fact that he is half-Sudanese and spent much of his youth in Khartoum—cleared away some of their alarm. But he and his colleagues have objected to the claim that Sudanese independence must include the right to join the British Commonwealth after the present three-year period of "Sudanization" of the administration is over.

The Sudanese may prove unable to govern themselves, the Cairo argument runs, and in that case they might appeal for British technical help. Whitehall would once again control the Nile Valley. This would be, of course, a most unexpected development in a world where nationalism is so anxious to have done with foreign control, but Egyptian suspicions of British motives are not based entirely on logic; they have been tragically increased by the conflict over the Canal Zone.

There must be a limit to the area covered in a book which started off with South Africa as its subject. Discussion of the Canal Zone would lead on to the whole problem of the Middle East, which, in turn, is affected by events in South East Asia. So I go no further than to remind the reader that Egypt controls not only the sea passage from the Mediterranean to the Indian Ocean but also the land passage from Asia to Africa. Its strategic importance is immense. The British may claim that, both in the Sudan and in the Canal Zone, wider considerations of policy have justified their attitude. The Sudanese, under British tutelage, had reached a far higher standard of living than had the Egyptians, under a selfish and corrupt monarchy. It would have been an immoral act to accept any settlement which brought them under the control of Cairo. And a strategic area of such importance to Western civilization as the Canal Zone could not be left entirely to the forces of Egypt, so clearly inadequate to defend it.

But nationalism is as little influenced as love by reason. The desire of Egyptian nationalists to control the Valley of the

Nile and to be the obvious masters over all their territory is as understandable as is the British desire to protect the Sudan of whose progress they are justifiably so proud and to retain some control over a military base on which they have spent roughly $1,400,000,000.

One way of steadying the water supply for Egypt is to build dams which will hold back the waters of the White Nile when the Blue Nile is in spate. This, indeed, is the sole reason for the Gebel Aulia Dam, built across the White Nile in 1937. But throughout the centuries the Pharaohs or their descendants have wanted to control Abyssinia—part of the ancient Ethiopia—for in Western Abyssinia is Lake Tsana, out of which flows the turbulent Blue Nile, carrying its great volume of life-giving silt. When its water is at its highest its flow is something like seven times that of the White Nile. A dam built at Lake Tsana might increase the population of the Nile Valley by millions—or, better but less probable—immensely raise the standard of living of the present population.

In the thirteenth century the Fatimite rulers of Egypt caused great casualties among the Crusaders, to the anger of the King of Shoa, in whose kingdom was Lake Tsana. He is said to have put hundreds of slaves on to the task of filling the valleys of two tributaries with rocks until they flowed southward, instead of northward into the Lake and the Nile Valley. And it may be that a subconscious memory of the disaster that then befell Egypt has something to do with the Egyptian fears that somebody will interfere with the flow of this river on which their lives depend. The mere threat by an Abyssianian king in the eighteenth century to take similar action sufficed at once to settle a serious dispute with Egypt in Abyssinia's favor.

But hitherto no Emperor of Abyssinia has allowed a dam to be built, for it would raise the level of the lake enough to flood a number of churches and monasteries, and the priests are extremely powerful—although the "Encyclopædia Britannica" describes them as "an ignorant body, teaching the scriptures in Giz,[3] a tongue understood by very few." And until recently the country has known such political chaos that the dam could not have been built even had an Emperor been prepared to sanction it, and had the funds been available.

Apart from Lake Tsana, however, Abyssinia has played an important part in Africa, since it is one of the very few countries in the continent with any kind of history, and men and ideas have made their way to other parts of it over this "roof of Africa" since very early times. The very name of Abyssinia is derived from an Arabic word meaning "mixed," and indicates its great variety of races and tribes. They are said to speak seventy different languages, and Amharic, the language of the Emperor, Haile Selassie, has 256 characters. Many Jews settled in Abyssinia during the period of the Captivity. The Greeks came here and, above all, the Christians. Whereas most Africans are pagans, who have heard of Christianity only within the last fifty years, large parts of Abyssinia have been Christian for fifteen hundred years or so. It has been identified with the legendary Christian kingdom of the legendary Prester John, the search for which inspired several Portuguese explorers from the end of the fourteenth century onwards.

The people vary in color from pale olive to pitch black, for the stream of immigrants from Asia Minor has met a countercurrent of slaves on the way to Asia. The black slave traffic to Asia Minor, indeed, continued even after Abyssinia had been admitted to the League of Nations. The Amharic tribes migrated from Asia Minor to the neighborhood of Lake Tsana a thousand years before Christ. Nobody who met the small but immensely dignified Emperor, and who heard his noble appeal for help made in the Assembly of the League of Nations during Mussolini's invasion of his country, could doubt that they are among the patrician peoples of the world. One felt that the

[3] More commonly written as Gi'iz. It was originally introduced into Ethiopia from the Yemen, but is now used only as the liturgical language of the Abyssinian Church.

legend of his descent from Solomon and the Queen of Sheba may indeed have been history. But men of his race make up considerably less than half the population of Abyssinia, maintaining an uncertain hold over the country only by ruthless, feudal methods.

Since Mussolini's invasion in 1935, the peoples of Abyssinia have had far more contact with the outside world than they had had in the previous ten centuries or so. The Italians, the world's best road-builders, opened up communications, even though they did so for such disastrous reasons. The country is no longer dependent for sea contact with the outside world on the Addis Ababa railway which passes through French territory before it reaches the sea at Djibouti. For in September 1952 the former Italian colony of Eritrea, ruled by the British since the destruction of Mussolini's empire, entered a federation with Abyssinia, and the 18,000 Italians who still live there and constitute the country's cultured class have thus come under the rule of Haile Selassie, whom their own ruler had attacked so ruthlessly and so needlessly. Somaliland, on the borders of which occurred the incident which provided the excuse for that attack, is an Italian Trust Territory under the United Nations (until 1960).

Eritrea, half Christian and Half Moslem, is very poor, and its particular brand of Coptic Christians are more closely allied to those of Tigre, the neighboring province of Abyssinia, than to those of Addis Ababa. Also Eritrea has a much more liberal constitution than Abyssinia. Eritrea may therefore help to break down the extremely rigid and reactionary system which still obtains in Addis Ababa. The Coptic Christians of Abyssinia, who easily outnumber the Moslems, are inordinately proud of the fact that they were converted well in advance of many Europeans. Even though they were subsequently, and for many centuries, isolated from the rest of the world by a circle of Moslems, they are inclined to behave with great intolerance toward foreigners. Their censorship remains amazingly severe, and two of the complications facing the editors of local newspapers are that they are not normally allowed to print news, and must on no account insert any name in an article before that of the Emperor.

This intolerance has hitherto made it difficult to estimate the wealth of the country, but the Italians, during their few years of conquest, did begin to exploit the considerable deposits of lead, copper, iron and other minerals. With the disappearance of the Italians, there is considerable confusion. The Americans are showing interest in the country's economic development, and the International Bank has given some help, but the Government turns most often to the British for political advice. The Belgians train the army and the Swedes train the air force. Even Russians are among its advisers, although there seems to be no truth in reports that the Soviet government has made Addis Ababa a center for Communist activity throughout Africa. It seems quite probable that Abyssinia will revert to its pre-war status of happy hunting-ground for adventurers. This is one of the countries which justifies the argument that, as Western Europe comes nearer to unity, much wider co-operation will be needed between its component states in the development of its African hinterland. And that co-operation will be needed in the interests of both continents.

15

EAST AFRICAN FEDERATION

East Africa is a convenient name for Kenya, Tanganyika and Uganda, but one doubts whether it is much more. These three countries share the same postage stamps and the same currency (with holes in the middle of the copper coins since most of the people who handle them have no pockets, and wear their wealth strung on string and tied round their waists). They have the same railway and harbor administration, although the railways of Tanganyika at no point come anywhere near those of Uganda and Kenya. And since 1948 they have had an East African High Commission, consisting of the three Governors and a small Secretariat, which co-ordinates a great number of medical and other technical matters. But, despite the fashion for federation, a much closer union between these three territories seems unlikely; their policies tend too much to diverge.

Kenya as we know it came into existence because the British Government began in 1896 to build a railway to Uganda.

167

And the British Government began to build a railway to
Uganda mainly because the Germans were becoming too active
in Tanganyika. That sounds confusing? But it is in these confusing ways that great empires come into existence. The British
Government did very little to encourage Cecil Rhodes when
he obtained a concession over the two Rhodesias. In the same
way, the British Government showed no interest when, in
1877, Bargash, Sultan of Zanzibar, offered to concede sover-
eignty, with very minor reservations, over his own island and
the coastal plain on the mainland to Sir William Mackinnon,
Chairman of the British India Line. Owing to the Government's refusal of support, the offer had to be refused, but some
years later, Mackinnon managed to form a company, the
Imperial British East Africa Association, to which the Sultan
conceded for fifty years all these territories that had not already come under German control. Thus a strip of East Africa
coastline ten miles wide came under British rule, and is still a
Protectorate leased by the British Government from the Sultan.

The Imperial British East Africa Association spread its activities inland and made trade agreements with such local chiefs
and rulers as it could find, but the maintenance of some sort of
order and protection for its agents was an excessive drain on its
capital—as had also been the case with Rhodes's British South
Africa Company. The members of the Association considered
themselves lucky when, after seven years of struggle and disaster, they sold all their rights to the Foreign Office for $700,000
—$28,000 more than their original capital. They had not done
much in the way of successful business, but they had taken
quite considerable steps to suppress the slave trade in the territory over which they had maintained a very tenuous control
—a territory then known as "Ibea," after the company's ini-
tials. For, believe it or not, many of the "Empire Builders" were men of the highest moral and religious standards.

The Foreign Office intervention was also caused by this joint
respect for the Empire and the Bible which, in that order,
played so great a part in British diplomacy in the second half

of the last century. Some twenty-five years earlier, Speke and Grant, while searching for the source of the Nile, had discovered a well-organized monarchy in Uganda. Thirteen years later, Stanley visited the court of King Mutesa, and was greatly impressed by the King's interest in Christianity. At his suggestion, the Church Missionary Society sent out its first missionaries. Mutesa died, and his son, Mwanga, showed a lamentable wavering in his faith, as one result of which an admirable man, Bishop Hannington, was assassinated and various African converts were massacred. For a short time the Catholic and Protestant missions even agreed to unite in opposition to the Moslems—for Arab traders were just as zealous on behalf of Mohammedanism as European traders had been on behalf of Christianity. And these small wars of religion naturally created a growing British interest in Uganda.

But during the same period the Germans had been active. They had acquired rights in Tanganyika, and on their behalf the famous Dr. Karl Peters promised Mwanga Germany's protection. Mr. (later Sir) Frederick Jackson, envoy of the British East Africa Company, had given a similar pledge on behalf of Great Britain, and the Company sent a young officer— later to become famous in Africa as Lord Lugard—to settle matters. He did so by an impressive blend of force and tact, and British control was reaffirmed. But the cost had been too great for the Company, and it announced its decision to withdraw from Uganda.

Only by such a threat could the British Government be aroused. It sent out Sir Gerald Portal as Imperial Commissioner and he took over the Company's responsibilities. A Protectorate over Mwanga's kingdom was proclaimed in 1894, and two years later the British Government began the construction of the strategic railway from Mombasa. Its estimated cost was $8,400,000, but its actual cost was nearly twice as much. A year later Ibea, the country through which this railway was to pass, was also taken over from the Company, and renamed the East African Protectorate. Not until 1920 was it to become known as Kenya Colony and Protectorate.

This railway created Kenya. Having built it, the British Government wanted to make it pay, it therefore gave every possible encouragement to settlers to establish themselves on the high and healthy ground which the railway had to cross. In almost every other case in colonial history, the flag has followed the settler; in Kenya, the settler followed the flag. The early settlers therefore have had the unusual advantage in Kenya of finding their communications laid on for them; they have had the handicap that the Government is inclined to look on them not as the chosen few in whose interests the country must be run, but as the smallest of the four communities under its care—Europeans, Africans, Indians and Arabs.

This railway also created one of Kenya's principal problems. The British Government brought in Indians to build it, and allowed them to settle in the country after they had done so. What with them and the Gujerati traders who had settled along the coast generations before the arrival of the British, the Indian population is now more than three times that of the Europeans. The Arabs are nearly as numerous as the Europeans, and their settlements along the coast date back for centuries. But they play very little part in politics. The Africans number more than five and a quarter millions—nearly a hundred and fifty times more than the Europeans. This Indian infiltration is looked upon by the Europeans as a great danger; it is equally a danger to the Africans, for those who do rise above the level of the mass find that the jobs they could fill are already filled by Indians. Nowhere else in Africa is one so driven to ask oneself whether it may not become a Brown Man's continent.

In a queer and involuntary way the Indians may do something to bring the Whites and the Blacks together. The young African returned from the war extremely self-confident, and ambitious in a way his father had never been. He had probably travelled as far from home as Burma. Not for him the quiet pastoral life, even if the land were available; he wants to drive an engine or to open a store or to become a clerk in a government office, and, he finds that the Indian has got there before him. At the other end of the scale, the sons of the white settlers cannot all make farming a career, and they are alarmed and annoyed to find so much Indian competition in business and the professions. It seems just possible that this common fear of a powerful Indian middle class may break the link between Brown man and Black which is forged by the White man's attitude in the color question. But at present the Indians form an even more energetic and ambitious community than do the Indians of Natal, and their policy is to win the co-operation of the Africans. More than two years before the Indian and African organizations in South Africa had decided to work together, the equivalent organizations in Kenya had begun to do so.

The white settlers of Kenya deserve kinder things than are generally said about them. The earlier arrivals were mostly genuine farmers in an expansive kind of way, and they love their land as did most of the squires and landowners of England before the First World War faced them with a mass of new problems they did not understand, and with which they could not cope. The proportion of ex-regular officers who spent their gratuities after the First World War on buying land in Kenya was fantastically high. They have been good settlers and they have a right to be proud of much that they have done for the development of such rather poor natural resources as Kenya possesses. But for them, Kenya would have needed to import a great deal of its food.

These genuine settlers are outnumbered and out-voted by town-dwellers and artisans, many of whom have had much less experience of dealing with people of another race. They have not made compromise much easier, and compromise above all is essential in a plural society. Such a man as Mr. Michael Blundell, leader of the European elected members of the Legislative Council, has done much to check wild and intolerant tendencies, and the Electors' Union, the chief organization of the Europeans, has become very much more moderate in the last three or four years. Nevertheless, the bitterness which burst into flame in the Kikuyu country in 1952 has been developing for many years.

Uganda, on the other hand, is a black man's country, and nobody disputes his claim to it. It is a gigantic Native Reserve, with practically no white planters. Its total white population, including government officials, is less than four thousand, as against five million Africans. There are some thirty-seven thousand Indians, but they create far less of a political problem than do those of Kenya, partly because most of them are followers of the Moslem sect of which the Aga Khan is the spiritual head, and his moderating influence has done much to check anti-British feeling—in any case, it is generally the Hindus who are politically active and discontented; the Pakistani Moslems in East Africa, like the Syrian Moslems in West Africa, prefer to spend their time making money. One of the amazing sights of Kampala—amazing, that is, to anyone who has followed the Indian press in East Africa—is a tablet in the finest park in the town announcing that it was the gift of an Indian in memory of "the glorious reign of King George the Fifth." The main problem of Uganda will be dealt with in a later chapter. It is the problem of conciliating the policy of indirect rule with the growing demand of the educated young African to play some part in the government of the country. And this is a problem between one black man and another which arouses little interest in the White Highlands of Kenya.

As for Tanganyika, that country has many problems in common with Kenya, but its government is determined to seek different solutions of them. The similarity of the problems, indeed, seems more likely to discourage federation than to promote it. For Tanganyika is the newest country in Africa, in that, as a mandated territory between the two world wars, it was shamefully neglected; now that its resources are being studied and developed, its government has some chance of profiting from the experience of other African states and of avoiding their mistakes.

There is also a question of prestige. Kenya has always been looked upon as the senior partner in East Africa; that status no longer goes unchallenged. It is true that in 1949 Kenya's total exports amounted in value to nearly $84,000,000, whereas those of Tanganyika amounted to a little under $59,000,000. But Kenya's imports were almost double those of Tanganyika, and only some $11,000,000 short of double her own exports. Sisal accounted for well over half Tanganyika's exports, and the price, already falling, may go a good deal lower, as other fibers come into the market. Even so, the officials in Dar-es-Salaam can claim that their financial and economic situation looks a good deal healthier than does that of Kenya.

There are roughly half as many Europeans in Tanganyika as in Kenya and two million more Africans. In other words, the European settlers are less able to check the Government's policy regarding the Africans and Indians, and even in the neighborhood of Mt. Kilimanjaro, where most of the politically-minded Europeans are grouped, only a minority is British. After the First World War, the expropriated estates of German settlers were sold very cheaply to any Europeans who came along, and most of them happened to be Greek. There is not the tough, diehard element that is found among the ex-Regulars of the White Highlands of Kenya. Much as these Europeans dislike the color policy of the Tanganyikan Government—and they dislike it quite a lot—they dislike still more any hint of interference by the Electors' Union of Kenya. They may share racial views of this Kenyan organization, but they have developed enough Tanganyikan national pride to resent advice from Europeans whose own policy in Kenya does not seem to have been very successful.

And possibly this question of prestige does not apply to the settlers alone. The Governor of Kenya presides over the East African High Commission. While that Governor was Sir Philip Mitchell, his reputation stood so high that his seniority could be accepted as a matter of course. But he has now retired and, although his successor is Sir Evelyn Baring, one of the most enlightened men in the Colonial Service, the Governor of Tanganyika, Sir Edward Twining, is also a most remarkable man. And so, too, is the Governor of Uganda, Sir Andrew

Cohen, who has probably done more, during his service in the Colonial Office, than any other man alive, to dispel color prejudice and to face up to the long-term problems of a plural society. If federation is seriously planned in East Africa, one of the most urgent steps would seem to be the appointment of a Governor-General with authority over the Governments of the three territories.

Thus in Kenya there is a strong demand for the maintenance of the white man's absolute domination; in Uganda there is complete acceptance of the fact that it is a black man's country; in Tanganyika there is an attempt, of which more will be written later, to gain acceptance from each of the three communities—European, African and Indian—that the other two are equally essential to the prosperity of the country. The geographical and economic advantages of a closer federation are obvious; one pities the men who have to overcome the obstacles to it.

16

DEVON IN AFRICA

I know no place more improbable than Entebbe, the capital
of Uganda. You look out, from the shady terrace of a fine new
hotel—owned by the State and built by the Colonial Development Corporation—across green lawns dotted with fine old
trees, and with flower beds the red soil of which makes you
think of Devon. The lawns slope down to the lake. The park
of some great house overlooking, perhaps, the estuary of the
River Exe. But fifty miles or so from the equator—no, it's too
absurd for words, especially for air passengers who boarded the
aircraft a thousand miles or so farther north, in the blistering
heat of Egypt or the Sudan.

Only after some minutes do you realize that the lake is
Victoria Nyanza; a lake larger than Belgium and Holland together; that the trees bear strange flowers and fruits and are
frequented by an extraordinary variety of birds that have
never seen the shores of England; and that the human beings

vary from tall, emaciated Nilotic tribesmen in rags more
picturesque and inadequate than those of any pantomime
Cinderella to stately Baganda women in brilliantly colored
robes down to their feet—for an earlier king of the Baganda
decreed that the display of a woman's calf was a crime to be
punished by death. Despite their habit of shaving their heads
and of wearing as many garments as possible round their waists
—for fatness is considered so desirable that some tribesmen
feed their young brides on milk until they cannot walk—the
women who walk bare-footed through the streets of Entebbe
and Kampala are among the most majestic I have ever seen.

Entebbe is the capital of the Uganda Protectorate, twenty-
one miles from Kampala, the capital of Buganda, whose people
are called Baganda and whose language is Luganda. An individual is a Muganda. (For these details I am indebted
to Elspeth Huxley.) And the Uganda Protectorate consists,
besides the Kingdom of Buganda, of the Western Province,
with the three small native Kingdoms of Bunyoro, Toro and
Ankole; and the Eastern and Northern Provinces, divided, less
romantically, into districts. The Protectorate so nearly runs
itself that Entebbe has a white population of less than 350.

This degree of self-government makes the Protectorate one
of the most interesting and contented countries in Africa.
But it has one grave handicap. After the British Government
had taken over control from the British East Africa Company
in 1893, it began to negotiate a series of treaties with the various rulers which promised them British protection with the
least possible interference with their existing way of life. Nowhere else has the policy of indirect rule been carried out with
greater care and greater success. But the policy itself contains
the seeds of disaster—this promise to leave the African rulers
free to run their own kingdoms automatically leaves them too
much freedom to resist healthy political growth and change.
Elsewhere, and particularly in West Africa, one has the fear
that change may be too fast; here in Uganda it may be too
slow, and the more loyal the British Government remains to its

original treaties, the greater its risk of appearing to support reaction.

The system has, in fact, worked out fairly satisfactorily, despite serious rioting in 1945. The British Residents have only given advice, but the Kings know it would be unwise to reject it, and they have made reluctant but very considerable concessions to democracy. The King of Buganda, known as the Kabaka, is a slender, civilized, neat young man with an attractive young wife, who was at school at Sherborne, Dorset. His English is admirable, and his desire to get back to Cambridge is intense. He complains—with great dignity—that he has to take responsibility without having power. The blame for unpopular British decisions falls on him, and he is constantly torn between the demands of the younger generation and those of the traditionalists who want government to go on in the same old way. It is difficult to remember that his grandfather distinguished himself by ordering one of the most comprehensive massacres of Christians in the whole history of Africa.

Uganda is one of the very few parts of Africa in which the early European explorers found a well-established system of government, and thirty-six Buganda kings have ruled from the Mengo Hill, on the outskirts of Kampala, where a high reed fence encloses a pleasant little white palace, the offices of the Ministers, and the Meeting Hall of the Grand Native Council, or Lukiko. The Ministers govern with the help of a Grand Native Council, or Lukiko, consisting of county (Saza) chiefs, notables approved by the Kabaka, and elected members. The chiefs are not chiefs in the old sense of the word—as in several other African colonies, they are in effect paid civil servants. And until early in 1953 only 40 of the 89 Members were elected; the number has now been increased to 60.

But democracy is on the march. The Executive Council—or government—now consists of 8 Official and 6 Unofficial Members, and of these Unofficials two are European, two African and two Asian—an approach to the seven-seven-seven system of Tanganyika described in a later chapter. The Legislative Council—or parliament—consists of 16 Officials and an equal number of Unofficial Members, of whom four are European, four are Indian and eight are African.

Kampala, like Rome, is built on seven hills. One is crowned by the Kabaka's palace; one, by the Anglican cathedral; one —on the place where my very distinguished predecessor, Stanley, met the King of Buganda in 1875—by a Roman Catholic cathedral, built mainly by African converts; one, by a wedding-cake kind of a mosque erected by followers of the Aga Khan; and one, by Makerere College, one of the few places where an African can get a university education in his own continent.

Makerere—accent on the second syllable—should provide the answer to the African's demand for higher education. It seems so much more sensible that Africans should go to such colleges as Makerere, Achimota (in the Gold Coast), Ibadan (in Nigeria), and Fourah Bay (in Sierra Leone) than to some university in the United Kingdom, even though the standard of education in an African college may not yet be so high as in an English university. The journey to Britain is so much more costly—but that probably worries only the government, for very few East African students could pay their own expenses. And the chances are so great that the student will be lonely in Great Britain and will have lost touch with his own people by the time he comes home again. I have suggested elsewhere in this book that there should be much less encouragement than at present to African students to graduate in a United Kingdom university; there should be much more help available for those of them who need to come on postgraduate courses.

But the Africans are not contented with Makerere. Each of them costs his (or her, for thirteen of the 270 students are women) government over $1,400 a year. But some of the governments concerned make a condition that the successful students for whom they pay shall later work for a specified number of years as civil servants, and many of these students could make much more money in private practice. Still more important, the students—with that suspicion of the white man's motives which is so devastingly prevalent in Africa—are convinced that they are being fobbed off with an inferior article. When I was there in 1950 there was accommodation for only 237 students, although Makerere exists to serve at least the three East African territories, with a combined African population of eighteen millions. Even so, the authorities have sometimes wondered whether they should reserve a few of these precious places for Europeans in the hope of diminishing these African suspicions.

There is one final point to be made about Makerere, and it applies to other African colleges as well. It is, of course, the reluctance of undergraduates to study agriculture, veterinary science and other subjects upon which depends the future of Black Africa. Elspeth Huxley[1] describes how, on a visit to Makerere, she found herself surrounded by students, who were disgruntled because they were not allowed to read law. On my visit I was amazed to find that there was not one person studying agriculture, although the need to get the Africans interested in the production of more and better food is so urgent that every book on Africa must come back to the subject with monotonous frequency. There was not even the possibility to study agriculture, since there was no professor on the subject, although Kenya has since founded a Chair of Veterinary Science with $140,000, from its Price Assurance Fund, which, like the Cotton and Hard Coffee Price Stabilization Funds in Uganda, is made up from the difference between the price paid to the African producer and the price received by the government from the foreign purchasers.

The main building of Makerere is flanked by two churches, outwardly precisely similar. But one is Roman Catholic and the other is Protestant, so that the rivalry between one Christian and another, which so bewilders the unfortunate African (especially when he is faced by such a variety of Protes-

[1] *Sorcerer's Apprentice* (Chatto and Windus).

tant missions) is emphasized here in stone. But however much one may deplore the effects of this rivalry, one must pay a tribute to the medical and educational work done by these missions. It is not their fault, but that of governments at home, if too much emphasis is laid on such subjects as English history and too little on social science and handicrafts.

One subject to which Makerere pays a lot of attention and which gives a poor financial return is that of art; yet it would be a tragedy if, for reasons of economy or what is so often miscalled common-sense, the art school were to be closed. For there are certain fields in which the Africans have rather to teach than to learn. Their influence on music, reaching Western civilization through the descendants of African slaves in the Southern States of North America, has, of course, been immense. So it will be, one feels on visiting Makerere, on sculpture and, perhaps, also on painting. And it can find expression only in Africa itself, for once the African artist has much contact with the work of non-African artists the temptation to copy the ways of the white man becomes almost irresistible. The art school at Makerere was the one place in Africa where I felt most strongly that a great contribution to civilization can be made by the black man.

"Tickle Uganda with a hoe and she will smile with a harvest." It is one of the few places in Africa where one finds the kind of jungle which, in my boyhood, I pictured all over the continent, with explorers hacking their way through the creepers that hung from trees full of leopards and snakes. In its forests are mahogany trees 180 feet high, containing twenty-four cubic tons of timber. But, since Africans do not grow vegetables and since so few Europeans own any land, there are practically no fresh vegetables in Kampala, and the hotel there gets them all the way by road from Kenya.

With these advantages of soil and climate Uganda would, in any case, be a relatively prosperous country. I have already mentioned its export of cotton. It exports well over three times as much coffee as Kenya. Bananas grow like weeds, and provide the people with most of their food and alcoholic drink. But it is as an industrial country that Uganda may best be known in the future. Copper, now so greatly in demand, exists in large quantities at Kilembe, not very far west of Kampala, and the railway to it, now about to be built, will ultimately reach to Ruwenzori and the Mountains of the Moon, and thereby open up a huge new area of Africa. There are rich deposits of such mysterious minerals as niobium, apatite and magnetite. But it is the Owen Falls Scheme which promises to produce developments in Uganda as startling as those of the Gold Coast and Nigeria.

I have written elsewhere of the Egyptian preoccupation with the water supplies of the White and the Blue Nile. Proposals made to Uganda to build a dam at Lake Albert were rejected years ago, for they would have flooded a thousand square miles of Uganda. Instead the Egyptians are taking part in a scheme much farther up the river. A meter added to the height of a dam near Jinja, on Lake Victoria, will give immense reassurances to the Egyptians and will enable Uganda to become a great industrial country.

Jinja is on the northern shore of the lake, where the surplus water, sweeping over the rocks of the Ripon Falls, becomes the White Nile and reaches the Mediterranean 3,500 miles away. A tablet records the fact that, on July 28th, 1862, Speke and Grant reached this spot and discovered the source of the Nile, sought by so many other explorers. Two miles down the river is a great pool called the Hippo Pool, and a little farther down again are the Owen Falls, where the great dam, when completed, will submerge the Ripon Falls as well, and will add quite a considerable new lake to the inland sea known as Lake Victoria. Large black and white birds shaped rather like cormorants flutter about the rocks—they are ibises, the sacred birds of Ancient Egypt. Hippos are so common here that the Jinja Golf Club is alleged to have special rules to cover the natural hazard created by one of these immense beasts strolling at night time across the greens.

Nearly fifty years ago, in "My African Journey," Sir Winston Churchill wrote of these falls: "It is possible that nowhere else in the world could so enormous a mass of water be held up by so little masonry." And the industrial possibilities of Jinja are immense. Cement is one of the great shortages in Africa, and most of it has to be imported all the way from England. The new cement works at Tororo, not far away, will soon be turning out half to two-thirds of the cement required for the hydro-electric installation and the housing of its workers. In due course, this installation will be able to supply power so cheaply that many new factories will be built. The Calico Printers' Association, which has had great experience elsewhere in training native labor, is establishing itself near Jinja and will probably make use of designs sent in from the Art School at Makerere. Near the Kenya border there is a mountain of phosphate which may go a long way toward checking the appalling impoverishment of the soil of Africa. Two hundred and forty miles of cable will carry power to the Kilembe copper mines, on the way to the Mountains of the Moon.

Uganda is certainly on the road to industrialization and prosperity. Of the cost of its ten-year development plan, $67,200,000 out of a total of $79,800,000 will be met out of its own resources—a greater contribution than that of any other British African colony except the Gold Coast. The plan may fill the Baganda with optimism. But it will end the patriarchal system by which the Kabaka and his Bahima ancestors have maintained a very successful rule over alien tribes. And people in Kampala face the certainty that their plans to create great wealth in the center of Africa will also create great social problems.

17

BACKGROUND TO MAU MAU

The first part of the road from Kampala to Nairobi, from Uganda to Kenya, crosses the plain round the shores of Lake Victoria. Dotted here and there in the mimosa scrub are the mud huts of Luo tribesmen, protected by circular stockades of sisal or thorn. Then the road rises over the foothills under the eastern wall of the Great Rift—the fantastic geological "fault" that runs northward to form part of the Red Sea, the Gulf of Akaba, the Dead Sea and the Valley of the Jordan—and you are at once aware of changed racial conditions; the large sisal estates are owned not by Africans, as almost everything is owned in Uganda, but by Indians. And as you climb toward the top of this great cliff, you see British names painted on the boards where tracks lead away to distant farms. This is the beginning of the White Highlands of Kenya.

Much of the country through which the road has passed carries far too dense a population. In the Highlands you drive through mile after mile of neatly-fenced and almost empty land. The contrast is too great, and it is not surprising that Africans, passing through this delectable country, should be filled with envy. Near Mao Heights, where the road climbs to over 8,600 feet, you drop in for lunch at the Highlands Hotel, the bar of which is so much like the bar of some very sophisticated golf club in Surrey that I had to concentrate my attention on the black barman in order to remind myself that I was in Africa—he was the only person who did not quite belong. This, the British will tell you, is the real Kenya—not Nairobi, although more than one-third of the Europeans in the country live there. There is even a pack of fox-hounds in the neighborhood.

And so, of course, it is the real Kenya in that some thousands of settlers have fashioned it to their taste, look upon it as their home and the home of their children, and would as readily fight to maintain their stake there as the Americans fought their War of Independence. They have proved, in two world wars, their passionate loyalty to the British Commonwealth (although most of them, I suspect, still call it the British Empire), but they have also a passionate loyalty to Kenya —*their* Kenya—and they are understandably impatient with Westminster and Whitehall, for no other British Colony has been made so much the victim of United Kingdom party politics. The variety of conflicting statements of policy made by successive Colonial Secretaries since the end of the first world war is shameful and shocking, and is the best argument I have discovered in favor of an all-party Colonial Affairs Committee in the House of Commons.

The favorite place for angry criticism of the misdeeds of the Colonial Office, the Fabian Society, the Indians and the Africans is the terrace of the Stag's Head Hotel at Nakuru. After all, one is told there, the Europeans farm less than five per cent of Kenya. The answer given by African politicians in Nairobi is that very little of Kenya is fertile land, but of the fertile land, more than one-half is in the possession of Europeans, although they are outnumbered by more than 150 to one. The Africans have far too little land. The Masai, for example, have one cow to every three acres, whereas each European cow has ten acres at her disposal.

Nonsense, they exclaim at Nakuru. The Masai are one of the few African tribes with a sufficient diet of proteins, since they live on a mixture of milk and blood from their cows. But they keep most of their cattle for prestige and not for food. The White Highlands will be producing first-class beef at the end of a hundred years, whereas the Masai will have turned their land into a desert. It's true, they add, that Native Reserves which were amply sufficient a generation or a decade ago are now dangerously overcrowded. But that is because those blank officials in London have so interfered with the natural cycle in Africa, by stopping tribal wars and curing disease, that the African population is growing much too fast, and will double itself within the next thirty-five years. At least one tribe is in steady receipt of famine relief, but the Government steadfastly refuses to conscript men in that tribe to work on the European farms in the White Highlands. And so on.

It is easy, but too misleading, to argue that the Africans of Kenya are poor because the white settlers grabbed their best land. There were injustices and mistakes when the White Highlands were set aside for European occupation, but even now the area of Native lands above the 5,000-foot contour is considerably larger than that of the Highlands. In any case, the Kikuyu, who have produced Mau Mau, lost land to the white men only in one small area near Nairobi; the real sufferers were their most bitter enemies, the Masai, who, as a pastoral tribe, were accustomed to graze their herds over immense areas of land.

Why, then, has Kikuyu discontent found expression in the fanaticism of Mau Mau (a word, by the way, of which nobody seems to know the meaning)? One reason is that, unlike most tribes, the Kikuyu had developed an intricate system of land ownership and tenancies under which they were unable to understand that white men who paid them for land were doing more than renting it. Another reason is that land which had been fully populated for some generations was temporarily empty, as the result of smallpox, rinderpest, drought and locusts at the moment of the arrival of British settlers. Such land quickly reverts to bush and, in any event, Kikuyu goats and sheep need bush rather than normal grazing land. Thus the British quite genuinely believed the land to be empty and the Kikuyu quite genuinely believed the British were tenants who would leave when required to do so. Land hunger is therefore very genuine, and is becoming much more acute, since so many Kikuyu squatters on European farms are no longer trusted and are being sent back to the Kikuyu Native Reserves.

The best analysis of Mau Mau has been written by Dr. L. S. B. Leakey,[1] the greatest expert on East African prehistory, who was brought up among the Kikuyu. From his book one realizes how profoundly the growth of Nairobi, on the outskirts of Kikuyu country, has disturbed the strict moral discipline imposed upon young people by all the tribal ceremonies through which they had to pass with other members of their age group. The oaths they took on such occasions could be broken only at grave risk not to themselves alone, but to every member of their families. Oaths, indeed, are so important that one understands the fear of those who have taken part in a Mau Mau oath-taking ceremony, even though the ceremony is incorrect by Kikuyu standards. There have been several cases of devoted Kikuyu servants asking to be dismissed, since they feared they would not have the courage to break their oaths if they were ordered to murder their white master.

The White Highlanders have some justification for pride in their contribution to the development of their new country. But there are two other Kenyas—the Kenya of the Asians and the Kenya of the Africans. The Kenya of 30,000 Europeans, the Kenya of 90,000 Asians, the Kenya of 5,250,000 Africans. And the road from Uganda has already provided a glimpse of

[1] c.f. *Mau Mau and the Kikuyu* (Methuen & Co. Ltd.)

the other Kenyas. I mentioned the sisal hedges round the Luo
farms and villages down on the plain near the shores of Lake
Victoria; I should have added that the growth of sisal by the
Africans is discouraged, except as windbreaks or as stockades,
because its selling price is so high that the Africans would
concentrate on its production, and grow still less food. Some
of the schools have started their own gardens in an attempt to
increase African interest in the land, but the masters are inclined to look upon the food grown there as their private per-
quisite and the boys are inclined to look upon the gardening
as a chore. Some of these plots are deliberately badly cul-
tivated, in the hope that the boys and their parents will profit
from the example. On one point at least there can be no doubt
or dispute—the District Officers, Agricultural Officers and other
civil servants in the field—many of them young ex-officers
who won high decorations in the last war—work with complete
devotion and great ingenuity to improve the lot of the Africans placed in their charge.

Wherever I have gone in British Africa—and this applies to
the Union of South Africa as well as to the Colonies—I have
been immensely impressed by the devotion these young men
show to their jobs despite so much discouragement. They
must at times feel that they are surrounded by enemies. First,
the enemy of bureaucracy. Just as there is still too little interchange of staff between the Colonial Office and the colonies, so
there is too little interchange between the Secretariat and the
men in the field in the particular Colonies. The men who are
likely to become governors and to retire with a title tend to
cluster round the Secretariat; it is astonishing how many
others prefer the less impressive, but certainly no less useful,
service in remote villages or towns as Agricultural Officers,
District Commissioners, Provincial Commissioners and so on.
Service which cuts them off from all contact with more than
a few dozen white men and from wider cultural interests about
which so many of them somehow remain so well-informed.
They want fewer contacts with the capital, not more. Their
greatest curse is the amount of interference from the Secre-

tariat, the amount of "bumph" that clutters their desks and keeps them from going on safari.

Those of them who work in a country with a large white population must necessarily find enemies even among their own compatriots, for their ambitions are basically different. The White Highlander, at most, wants paternal control now with possible partnership in the very distant future; the official wants partnership now in preparation for the probability of the black man's predominance in the distant future—although not nearly as soon as do some of the politicians in Westminster. In many parts of Africa the patient propaganda of the District Officers is at last having effect—the Africans are being persuaded that they would be better off if they would sell some of their cattle. But in Kenya much of that cattle cannot reach the Nairobi market unless it crosses the White Highlands, a clean island in a sea of degenerate and degenerating stock. Cattle lanes can—at great expense—be wired across this country, but ticks and flies cannot be excluded as easily as all that. And who can blame either the angry official who explains that his tribesmen must be able to sell their surplus cattle which are ruining the soil or the angry White Highlander who has spent all his own money, and probably a lot of the bank's as well, in order to build up a fine pedigree herd, and who sees it threatened by the passage across his land of a lot of diseased and undersized scrub cattle?

But the District Officer's most unexpected enemy is often the African himself. Not so much the ordinary African peasant—even members of the Kikuyu, one of the most fanatically political tribes in all Africa, will in normal times greet a white man with deferent friendliness in the countryside. The opposition comes mainly from the urbanized African, but the development of Mau Mau shows how easily the Nairobi African politician can work on the most superstitious and ignorant of his fellow-tribesmen. And the Government's greatest difficulty is to take action which is strong enough to crush a dirty and dastardly campaign but not so severe that it drives the moderate African to support immoderate policies.

Some years ago I went out to see an African chief near Fort Hall—distinguished from his fellow-men not by some grand robe or head-dress, but merely, as is unfortunately the way with chiefs in East Africa, by a topee and a gilt badge. With great and justified pride he showed me round his land, with its neat terracing and contour-ploughing, designed to prevent the rains from washing away the top-soil. An admirable example to the neighboring villages. But this was Kikuyu country, and the neighborhood where Mau Mau was subsequently to gain so much influence. And the African politicians in Nairobi had decided that such schemes must not succeed—the only schemes that can possibly save the soil of Kenya and thus feed its people—and the peasants were encouraged to pull down the grass banks of the terraces. The white man, the peasants were assured, wanted these changes for some selfish purpose of his own. Since the selfish purpose was unusually difficult to discover in this case, the rumor was put around that the British Navy had objected to the discoloration of the sea by the immense and tragic red patches of topsoil washed down by Kenya's rivers!

The human population is increasing. The cattle population is increasing. The acreage of uneroded land is decreasing. "We are getting near the stage," one disillusioned scientist said to me, "when erosion will have become so bad that cattle will die of starvation as fast as formerly they died of disease. The only difference will be that the different cause of death will have ruined the land and have intensified the jealousy of the black man toward the white man who won't hand over more land to be destroyed."

But a good deal is being done from Nairobi. The District Officer in the villages is trying, against great handicaps, to teach the Africans to conserve their soil—the greatest handicap is that, even if he could persuade them of the necessity of allowing land to lie fallow, there is so seldom any other land available to grow their food for them in the meantime. The central government has to try to teach the Africans a sense of responsibility. I have mentioned in an earlier chapter that a European engine-driver in Kenya gets about three times as much pay as an African driver and twice as much as an Indian one. But for this there is more reason than the African will admit—he is much the least dependable of the three, and is still quite likely to disappear without warning from his work for weeks at a time if some tribal celebration promises to be interesting. The whole African labor force in Kenya is changed entirely in the course of twelve months.

One effort to check this instability is the Kabete Technical and Trade School, near Nairobi, where young Africans are taught to be carpenters, welders, shoemakers and so on. They pay $5.60 a term for their board, lodging and training, with a $28 deposit as a guarantee that they will stay the course. They come on probation for three months, and most of them work with enthusiasm. After a three years' course they are generally able to compete with the Indians on whom their villagers would otherwise be dependent, but the instructors were unanimous in saying that even these selected Africans needed constant supervision and showed very little initiative. I also visited a similar training institute in Kaduna, Northern Nigeria, where the standard of work seemed to be very much higher. But again there were complaints about the lack of initiative and concentration. In any case such schools can deal with only a few hundred students at a time, thus it will be many years before any considerable proportion of the Africans can be trained either as local craftsmen—of which there are astonishingly few when one compares them with even the most primitive peoples of Asia—or as workers in industry.

The other main effort to give the African greater stability and reliability is by the development of local government, which should in time lessen the baneful influence of the worst demagogues in Nairobi. The system in Kenya is less complicated and complete than that in Uganda, but the emphasis is also on encouraging the Africans to govern themselves. There are, for example, African District Councils, in most of which there is a majority of unofficial members. Some of these are elected with the help of the ballot box, but on the whole the better men are generally those chosen by the village elders, sitting under their chosen tree.

A session of an African District Council will probably be opened by the local District Commissioner, who is its president. On the first day he will run through the items on the agenda, give his opinions on them, and explain the reasons for these opinions. But then he will withdraw, and leave the Africans to discuss freely under the chairmanship of an African Vice-President. On the third day he will consider and discuss the Council's conclusions, and in the case of any serious difference of opinion the matter will be referred to the Chief Native Commissioner in Nairobi. On the whole this system seems to work well.

But there is also the authority of the chiefs to be considered. It would seem unwise to put an end to indirect rule, at least until far more Africans have been trained through the schools and these African District Councils to understand and accept responsibility. And yet the younger Africans have no respect for the old system whereby the chief had unlimited authority in his limited sphere. Besides, in the case of the Kikuyu, the tribal customs, which were unusually democratic and decentralized, have been so disturbed that the existing chiefs are not generally considered as men to whom heredity has given a traditional authority; they are looked upon as officials of the white man's government. Therefore there are now a couple of dozen Location Councils, each with some fifteen to twenty members, to advise the chiefs. These councils may cover a population of 20,000 and they seem to the visitor to be as useful a training in the machinery of democracy as can now be devised. But it does not at all satisfy the African politicians in Nairobi.

What would satisfy them? While making every possible allowance for a natural and ebullient nationalism, accentuated by an equally natural dislike of being governed by people of a different color, it is difficult to find excuses for the deliberate

way in which some of these people block the progress of their
more backward compatriots—for the destruction of terraces
that preserve the fertility of the soil is only one of so many
examples. Their behavior is appallingly destructive and irre-
sponsible.

The chief African industrial and political organization in
Kenya is K.A.U., the Kenya African Union, which I found
in one room in a grubby building in the Indian quarter of
Nairobi. Outside the grubby offices of Indian lawyers were
grubby African clients awaiting their turn to waste some of
their small capital on legal fees. Opposite the K.A.U. office
was a bookmaker's den called the City Turf House. But, I reflected, revolutionary changes are planned more often in such
surroundings than in swagger offices with a doorman and a lift.

Jomo Kenyatta, the redoubtable president of the Union, was
away, running his Independent Teachers' College, which the
Government believed to be one of the main channels for
spreading Mau Mau ideas in the villages. A man of considerable culture, he was Secretary-General of the Kikuyu Central
Association, or K.C.A., which was banned during the second
world war on account of its subversive activities. Kenyatta
spent thirteen years in England, and for a time during the war
he worked as a farm laborer in Sussex. Many of his friends at
that time were Communists. Even without any Communist affiliations, however, it is not surprising that a man so ambitious, so histrionic, so brilliant and so frustrated should become a bitter opponent of European rule, even though, since
his arrival as a small orphan at the Church of Scotland mission near Fort Hall, almost every opportunity of advancement
came to him from British benefactors.

While Kenyatta was in England during the war he became
President of a Pan African Federation, of which Dr. Nkrumah,
now Prime Minister of the Gold Coast, was General Secretary.
This federation, of course, brought him into contact with
other African leaders, so that his trial and sentence to seven
years imprisonment have stimulated African nationalism
throughout the continent; inside Kenya itself, his reputation

was immense for his college had supplied many teachers for Kikuyu schools, and some of them had taught their pupils to look upon him as a black man's Christ. The membership of the Kenya African Union was estimated to be about a hundred thousand, most of whom belonged to the Kikuyu tribe, which makes up about one quarter of the country's Africans. Since Kenyatta and other prominent members of the illegal K.C.A. later became prominent in K.A.U., and since Mau Mau methods so closely resemble those of K.C.A., especially in its misuse of Christianity, it is not surprising if most Kikuyu see very little difference between the three of them. And Kenyatta towered above them all. With him out of the way, the authorities have some hope of destroying Mau Mau.

One man I met in the K.A.U. office was its mild-mannered Vice-President, Tom M'botela. He told me in a gentle voice that his people intended sooner or later to run their own country, in which Europeans would be welcomed as long as they obeyed African laws. But even he was too moderate for the Mau Mau fanatics, and he was found murdered and mutilated in the Burma Market in Nairobi. There is now so little room for moderation on either side.

The Mau Mau campaign will, one fears, check progress in Kenya for a long time to come. In such an atmosphere it is very difficult for the government to remove the genuine causes of discontent. One cannot exaggerate the shock to the white settlers to discover murderers and plotters among Kikuyu servants whose loyalty would no more have been questioned a few years ago than would that of the old family retainer in 19th century England. Indeed, it is a high tribute to Michael Blundell and some of his colleagues that the Europeans have shown so much restraint.

On the other side, many of the methods used by the government must accentuate long-term problems even though they be obviously necessary during the emergency. The removal, for example, of many Kikuyu farm workers from the White Highlands back to Kikuyuland could not have been avoided. But it has increased the over-crowding and discontent in the Native Reserves. The Kikuyu on the land are bewildered by the police raids against themselves and their cattle; the Kikuyu in the towns are frightened and embittered by the increased police interest in their activities. Among the African leaders, the few who had the courage and integrity to condemn the Mau Mau appeal to the basest superstitions and most primitive instincts of their fellow-tribesmen feel with some reason that too little use has been made of them; in such a crisis, authority tends to prefer police methods to psychology, and it has been very difficult to decide whom one can trust.

Lastly, the crisis has not led to an improvement in the relations with the third race in Kenya. The Indian community has even more reason than the European to be alarmed by African terrorism; it is much less able to defend itself, and comes much more into genuine competition with the Africans. But there is among the Europeans a deep suspicion that the Hindus have stimulated the African hostility. The government has therefore done very little to associate leading Indians with the campaign against Mau Mau, and they resent it.

Kenya is larger than France. Its capital has grown in sixty years from a stores and repair depot for the Mombasa-Uganda railway to a city with 140,000 inhabitants, of whom rather more than half are Africans. It is by far the best known of British African territories, and its white community, although to a much smaller degree, has struck roots in the White Highlands as deep as those of the Europeans in South Africa. How can Kenya solve the problems of a plural society which have now become almost insoluble in the Union? Are the problems not even graver than those of the Union, since the white community forms so much smaller a proportion of the population, and yet is quite as determined to stay where it is?

There is an exceptional number of British aristocrats in the White Highlands. These people might with profit ask themselves how the British aristocracy has retained its status and power in England for so many centuries. Surely by picking out and promoting men of exceptional energy, promise and ability from other levels of society? In this way fresh blood has been brought in to sustain old titles, and the interests of the aristocracy have in fact more nearly coincided with those of the nation than, perhaps, in any other country. Nowhere else have so many aristocrats supported social reforms, even though they may be the first to suffer from their application.

It is, of course, more difficult for the White Highlanders to adopt a similar policy of integration, for they are expected to welcome men of ability not only of another social class, but also of another race and another color, and color prejudice is notoriously difficult to overcome. But to the visitor there seems to be no other solution. However high the qualifications of intellect and wealth demanded of the voter may be, once they are made the same for everybody, irrespective of color and creed, much of the discontent that causes revolutions is removed.

The color bar has done more than anything else to lose the British their predominant position in Asia. So many of the leaders, from Gandhi downwards, of the nationalist movements have been men who have been embittered by some hurt they have received on account of the color of their skins. That same color bar is in process of losing us our predominant position in Africa, and one will not feel confident that the White Highlanders are there to stay until Europeans, Indians and Africans may be seen drinking their "sundowners" together on the terrace of the Stag's Head at Nakuru while they discuss the problems they have to solve, as the members of Kenya's ruling class. A black man drinking at the Stag's Head? Well, stranger things have happened since the war.

18

SEVEN-SEVEN-SEVEN

Tanganyika is the most stimulating country in Africa. More stimulating than British West Africa, which is admittedly a black man's territory. It is the one country in which the problem of a plural society is being deliberately faced. From the white man's point of view the situation looks even more difficult than in Kenya, for there are only 15,000 Europeans to 72,000 Asians and 7,600,000 Africans. And yet it is the only country in Africa—at any rate, in British Africa—which may supply an alternative to "apartheid."

Between the two world wars Tanganyika suffered from every disadvantage. As a former German colony nobody knew what its future was to be. Mandated territories were not to be treated as colonies, and there was no incentive to spend money on their development. Whatever the government did was sure to arouse criticism in Geneva, and therefore the most sensible thing was to do nothing.

This hesitation has been Tanganyika's greatest blessing. During the war the country inevitably became much more closely linked with Kenya and Uganda to the North and Nyasaland and Northern Rhodesia to the South. And after the war, with the growing, and sometimes exaggerated, estimates of the potentialities of Africa, it became absurd to leave so large a territory undeveloped. The Overseas Food Corporation chose it as the scene of its most ambitious and most disastrous experiment, which nevertheless provided some communications and a lot of experience. The world shortage of sisal brought in a lot more capital. Above all, Tanganyika has had the chance to benefit from the mistakes of other and more advanced territories; thanks to the energy of an exceptional Governor, it has done so in the most encouraging way. When the British received the mandate for Tanganyika after the first world war, the budget provided for an expenditure of under $2,800,000; expenditure now amounts to nearly $56,000,-000. In 1921, there were 3,800 African school-children; in 1951, there were 227,000.

In 1884 that very remarkable German, Dr. Karl Peters, formed a Society for German Colonization, and went inland from Bagamoyo to make agreements with as many of the tribes as he could find. It was from this same little port, forty-four miles north of Dar-es-Salaam, that Stanley had set out thirteen years earlier in search of Livingstone, to whom he gave his famous greeting at Ujiji, on Lake Tanganyika (the surface of which is 2,500 ft. above sea level and the floor, 2,000 ft. below it). And it was to Bagamoyo that Livingstone's devoted carriers brought his body after his death. Although they disguised the corpse as a bale of goods, their journey with it through hostile and superstitious territory is one of the greatest tributes ever paid to that amazing man. Lastly, Bagamoyo was the end of a sandy track, still known as Caravan Road, down which came hundreds of gangs of chained slaves to be shipped overseas, and the name of the town is said to mean: "Here we lay down our hearts."

Karl Peters found more sympathetic listeners in Berlin than

did Cecil Rhodes and William Mackinnon in London. The British were surfeited with colonial problems and still so easily able to find markets and raw materials elsewhere; they wanted no more territory to be painted red on the map. The Germans, on the other hand, were just beginning to reach out for colonies. Although, as we have already seen, the British Government was driven to declare its rights over Uganda, and to build a railway from Mombasa to enforce them, it had for several years paid scandalously little attention to German penetration in Africa which cut across Cecil Rhodes's proposed line of communications from the Cape to Cairo.

How well or badly the Germans colonized the territory, the passing visitor cannot tell. They were certainly very harsh, and 120,000 Africans are said to have died as the result of one rebellion against them—the Maji Maji Rising of 1905. On the other hand, the "no nonsense" policy was one the Africans could understand and respect, and the traditional thoroughness and industry of the Germans did much to help the subsequent development of the country by the British. It was a German, Dr. Hindorf, who imported 1,000 sisal plants from Florida, of which 300 survived by the time they reached Hamburg and only sixty by the time they reached Tanganyika —but from those sixty plants has grown the sisal industry which now produces some 180,000 tons of the Territory's most valuable export.

Most of the few European settlers in Tanganyika are grouped along the slopes of Kilimanjaro and the neighboring mountains. Arusha and Moshi give one as strong an impression of British influence as any towns in Africa. I came to them by road from Nairobi, and stopped, some forty miles short of Arusha, to ask something of an old lady in a white bonnet such as one sees in early Dutch paintings. She could answer me only in Dutch, for one finds quite a number of Boers whose wanderlust has driven them as far north as Tanganyika and Kenya, and her family had left South Africa in the days before Afrikaans had displaced High Dutch as the language of the Boers. In Arusha there is a signpost proclaiming that the town is exactly half way from the Cape to Cairo, so these descendants of Van Riebeeck have travelled quite a distance.

But the nearer I came to Kilimanjaro, the more non-British Europeans I met. When the Germans were turned out during the second world war there was very little competition among the few British settlers to take their place. Nor did the government encourage them to do so. Nobody knew what the future status of Tanganyika would be, and for a time the Government would grant leases of land for only thirty-three years, which attracted the type of farmer who was ready to take all he could out of the land but to put nothing back. Also, it would not look too good to members of any future Mandates Commission if the best non-Native land in this Territory, which was supposed to be governed in the interest of all nations, were to go to settlers from the United Kingdom. Thus it happens that the Greeks and the Indians bought up many of the German estates along the slopes of Kilimanjaro and the neighboring mountains. Even in this British-looking town of Arusha the Indian quarter houses 41,000 people to the square mile, as against 35,000 in parts of London, where at least there are sanitary arrangements. And in the country as a whole there are more Greeks than people from the United Kingdom.

In the plain, below the European farms and coffee plantations, live the Masai with their cattle. On the mountain, above the Europeans, live the Chagga, who were driven there in the first place to escape from the Masai and who now make so much money out of growing coffee that their number has increased from about one hundred thousand in 1919 to over a quarter of a million.

The Chagga are one of the most intelligent tribes in all Africa, and, under the guidance of one European, Mr. A. L. B. Bennett, they have organized the Kilimanjaro Native Cooperative Union, now twenty years old with twenty-nine affiliated societies, which is the most successful experiment of the

kind anywhere in the Continent. The export of coffee comes
second only to that of sisal—although a very long way behind
it—and the Africans now grow much more of it than the Europeans. Between $3,220,000 and $3,500,000 is the average annual
local value of the crop grown by the members of the
K.N.C.U., which means that the Chagga, by African standards,
are extremely wealthy and by any standards, quite well-to-do.
The three chiefs of the tribe each get $1,680 a year salary, but
many of the growers earn very much more. They are so anxious
to make money out of coffee that they have too little land for
the bananas which provide most of their food, and their desire
to get land in the middle belt of European settlement, rather
than to go to land which the government has prepared for
them in the plains causes a good deal of friction. Their reluctance to go down to the plains is all the more understandable
because it takes about three generations before they are accustomed and relatively immune to malaria. And they cannot
go farther up the mountain without destroying the forest belt
upon which the rainfall depends.

The headquarters of the K.N.C.U. is at Moshi, a pleasant
little town at the foot of Kilimanjaro, which towers almost
20,000 feet above sea level. And this building is, in its own
way, as remarkable as the coffee co-operatives that have made
its construction possible. It is an international community
center as well as an office, and will have cost about $560,000
when it is finished. It has well-equipped bedrooms, each with
its own bathroom and lavatory, a printing press, a large library,
a reading room, a roof garden, its own shops and a laundry.
The part still to be finished will contain an assembly hall to
seat 750, a restaurant to seat 250 and a museum. This center
had been built entirely on Chagga initiative and with Chagga
money. A distinguished Colonial ex-Governor, Sir Charles
Dundas, living in retirement in Cape Town, was invited to
lay the foundation stone because, as the first British administrator in Moshi after the Territory had been taken over from
the Germans, he persuaded the Chagga people to grow coffee.

One could not exaggerate the patient efforts made by Mr.

Bennett in teaching these Africans the value of co-operation, but this center was not built at his suggestion; it is the proof, given spontaneously by Africans, that black-white partnership is not necessarily an empty phrase. Other similar, but less ambitious, attempts to cater for a plural society which I have come across have nearly always been the result of European initiative and all over Africa these welfare centers, if imposed from above, are unlikely to serve the purpose for which they were intended. They tend to become "snob clubs," from which the masses feel they are excluded because they have not the necessary intellectual attainments to understand the impressive publications that lie around in them; often they provide centers in which the better-read Africans meet to grumble that so little opportunity is given them to make use of their learning. But the Centre at Moshi, one of the finest buildings in East Africa, is entirely an African affair.

The K.N.C.U. printing press is the only one in Moshi and work of every kind comes its way. I asked one of the African managers—for it is entirely independent of European control —what he was printing at the moment. With a smile almost entirely devoid of malice, he showed me the latest edition of the rules of the Moshi Club, with the usual insistence on its exclusively European character. The K.N.C.U. has sent eight Africans to study in England, and one of the worries of Mr. Bennett, when I met him, was whether, on their return, they will be able—will be allowed—to get jobs good enough to prevent them from becoming embittered.

The progress of this remarkable organization has not always been smooth. In 1937 the Chagga found it so difficult to understand that co-operation involves giving as well as taking, discipline as well as dividends, that they revolted and burned down some of their own warehouses. As happens only too often in these cases, the trouble was accentuated partly by African agitators who grew no coffee themselves and partly by Indian lawyers. And one needs to remember that in the early days of our own industrial revolution the Luddites destroyed the machines that were ultimately to give them their chance of political and economic freedom. That short-sighted protest did not denote a congenital British inability to face facts, and there must now be very few Chagga who fail to realize the great benefits of the K.N.C.U.

There is another striking example in Tanganyika of what can be done by genuine partnership. This is in Sukumuland at the south-eastern corner of Lake Victoria and just south of that most famous of game reserves, the Serengeti Plains. In the course of ten years an area of uninhabited and tsetse-infested land nearly as large as Wales will have been made safe for human habitation. Roughly one million Africans now living in crowded conditions on land that is decreasingly able to support them will be able to spread out over this new area. And this change, at every stage, has been carried through with the full support of the Africans.

The first stage was to create a Sukumuland Federation which was in itself an important achievement since some fifty tribes were involved, and much patience was needed to persuade their different chiefs to co-operate. Their co-operation now is all the more remarkable because the Federal Council, in which they all meet, also includes a number of "people's representatives," so that the second stage—that of widening the basis of power—has also been accomplished. Further, the members of the Federal Council, which meets twice a year, have relegated some of their responsibility to an Advisory Council with only fourteen members.

The next step was the arrival of government experts who set up their headquarters near the offices of the Federal Council. The team of experts on water conservation, forestry, agriculture, veterinary science, and so on discuss each proposed new step with the team of chiefs and all kinds of experiments are being tried out. As everywhere, the great difficulty is to persuade the Sukumu people to keep their cattle down to numbers the land can carry, and in the early stages of the scheme a drought took the unpopular decision out of their hands by killing off more than half a million of their beasts. But by degrees the peasants are realizing, on a far wider scale than anywhere else in British Africa, that some kind of group or collective farming, with some degree of mechanization and the sale of surplus cattle to a meat-packing station can give them a prosperity and a security such as they had never known before.

Tsetse fly has made about two-thirds of Tanganyika uninhabitable. If the Sukumuland scheme is fully successful the Territory will have set an encouraging example to every other African country with too many peasants and too many cattle on too little land. And that means to almost every country in the continent.

The chief of the Sukumu is a young man named Kidaha Makwaia, who is the first African member of Tanganyika Executive Council and the one African member of the Royal Commission studying conditions in Kenya. Colin Legum[1] has quoted him as saying: "It would be a very bad thing for Africans to lose the great advantage which white settlement has brought to the Territory. But white settlement would not be secure if the great mass of Africans came to feel that they were being denied fair play. It is as much in the interests of the Whites as of the Africans to see that they are fully considered." And, on the other side, Mr. E. Hitchcock, the most important man in the Territory's sisal industry, has said: "It is my view that an imposed white leadership is to-day an anachronism and will surely defeat its own objects. Leadership, whether by Europeans, Asians or Africans, will emerge on its own merits."

That kind of attitude is very unusual and refreshing in Africa. It is due partly to the fact that Tanganyika has been a Mandated or Trust Territory since the end of the First World War, and everybody has been on his best behavior because so many foreigners were looking on, through the windows of the Mandates Commission or the Trusteeship Council. But also it must be due in great part to the personality of Sir Edward Twining, appointed Governor in 1949.

A very large man whose stomach adds greatly to his dignity,

[1] *The Listener*, July 31st, 1952.

with a robust and earthy sense of humor and an ability not
to hurt fools too much when he fails to suffer them gladly.
Had he not chosen the army as a career, he might have made
music hall audiences rock with laughter. But his choice of the
army was a valuable one for a future occupant of Government
House in Dar-es-Salaam. For it gave him a respect for display
and discipline, for one of which the Africans have a great
liking and for the other, a genuine respect. He goes off to
remote parts of his huge territory, appears in full uniform with
the maximum of pomp and circumstance. Having thus impressed the Africans with his own great importance as the
representative of a very important Queen across the seas, he
changes into more ordinary clothes and sits with the chiefs
under their favorite tree, discussing their problems and sharing
their drink. One doubts whether any other type of man could
serve the Territory so well, although his seven-seven-seven policy has made some bitter enemies for him among the white
settlers, especially in the Kilimanjaro area.

Seven-seven-seven? This is the magic number of unofficial
members from each of the three main racial communities whom
it is proposed to appoint to the Legislative Council. Seven
Europeans representing the 15,000 Europeans, seven Indians
representing the 72,000 Asians and seven Africans representing the 7,500,000 Africans.

This is the unanimous recommendation of a Constitutional
Development Committee which spent many months discussing the future of the Territory, and there is no doubt that the
recommendation fits in very closely with the desires of the
Governor himself, who is apt to show great impatience with
any member of one of these communities who forgets that he
should look upon himself, first, as a Tanganyikan and only in
the second place as an Englishman, an Indian or an African.
And the most remarkable feature of this recommendation is
that no unofficial European members on the Committee opposed it. Perhaps, in view of the very small European population, you would not expect them to object to this equality with
much larger communities, but the tradition of European over-

lordship is so deeply ingrained that it is only from this smallest of the communities that any complaints have come. There are a good many white settlers around Kilimanjaro, spiritually and geographically much nearer to Nairobi than to Dar-es-Salaam, who consider the seven-seven-seven agreement as an act of treachery. Their conviction is deepened by the fact that both Indian and African communities, despite their numerical preponderance over the Europeans, have accepted it with enthusiasm.

The Indian community in Tanganyika deserves a special comment. In one of the side streets of Dar-es-Salaam I came across this inscription on the side of some temple: "The sole owner, master and proprietor of this Jamat Khasa is H. H. Rt. Hon. Sir Sultan Mahomed Shah Aga Khan, P.C., G.C.V.O., G.C.S.I., G.C.I.E., L.L.D." The swarming Indian tailors and shop-keepers must, of course, be completely bewildered by all these titles and letters, but their bewilderment probably increase the enthusiasm with which they hang the most frightful colored portraits of him on their walls. It is to this city that he comes to be weighed against diamonds, for Dar-es-Salaam is the headquarters of his Ismaili sect. And his close connection with Great Britain has done much to make the Indians of Tanganyika more accommodating and contented than are the Hindus in Kenya or Natal. Indian feeling in Tanganyika toward the British—or, at least toward British officials—is so good that I once saw the Governor, at a Government House garden party, looking on with calm and confidence while an Indian schoolgirl, with a bow and arrow and unbelievable skill, shot apples off Lady Twining's head for the benefit of Red Cross funds.

The white settlers hate the extent to which the Indians have been allowed to buy sisal and other estates. The Africans complain bitterly of the business morals of the Indian middlemen with whom they have to deal. But without the Indians there would be nobody to give the African's wife the incentive to persuade the African husband to work harder. It is the Indian who brings the vivid cotton cloths of Lancashire (and

Japan) to the remotest areas. It is the Indian who does all
the jobs that are beneath the dignity of the European and
above the ability of the African.

The Europeans supply most of the capital and the political
and technical experience, but it must be admitted that they
will be lucky if the other two communities agree for very long
that these assets are adequate compensation for their small
fraction of the population. As for the Africans, their value
in supplying the labor force should be too obvious to require
mention. Even though few of them work for more than five
hours a day, the whole economy of the country depends upon
them; they are, indeed, so important that the sisal industry
sends motor buses to recruit them all the way to the Belgian
Trust Territory of Ruanda-Urundi.

But partnership is a difficult pill to swallow. Two quotations
will give the white and black points of view. On February 3rd,
1951, the *Kenya Weekly News* wrote: It is idle to suppose
that settlers of Kenya can stand by, disinterested and idle,
while the Colonial Office and the government of Tanganyika
play ducks and drakes with the constitution of a Territory
which is an integral part of the East African economic basin."
Meanwhile the Tanganyika Africa Association was declaring
that: ". . . leadership . . . is understood by Africans to mean
British government guidance under United Nations Trusteeship, and *not* the leadership of some British, European or any
other immigrant elements whose only qualification is their own
free choice and decision to live here." What peaceful solution *could* there be in Tanganyika but "seven-seven-seven"?

Tanganyika is remarkable in one more respect. It was here
that the Overseas Food Corporation carried out its first great
experiment in large-scale food production. So this is the obvious
place in a book for a few comments on future methods of
African development.

The groundnuts scheme started with handicaps for which
people in London rather than in Tanganyika are to blame.

In the first place, it was a grave mistake to put it in the hands of the Ministry of Food instead of the Colonial Office. There could be no more obvious way of impeding co-operation with officials on the spot, no more likely way of finding oneself landed with the wrong sort of personnel.

In the spring of 1947 I found myself in the bar of the Dar-es-Salaam Club. It was a Saturday morning, and the place was therefore packed and cheerful. Another guest there was a very high official of this new groundnuts scheme, and as soon as he went out the comments began. Old So-and-so, who had failed in every job, had been offered a fabulous salary to do something at which he was sure to fail again. Somebody else, who knew Tanganyika like the palm of his hand, had volunteered a few details about the climate and the soil, and had been snubbed for his pains. Somebody else had complaints to make about the way in which the Native labor was being recruited, regardless of the requirements of existing farms and estates. I had never heard so many people condemning a scheme for so many diverse reasons.

In one respect the people in London were unlucky. They *did* take the advice of a man who had been an agricultural expert in the Tanganyika Administration, and that advice turned out to have been bad. But in most other respects they deserved disaster, and the resentment of many of the men in the field. There was so little attempt to win the co-operation of men who had gained their experience of the soil and climate the hard way. There were no pilot schemes. Recruits selected in London were hopelessly unsuitable. One hears of a waiter, a photographer and others who were sent out as tractor drivers but who had never previously driven tractors in their lives; of scores of officials with high salaries hanging about at Lindi and Dar-es-Salaam with no work to do; of men who had never employed workers of another race and color being placed in charge of African labor. In these circumstances, the wry jokes about the scheme are not surprising—what is the difference, one was asked, between the Overseas Food Corporation and the B.O.A.C., and the answer was that the O.F.C. carried more passengers. Or one was told about the man who came into a bar in Dar-es-Salaam, ordered a beer, put two groundnuts on the counter and asked for change.

The 2,400,000 acres of Tanganyika which were to have been prepared for agriculture were reduced in 1949 to 600,000, to be developed by 1954; even this scheme had to be abandoned, and in the end only about one tenth of the 2,400,000 acres will be used for agricultural purposes; the Overseas Food Corporation has been handed over by the Food Ministry to the Colonial Office, and the emphasis will henceforward be placed rather on the best ways to develop African resources than on those of meeting United Kingdom needs.

But that other organization which also aroused such hopes, the Colonial Development Corporation, is still responsible for half a hundred schemes in different parts of the Colonial empire, and many of them are doomed to fail. For it continues to show the same symptoms of incompetence and incomprehension. Until he had held his appointment for over two years, the Chairman, Lord Reith, did not make one journey overseas to study on the spot the difficulties with which his employees were faced, and—perhaps above all in Africa—the soil, the climate and the workers fail to conform to plans drawn up in London. There is still the absence of pilot schemes, of full co-operation with the local governments, and of experience in dealing with African peoples.

And yet there is no future for the African with his hoe, even with a number of wives to do his work for him. Soil erosion and the elimination of diseases and tribal warfare have between them so decreased productivity and increased populations that the old methods are inadequate even to keep people healthy, let alone to give them the few luxuries which they are so rapidly coming to look upon as necessities. Large-scale development is essential, and it would be a great tragedy if the kind of development which the O.F.C. and the C.D.C. were designed to assist were to be condemned because of their failures.

Driving one day from Moshi toward the coast, I came

suddenly to the sisal estates. To the north of the road there was the abominable, useless and monotonous thorn scrub that covers so much of Africa; to the south of it, for mile after mile, stretched neat rows of sisal plants. And the contrast provided one of the most impressive sights I have ever seen. This is what can be done with plenty of capital and a product for which there is a great world demand.

But the plantation system has many social drawbacks even when, as in the case of the sisal plantations, the villages built for the African workers are adequate. I have already shown how it makes the population far too dependent upon the fitful and eccentric demands of people on the other side of the world, and how it often leads to such a demand for the best available land that it results in definite malnutrition. Also it gives the Europeans who run these plantations a political power which cannot easily be justified even though many of these immense organizations, such as the United Africa Company in West Africa, make generous gifts toward African education and welfare. Lastly, the recruiting of the necessary labor force gives rise to increasing difficulties—in South Africa, for example, it led to the problem of the Indians in Natal, and, even where Africans themselves are called upon to supply the labor, the general consequence is to hasten the destruction of family or tribal life before any alternative system has been developed.

The problem seems to be to find a formula which equates African labor with European or international capital. "If the Tanganyika groundnut scheme had been conceived in 1925," wrote Professor Arthur Lewis,[2] "it would have provided for 200,000 indentured Indian immigrants and very little machinery. Instead, conceived in 1946, it provided for $70 millions of capital, at the rate of $1960 per worker, and is to be probably the most highly capitalized agricultural undertaking in the world. . . . We can provide $70 millions for one of these schemes, or $140 millions for two, but it is quite out of the question to do very much development of this type. . . . If

[2] *Attitude to Africa* (Penguin Books).

new plantations fade out of the picture, the development of peasant agriculture becomes the principal means of expanding the colonial output, and this involves a complete revolution in our approach."

That revolution is taking place in Tanganyika; for that reason the country is so stimulating. Sisal—which is a plant with long, spiky leaves such as are sat on by people in slapstick comic films—cannot be grown except in plantations, for the process of extracting the fiber from these leaves is a very complicated and expensive one. But coffee grows all along the branches of coffee trees, and the output of the K.N.C.U. on the slopes of Mount Kilimanjaro is an important agricultural and financial asset to the Colonial Empire. The Sukumaland scheme, to which I have also referred earlier in this chapter, is bringing thousands of acres of completely undeveloped land under cultivation, but only because European capital, skill and knowledge are combining with an African readiness to learn new methods of agriculture. In the Gold Coast and other parts of British Africa, there are schemes which give new land to the African, with water, good housing and roads, in return for his agreement to use new farming methods, and there can be no doubt that the success achieved by a few such undertakings is doing far more than any amount of white man's propaganda to check the destruction of Africa's thin layer of topsoil.

The fundamental defect of the Colonial Development Corporation, then, seems to be that it is ill-suited to encourage the development by Africans themselves. London is not the place in which to plan schemes which depend for their success on the energy and understanding of an African peasant living in a round hut thatched with grass or palm leaves. The capital available for development is still terribly inadequate; it is tragic that any of it should be wasted on schemes, however well-meaning, which do nothing to convince the black people of Africa that they are genuinely the partners of the white people. And such schemes grow slowly, nurtured by experts who have spent years studying the ways of the Africans. The most effective way in which the British taxpayer can help them would seem to be not by subsidizing the large staff of a Colonial Development Corporation, however keen and competent, but by developing new supplies of water and water power, new air, road and rail communications. Trade follows the railway.

19

CENTRAL AFRICAN FEDERATION

In Mbeya, near the Northern Rhodesian border of Tanganyika, they decided I should go to the hospital. My foot, for no apparent reason, was turning from pink to red, from red to blue, from blue to black. But there are only three hundred and thirty-three qualified nurses of any race in the whole of Tanganyika, and Mbeya's one white nurse had been married on the day of my collapse, and all I saw of her was her marriage lines which she had forgotten in the doctor's car.

There were, I learned, two doctors in the town, which was an impressive change after the Southern Highlands, where I had stayed the night before. There they had told me there was a doctor just down the road. How far? At Iringa, about sixty miles away. One of the Mbeya doctors ran two hospitals, one European and one African. The other was Medical Officer for two provinces, with an area 600 by 400 miles under his control. There was trouble at a leprosy station at the other end of his area, and he had to spend much of his time driving along roads that are so dusty in dry weather that there are frequent collisions in the dust clouds when one car is following another, and so slippery after each storm that every car carries chains and a spade. In 1950 there were fewer than three hundred doctors of all races in a country nearly four times the size of Great Britain and roughly one-fifth of the size of the United States. This was my first opportunity of discovering how devoted and overworked are the medical staffs in Africa.

I did not enjoy the interval between the departure from Dar-es-Salaam and the arrival in hospital in Fort Jameson, Northern Rhodesia, sixteen days later. I saw practically nothing of the Southern Highlands of Tanganyika (but enough to convince me that, if I were to settle as a farmer in Africa, I should prefer them to the White Highlands of Kenya). I failed to visit the Lupa gold mines. I missed a motor drive through Nyasaland. But in retrospect I am grateful, for I learned quite a lot about Africa which would in other circumstances have escaped me. The difficulty, for example, of getting from one place to another if one is too ill to travel by road. The nearest railway was more than four hundred miles away, and its train would have taken me back to Dar-es-Salaam. The only aeroplane was an occasional one to two unwanted and remote destinations, and there were immense difficulties about chartering an aircraft of the size we should need.

I learned, too, quite a lot about the African orderlies while I was in Fort Jameson hospital. Their response to broadcasting, for example. The Northern Rhodesian Government has gone to immense pains to find a cheap battery radio set and to provide the kind of program to which the Africans will listen. Although there is still no Central African Federation, there has for some years been an agreement whereby Salisbury broadcasts in English to the two Rhodesias and Nyasaland, while Lusaka, the capital of Northern Rhodesia, broadcasts in various African languages to the three territories. And the Africans listen. Sometimes, for the most urgent needs, I

would ring the hospital bell with no result; I had only to
switch on the radio to a program of African music, and the
whole African staff would find that there were important jobs
to be done in my room, and I could be rid of them only by
switching off again.

I learned a little of the responsiveness of the African. The
first time I was allowed to have a bath, the business of getting
me into it was so painful that I was on the verge of tears,
and the orderlies looked as though they shared my misery.
Fortunately, the idea of three Blacks trying to lift my pink
and podgy self into the bath struck me as so unexpected and
comical that, instead, I burst into rather hysterical laughter.
The result was terrific; the Africans laughed even more loudly
than I, while the matron knocked on the door in shocked bewilderment.

I even began to learn the local African language, Chinyanja,
in order that I could say "buinobuino," which means "carefully"—literally "good, good"—when the orderlies were making
my bed. I discovered that a mosquito is "oodzoodzoo" and a
machine-gun, not surprisingly, is "bombom." But a bullet for
some reason is "cipolopolo." "Mzungu" is a European, but
"Dzungu" is a pumpkin. "Bingu" is an earthquake, and when
one occurs you run "balála balála," or helter-skelter, out of
your house. "Kalilole" is the charming word for a mirror, and
to commit adultery is pronounced "Kuchita chigololo."

I learned that the hoopoe pottered about under the tree outside my room only very early in the morning, and that it spent
most of its time with its magnificent crest folded up like a
closed fan. I learned to expect the cloud of cigar birds—very
small, brown birds with ash-colored heads—a little before dusk.
I learned that during the heat of the day hardly a bird was to be
seen or heard. I learned at what time to expect the party of
African prisoners wheeling the trucks with buckets of night
soil from the town to some unknown destination. And when
I got better and could be moved to my son's tobacco farm
some miles away, I learned to think with real affection of the
five or six Africans who carried my bed through the orange

grove to the river bank. No Roman emperor was ever carried in his litter by so cheerful a bunch of bearers.

This affection for the Africans still prevails among the white settlers of Northern Rhodesia, and the history of their new homeland differs sufficiently from that of Southern Rhodesia to explain why union between these two countries would be impossible and federation will be difficult. But the young men in wide-brimmed hats, corduroy trousers and bright check shirts from the tobacco farms or the mines of the two Rhodesias impress one as being far more self-confident than the white men in most other parts of Africa. With the examples of the Gold Coast away to the north and of Malan's "apartheid" away to the south—the one so ready to criticize the Europeans, the other so ready to criticize the Africans—they are determined to mold their own futures themselves. The British Government has already lost almost all control over Southern Rhodesia; the Colonial Office has to deal very carefully with Northern Rhodesia, even though it became a colony as recently as 1924.

Those Europeans in Tanganyika who are not officials or merchants in Dar-es-Salaam live for the most part on the slopes of Kilimanjaro and neighboring mountains or in the Southern Highlands. They have added considerably to the wealth of the Territory, and they live in a beautiful part of Africa. But there are only 15,000 of them all told, and they are nowhere near to agreement amongst themselves about the political future. Even in Kenya the total white population is less than that of Dover. Elsewhere in British Colonial Africa all but a very few officials and business men plan one day to return to Europe and to live on their pensions. But the white population in Northern and Southern Rhodesia already outnumbers that of Kenya, Tanganyika and Uganda by about three to one. It is expanding so rapidly that it has doubled in just over ten years. Lusaka and Bulawayo are boom towns such as one might have found in the Far West at the beginning

of this century and as one might find now in parts of Siberia
if one were allowed to go there. With immense resources in
water power, iron ore, copper and coal, the two Rhodesias are
bubbling over with self-confidence.

How did these huge territories become part of the British
Commonwealth? Not by any action ordered from Whitehall.
The copper of Northern Rhodesia is one of the greatest dollar
earners, and had Rhodes been backed up by an enthusiastic
British Government, he might even have added to the assets
of the Commonwealth the uranium that is now bringing so
much wealth to the Belgian Congo. But successive British
Governments were as anxious to avoid obligations in Central
Africa as they had been in Kenya. The best the Colonial
Office can now say is that the British public was not called
upon to contribute a single soldier or a single shilling in the
conquest of the Rhodesias.

Northern Rhodesia was not in fact conquered, and such
fighting as occurred in Southern Rhodesia was mainly the
affair of Cecil Rhodes' Pioneer Column. In 1888 this extraordinary man obtained a concession from Lobengula, a chief
of the Matabele, for the minerals that might lie somewhere
beneath his land. He formed the British South Africa Company, which was granted a Royal Charter in the following
year, "to promote, under the supervision of the High Commissioner for South Africa, trade, commerce, civilization and
good government in the area bordered on the south by the
Transvaal, on the east by Portuguese East Africa and Nyasaland, on the west by South-West Africa and on the north by
the Belgian Congo and Tanganyika Territory."

The price paid to Lobengula for this concession was £100
($280) a month, and 3,000 rifles. There was also to have been
a gunboat on the Zambesi, but it never arrived. At the time that
the concession was granted, the Matabele dominated much of
what is now known as Southern Rhodesia, and they were
frequently at war with the Mashona tribes farther east. They
also provided a constant threat to the Barotse, north of the

Zambesi, who occupied most of what is now known as Northern Rhodesia.

To maintain order in this immense area, and to develop its resources, the famous Pioneer Column of 187 Europeans and 150 Africans left Kimberley in 1890. Lobengula found that he had signed away more than his tribesmen were prepared to grant, and only three years after the Pioneer Column arrived there occurred the Matabele war and the occupation of Matabeleland. Then came the Matabele and Mashona Rebellions, which were put down in 1897. Since that date, no African has been killed by government forces in maintaining law and order in Southern Rhodesia.

In fear of the Matabele, the Paramount Chief of the Barotse asked in 1890 for the protection of the British Government. Nine years later, he granted the "Barotse Concession" to the British South Africa Company, which has since formed the basis of British administration in Barotseland. This Concession was to be considered as "a treaty or alliance" between the Barotse nation and the Government of Queen Victoria. Although Barotseland is now part of Northern Rhodesia, the constitutional powers of its Paramount Chief remain.

As for Nyasaland, the proclamation of a British Protectorate in 1891 put an end to civil wars and the slave trade. It has remained almost entirely an African territory, with some 4,000 Europeans out of a total population of 2,350,000. There is a less rigid color bar than in the Rhodesias and a remarkably high standard of African intelligence—perhaps higher even than that of Uganda, although it has not the same highly developed monarchical system which so impressed Speke and other early explorers in search of the sources of the Nile.

Thus, Southern Rhodesia was to some extent a conquered territory, in which authority was imposed, and Northern Rhodesia joined the British Empire of its own free will and retained its tribal chiefs and customs. And this contrast between direct and indirect rule has led to notable differences in the development of the two countries. The whole emphasis in Southern Rhodesia has been upon the economic development of the African, to the extent which the European has thought expedient; in Northern Rhodesia it has been upon the African's political development. Southern Rhodesia can rightly claim in many ways to have done more for the welfare of the ordinary African than Northern Rhodesia has done; its expenditure on social services is, in fact, greater than that of Northern Rhodesia and Nyasaland put together. Northern Rhodesia, on the other hand, has tried at every stage to give the African a sense of responsibility for his own affairs.

The results have been startling different. In Northern Rhodesia and Nyasaland, the Africans play a considerable part in local government and have their own Native Authorities which are far in advance of the Native Councils in Southern Rhodesia. They have more chance of reaching high ranks in the Civil Service, and there is far less tendency to accept the idea that the white and black races must grow up in two entirely separate compartments.

One needs to remember how many of the earlier settlers, especially in Southern Rhodesia, came from South Africa. Many members of the Pioneer Column were murdered on outlying farms or killed in the fighting during the Matabele and Mashona rebellions. The link between Southern Rhodesia and South Africa would not be very strong even if the Europeans in both countries were not faced by a similar color problem.

Northern Rhodesia is in many ways a typical British African colony. Only about one-fiftieth of the land is occupied by Europeans. More than one-fifth of the country consists of Native Reserves, where no European may settle. Two-thirds is Native Trust Land, which is kept for African development, but of which part can be alienated in the interests of the country as a whole, for such purposes as the making of a new forest reserve, the building of a new town, the construction of roads or the conservation of water. There is still some Crown land, but not nearly enough of it is made available to Europeans to please the tobacco planters, who need a lot of land to lie fallow and to supply the timber with which to dry their tobacco. And not nearly enough to please the Afrikaners trekking up from the Union.

These Afrikaners face the Colonial Office with a problem that is, I think, unique in a British colony. One day in Cape Town I mentioned to Dr. du Plessis, the Director of the State Information Office, the astounding fact that the Union, in the middle of its industrial revolution, had a decreasing white population. More Europeans were then leaving the country than were coming into it (although this tendency was reversed in the latter part of 1952). He agreed that this was due in part to the small encouragement given by the present Government to all immigrants except those who are highly skilled, but he added, with every appearance of satisfaction, another reason, which was that so many Afrikaners were trekking northward. These men, he explained, would be able to spread Afrikaner methods of dealing with the growing danger from the Blacks. These men are hard workers and they are tough, but many of them believe in complete segregation of the Africans which the Colonial Office has rejected in favor of "partnership." In the second quarter of 1952, for the first time since the war, more immigrants into Northern Rhodesia came from the United Kingdom than from South Africa.

Northern Rhodesia has a white population scarcely larger than that of Kingston-on-Thames, but it is a country large in size and prospects. It is a thousand miles by road from Livingstone in the south-west, to Abercorn in the north-east and its area is roughly three times that of Great Britain. So far, there is a much friendlier relationship between European and African than in Southern Rhodesia or Kenya. It seems to be one of the territories in which, as in Tanganyika, a genuine partnership might still be devised, and the African's hesitation to discuss federation is very intelligible, even though it may be unwise. In most colonies in Africa one finds that far more money is spent on the education of a few hundred Europeans than upon hundreds of thousands of Africans; in Northern Rhodesia, on the contrary, roughly two and a half times as much goes to African, as to European education. In 1927, expenditure on African education was $19,600; in 1937 it was $80,220; in 1947 it was $687,506. By 1950 the figure had risen to $957,600.

This increase, however, is due less to any remarkable change in the Black-White relations than to the riches that have poured into the country in payment for its copper. The national revenue in 1951 was almost exactly ten times that of 1939. It would have been even greater if communications were better. All the coal has to come by rail from the Wankie Colliery, in Southern Rhodesia, and not enough of it is available although the railway is the only one I know on which coal trucks have absolute priority over passenger trains. When coal is short, wood has to take its place. In one year 20,000 acres of forest had to be felled for the copper and zinc mines. Although Northern Rhodesia has a greater relative area of forest than any other British African territory, this destruction of timber, considerably aggravated by the tobacco planters, may end up by altering the rainfall, upon which European and African alike depend for their livelihoods.

Politically the extent to which the African has advanced in Northern Rhodesia is shown by the fact that two of the four members representing African interests in the Legislative Council are themselves Africans, whereas no African yet sits in the Southern Rhodesian Parliament. To the Executive Council— the Government—the door is left open for African members "when they are ready for it."

But, despite these first steps toward "Partnership," the European "unofficials"—settlers, tobacco growers, miners and others—have much more power than one would expect in a colony where they are so heavily outnumbered by the Blacks and so restricted in their ownership of land. For there is a gentleman's agreement that, subject to his own right in the last resort to appeal to the Colonial Secretary, the Governor will accept any measure on which the elected members of the Executive Council are unanimous. But one of these elected members is there to represent African interests, and it is therefore unlikely that—even with the able and vigorous Roy Welensky, ex-boxer, ex-barman and ex-engine-driver, as their leader—the "unofficials" would be able to push the Government into some action contrary to the final policy of partnership. Nor is it at all likely that Welensky would push them in that direction.

In the very important matter of housing, the Northern Rhodesian Africans are also better off than most of the Africans farther south. In the copper mines, the owners have built whole villages for their workers, so that there is not the tragic break with family and tribal traditions that one finds in the gold mines of Johannesburg. In South Africa, and in a slightly lesser degree in Southern Rhodesia, the fiction is maintained that the African who comes to town will sooner or later return to his Native Reserve, and in consequence very little is done to give him the ordinary and reasonable amenities of an urban home; in principle, the African of Northern Rhodesia can build his house in a town on the same terms as the European.

There is, it must be admitted, a very wide gap between principle and practice. For example, in most shops the African is served through a special hatch. The usual excuse for this discrimination is that if the African comes inside the shop to make his purchase he will bring all his family with him and they will be there all day fingering the materials while he tries to make up his mind. But this excuse can hardly justify the use—even though it is diminishing—of a similar procedure in post offices and banks. Again, there is a vigorous trade union movement in Northern Rhodesia, which the Government has helped to organize and which has managd very considerably to raise the miners' wages in the copper mines. There is still a wide discrepancy in pay between the skilled worker, who is always European, and the unskilled worker, who is always African—the Northern Rhodesian Government's report for 1950 gave the average monthly basic wage in the mining industry for Europeans working underground as $143.20; the average monthly basic wage for Africans working underground totaled about $11.20, plus their food. But at least the principle of trades unionism is given official encouragement in Northern Rhodesia; it is definitely discouraged south of the Zambesi.

In two other respects the Northern Rhodesian African is better off than the African farther south. An African co-operative movement is developing under official sponsorship. Most of the Europeans look on it with much the same disfavor as their compatriots showed in the early years of the coffee co-operatives on Mount Kilimanjaro, but the system is nevertheless on the way to success. And, lastly, the Northern Rhodesian Government is encouraging a system of group-farming under which—as in the Gold Coast and some other colonies—an African is given some thirty acres of land and facilities for farming it on the condition that he follows the advice of the experts. The country is short of food, and is likely to remain so for years to come, partly because few of the tobacco growers yet go in sufficiently for mixed farming even to feed their own employees, partly because the increasing demand for copper leads to an increasing demand for food for the miners, but, above all, because the Africans experience the same temptation to leave the land in order to go to the towns that the English rural worker experienced during the industrial revolution.

This drift from the land is one of Northern Rhodesia's greatest worries. It means that more than half the men are away from the villages at any one time. Some of them go to work on the tobacco farms round Fort Jameson (where the last caravan of slaves on its way to the coast was intercepted by the British in 1898). In that event the men are probably not too far away from their Reserves. But the tobacco planters themselves find it increasingly difficult, despite rising wages, to keep their workers, who drift either westward to the Copper Belt or southward to Johannesburg. The Nationalists in Pretoria, in defense of their color policy, can always point out that the Northern Rhodesian Government has to impose strict regulations to prevent too many of its Africans from going to work in the Union.

One handicap of this migration is that it makes Northern Rhodesia too vulnerable to economic blizzards. Too few people are producing food; too many are helping to mine copper and lead or to grow tobacco. More than half of Northern Rhodesia is infested with tsetse fly, and it can therefore supply only about three-fifths of its meat demand (for the African worker expects much more meat—of a sort—than does the average worker in Great Britain). Should there be a sudden fall in the world price for copper, the resulting crisis would be much more severe because the country cannot produce all its own food.

The European population of Southern Rhodesia is three and a half times greater than that of Northern Rhodesia; its Government is not under the control of the Colonial Office; although any bill which might seem to discriminate against the Africans must be submitted to the Secretary of State for Commonwealth Relations before it becomes law, no such bill has in fact been rejected in London; and geographically and sentimentally, Southern Rhodesia is much nearer than Northern Rhodesia to the Union of South Africa.

These facts help to explain why there is so much opposition among the Africans of Northern Rhodesia and Nyasaland to the proposal for federation with Southern Rhodesia, even though, in that country, more money is spent on African education, health and agricultural development. Events in the Union provide a strong argument in favor of a Federation; they also strengthen the opposition to it. And the distrust of change is not confined to the few Africans who are politically conscious. To their fear that the Europeans will do them down, one must add the traditional and universal conservatism of a peasant people. Should federation of the three Central African territories (which, incidentally, are nowhere near the center of Africa) have been forced through, as being good for the Africans, like contour-ploughing or injections against

sleeping-sickness? Or should it have been delayed in the rather
vague hope that, in due course, the Africans would decide
that they would like it?

One political argument that federation would be a retro-
grade step is based on the fact that Southern Rhodesia has
no Africans in its Legislative Council, whereas the other two
territories each have two African members. But this is of relatively small importance, since the federal proposals in no way
affect the composition of the three existing legislative councils, whereas they do provide for six Africans in the proposed Federal Assembly. The real objection lies elsewhere.
It is that the discrimination against the Africans north of
the Zambesi is enforced not by law, but by social prejudice
and may therefore be more likely to disappear than the legal
discrimination one finds in Southern Rhodesia. The attitude
of the European workers on the Copper Belt has been selfish
(although there seems to be far more excuse for it than for
the attitude of mine-workers in Britain in 1952 toward
Italian miners) but there are not the same legal restrictions
in Northern as in Southern Rhodesia against the economic
progress of the African. The urban African is annoyed by
pass regulations in both the Rhodesias; in Southern Rhodesia,
however, he needs more passes and they are more strictly con-
trolled. The African in Lusaka or any other town in Northern
Rhodesia is unlikely to be able to build himself a house in
the middle of the European area, but there is no law against
it, as there is in Salisbury or any other Southern Rhodesian
town.

It is quite true that the Black-White relations in Southern
Rhodesia are very much better than are those in the Union,
just as they are better north of the Zambesi than they are
south of it. But the Africans are far less crowded in Northern than in Southern Rhodesia, and far less again in Southern
Rhodesia than in the Union. The more one studies legislation
in Southern Rhodesia, the more one is driven to the conclusion that racial relations are better there than in South Africa
because the European's feeling of insecurity is not yet so

pronounced, and not that there is less feeling of European insecurity because racial relations are better. Legislation so far is much less harsh, but there is no guarantee that it will never become so.

But there is one respect in which legislation in Southern Rhodesia is markedly different from that in the Union, and, although I referred to it in the South African section, I return to it, because it introduces so important a principle. There is a common voters' roll; providing he has certain property qualifications, every adult Southern Rhodesian has the vote, irrespective of the color of his skin.

In practice, this may not mean very much, and already the law has been amended in such a way that much of the value of the principle has been destroyed. Originally the qualification, apart from a very rudimentary knowledge of English, was the possession of an income of £100 ($280) a year or of property of £150 ($420); in 1951 the respective figures were raised to £240 ($672) and £500 ($1400), and, although this was explained as a result of currency depreciation, most people interpreted it as a measure to keep down the number of Africans who might vote. There are fewer than 500 Africans on this roll (although probably four times as many have the necessary qualifications but do not apply to be enrolled, either because they are too lazy or because they would not like the tax-collector to know how much they possess).

The economic advantages of federation are fairly obvious. For example, the Copper Belt in Northern Rhodesia has to depend for its coal on the Wankie Colliery, in Southern Rhodesia. The present frontiers are entirely artificial, and they divide peoples, black and white, whose problems are similar. Above all, there is not much chance of progress in the Kariba Gorge scheme without some kind of federal authority, able to decide what should be the responsibilities and financial burdens of each territory.

The Kariba Gorge is nearly three hundred miles below the

Victoria Falls. A dam across the Zambesi here will ultimately have a hydro-electric capacity of one million kilowats, twice that of the Volta River scheme in the Gold Coast. The "immediate potential load" of the Copper Belt is put at onetenth of this total, while Salisbury and the area round it would take about 300,000 kilowatts. The initial scheme, producing 385,000 kilowatts, would cost at least $121,853,200, and would be in operation in "1960 or as soon thereafter as possible." The final scheme would cost an estimated $208,611,200.

All these estimates have been prepared by a commission which was set by the Central African Council, and which reported in May 1951. But the Zambesi divides the two Rhodesias, of which one governs itself and the other has to depend on decisions reached in London. What does each country need in power? How to meet the irrigation needs of each? How much must each pay? Such questions may receive no answer for years unless they can be discussed in a federal parliament. A much stronger unifying force is needed than that provided by the existing Central African Council.

There is a far more important argument for federation. Undoubtedly the Europeans who favor it do so because they want to strengthen their own position. But not only *vis-à-vis* the African. If the Native policies of Northern Rhodesia and Nyasaland differ too widely from that of Southern Rhodesia, the latter will almost certainly turn more and more toward "apartheid" and the Union. The final Scheme, published in February 1953, leaves the three territorial legislatures in control of all regulations concerning the ordinary daily routine of the Africans in their respective territories; when some federal change of policy is under consideration, the African Affairs Board, half white and half black, comes into operation. Any proposed federal legislation which, in its opinion, differentiates between Europeans and Africans, has to be referred to Westminster and Whitehall for approval. The safeguards are as complete as they could be—but there is not much that London can do if they are not respected. These white Rhodesians may still be guided; one doubts whether they could be coerced.

There are, then, three reasons why federation seems to be advisable. One, the influence of the Secretary of State over Southern Rhodesia is still considerable. Although he has not, in fact, vetoed any legislation in Southern Rhodesia, this is because the proposals have been modified, on Whitehall advice, before they have reached the public. Two, there is, among the white men in all three territories, a kind of nostalgic affection for the Old Country about which it is very easy to scoff (as it is, indeed, about any deep emotion) but which shows its strength and value whenever the United Kingdom becomes involved in war. If that tie of affection were ever to snap, it would be mainly because we at home had failed to appreciate the genuine problems of ordinary, decent folk in Central Africa. And, lastly, the more one travels in Africa, the more one realizes that the emancipation of the African will come not through some startling conversion of the Europeans to a "Fabian" kind of policy, but through the force of economic circumstances. New factories, new mines, new large-scale methods of agriculture require skilled labor, and only the Africans will be able to provide it. The capital for such undertakings is more likely to be forthcoming if there is a federation than if the three States remain divided.

In Nyasaland, where opposition to federation is strongest, Blacks outnumber Whites by more than six hundred to one; it is not therefore surprising if their political leaders dream of following the Gold Coast and Nigeria toward self-government. But these leaders, who are among the more intelligent Africans, must be aware of the smallness and poverty of their country. It has some coal but few other minerals. The chief export of the Gold Coast is cocoa, wanted all over the world; that of Nyasaland is young men, leaving in search of work in Johannesburg or on the Copper Belt.

Nevertheless, even the keenest supporters of federation have to admit that African hostility to it is much more widespread than they had expected. More than a hundred Chiefs, including such important ones as Chitimukulu of the Bemba and Mpezeni of the Ngoni, have signed a petition against federation organized by the African National Congress of Northern Rhodesia. There have been equally significant developments in Nyasaland. I am one of those who have come to support federation because I believe the Europeans who will have to carry it out—those on the spot—are more likely to behave well if they have this evidence that the British government has shown confidence in them than if they are constantly accused of irresponsibility by people in Westminster. The assurance that the proposed university for Central Africa will be open to students of all races may be only the first of many measures to lessen African distrust of federation.

Apart from the official plan for a Central African federation, there is the unofficial plan, put forward by the Capricorn African Society—headquarters, Salisbury—for a still wider federation which would link the two Rhodesias and Nyasaland to Kenya, Tanganyika and Uganda. And, although this plan is mainly the work of one man, Colonel David Stirling, who started the Special Air Service during the war, it deserves a section to itself as the most interesting proposal yet produced in British Africa.

To the distress of many Europeans in the Union, on the other side of the Limpopo River, this Capricorn Society opens its Declarations, first published in December 1952, with the affirmation that "all men, despite their varying talents, are born equal in dignity before God, and have a common duty to one another. . . . We emphasize this simple precept of Christian teaching . . . because we want to dissociate ourselves from barren philosophy which determines racial relations in lands beyond our boundaries." Which is a relatively polite way of rejecting the "apartheid" of Dr. Malan. European leadership, necessary at the outset, "will not endure, nor deserve to endure, unless it encourages the participation of other races.

. . . All Africans who have attained the necessary social and intellectual standards must be accorded the responsibility of franchise, and be given no less opportunity than their European fellow-citizens to play their part in an expanding civilized community."

The Capricorn Society is not, however, naïve enough to suppose that many Africans are yet ready for this equality of opportunity with the Europeans. It claims that there must be a kind of "apartheid" but one which is designed rather to protect the African than the European. There must, in other words, be Native Development Areas and Open Areas. The former would include Uganda, Nyasaland, the Barotseland Protectorate in Northern Rhodesia, and, roughly, the existing Native Reserves in Kenya, Southern Rhodesia and Tanganyika. In these Native Development Areas only Africans would own land; in the Open Areas "the paramount interest will be that of civilization itself, not the interest of any one race, color or creed." The Africans who chose to live in these Open Areas would in fact be those who were sufficiently advanced to compete with the Europeans.

The plan is still vague in many respects. Intentionally so, for it could not otherwise win support from important members of all three racial communities. In order to soothe the White Highlanders, it provides that non-Europeans in the Open Areas would be allowed to own only urban land. It does not make clear what kind of test the Africans would have to pass before they were accorded "the responsibility of franchise," but the important fact is that Africans, Indians and Europeans—some of them—see in the Capricorn Declarations the possibility of breaking away from a negative policy based upon fear. They plan to hold a multi-racial conference in 1954, one object of which will be to discuss how to define "civilized men" to whom, Cecil Rhodes claimed, equal rights should be guaranteed, whatever the color of their skins.

Many of the Europeans who support this plan do so because they have come to realize the most important fact about British Africa—if the white man is to retain his influence there the concessions to the Africans must be made, not by the Colonial Office but by the European settlers. Otherwise, the Africans will think more and more of the Colonial Office and the House of Commons as their protectors and the white settlers, who are their neighbors, as their enemies. The African opposition to the idea of Central African Federation shows how far this tendency has already gone. It may be that the blame rests principally with the white settlers in that they —in common with almost all human beings in similar circumstances—give too little and too late. But, all sentimental considerations apart, many of those parts of the British Commonwealth where there is a plural society are of such immense economic value that the House of Commons must also appreciate the dangers of making concessions to the Natives faster than the Europeans on the spot can accept them. We shall neither hold the Commonwealth together nor give the African members of it a chance to catch up with the rest of the world if people in the United Kingdom find themselves encouraging the Africans to become enemies of those white immigrants who have made Kenya, Tanganyika or the Rhodesias their permanent home. The Capricorn Society is important above all because it is an attempt by some of those immigrants to turn into a reality the Colonial Office theory of partnership.

20

BLACK MAN'S CONTINENT?

There are, as we have seen, many different attitudes to the Africans. The absence of a color bar in Egypt and the Portuguese colonies; the assimilation policy of the French; the defensive oppression by the Afrikaners; the "creative imperial abdication"—to quote a phrase used by J. H. Huizinga—of the British Colonial Office; the managerial revolution of the Belgians. But at the back of all these policies is the realization that the black man is awaking from a sleep as long as history, and there is a flavor of Lilliput about our efforts to cope with him.

If we hand over to him the seals of office almost before he can begin to ask for them—as the British are doing in West Africa—will he be grateful for all we have done for him in the past and be prepared to co-operate with us in the future? If we give him exceptional opportunities of economic development—as the Belgians are doing in the Congo—will he be content to forego any claim to political rights, and leave gov-

ernment in the hands of Europeans? If we make small political concessions when the only alternative is public disturbance—as the British do in those colonies where there is
a white settler population—will some solution of the problem
turn up? If we allow no nonsense about Native readiness to
take over control—as do the Afrikaners—shall we be able to
maintain our position without too much resort of force?

There are clearly two major considerations to keep in mind.
One is that the continent belongs to the black men. In earlier
times they appear to have come down from Asia, and are
therefore themselves intruders. But that was a long time ago
and the original inhabitants are nearly extinct; except for
the strip of territory between the Mediterranean and the Sahara and for at least a part of the Union of South Africa,
the Blacks obviously have a far better claim to Africa than
the Whites. Perhaps the greatest danger to both of them is the
growth of the Indian population, steadily reinforced by fresh
arrivals from that over-crowded sub-continent.

But the other consideration is that our civilization cannot
afford to leave immense areas of the world undeveloped.
Even if the inhabitants of these areas were anxious to go on
living as their ancestors have lived for centuries, we should not
allow them to do so. And so little are they anxious to go on
living in that way that the demands of the backward masses
in Europe, Asia, Africa and South America for all the amenities, good or bad, of western civilization have plunged us into
the most momentous series of revolutions in history. Had the
missionaries and the merchants left the Africans alone, they
would have spared them many forms of bewilderment and
frustration, but the more one travels in Africa, the more one
is horrified by the conditions of disease and terror in which
many tribes used to live. The missionaries have given them
an ethical standard by which to live but, by and large, the
white race has for centuries dealt with the black in a shameful way; it would not have been astonishing if the African
had developed an ineradicable loathing for the Europeans,
the Americans and the Asians who raided his continent in

search of slaves. But the black man, ignorant of any method of writing, has had a blessedly short memory, and the white man has begun to make amends during this century. Even when his motives have been obviously selfish, the hardships he has imposed have been probably far less severe than those to which the African was accustomed before his arrival.

What happens in Africa is of particular importance to Europeans, for the one continent is geographically so closely linked with the other. They are complementary, as are North and South America. The Mediterranean lies between them, but the Mediterranean has linked peoples more often than it has divided them. A more serious barrier is the Sahara— more formidable as a desert than when a large part of it was a sea—but communications across it and around it improve every month. The men who first explored the coasts of Africa were seeking easier access to the silks, spices and other products of Asia. But Asia has, for political reasons, become almost a closed market even in this uneasy period we call peace; if another world war were to break out, very few of its exports would reach Western Europe.

The Russians are said to have learned the lessons of the last war, and to have concentrated on the construction of submarines. The Atlantic would be a still crueller sea in another war than it was in the last one. In any case the Western European nations are likely to be increasingly resentful of their dependence upon the goodwill of the United States, which subjects a genuine friendship to an unhealthy and intolerable strain. And, even if we had the money available, we should find that the rising standard of living in the South American countries had greatly reduced their readiness to sell us food in large quantities and at low prices. We have had bitter reminders since the war that Africa is, agriculturally speaking, a desperately poor continent. Its output of foodstuffs can and must be immensely increased by modern methods, but, even so, it will never be able to export much; its own people need so much more food themselves. But the African continent, as we have already seen, contains huge supplies of electric power and minerals—both essential to the highly industrialized states of Western Europe.

Thus the African has decided to raise his own standard of living, and we have decided that we cannot raise ours, or perhaps even maintain it, without the help of Africa. Even the most backward Native now wants something a little better than mere subsistence, enlivened by the occasional beer drink, to which he was accustomed. His ambition for the moment may not soar much above the acquisition of an empty gin bottle, but his son will want to go to school and to become an office worker. And yet he cannot acquire even the gin bottle without European help, and—with the steady erosion of the soil—the white man's skill and capital are needed to keep the present population alive, let alone to meet its demands for some of the white man's comforts and luxuries. Nor can the European benefit from the resources of Africa, so many of which come from the tropics, unless he has the co-operation of Native labor.

Very roughly, the population of Africa south of the Sahara —and nobody would dispute the claims of the Arab peoples, independently or under European control, to be the rightful inhabitants of the area to the north of that desert—consists of nearly three million Europeans, half a million Asians and a hundred and thirty million Africans. It is surely unrealistic to imagine that, with so large a majority, the African will not ultimately achieve at least equality with the European, and probably domination over him? The Colonial Office may be helping him to acquire control before he is sufficiently trained to merit it; the South African Government may be going to dangerous lengths to postpone that acquisition. But the European's problem, if not its solution, can be set out very simply —how can he become the partner of the African?

"Partnership" is a word which has been devalued by misuse. But there are places in Africa where it is being put usefully into practice. The Kilimanjaro Native Co-operative

Union, for example, is now entirely a black man's concern, but European help and advice in its development has been so wise and generous that it has left a balance of African goodwill. The West Africans are, for the moment, so excited by their ebullient nationalism that one must sometimes wonder whether they will allow it disastrously to delay their progress, but it seems that they are beginning to realize the close link between foreign capital to develop their resources and the means to educate enough of them to run their country. The Gezira Scheme in the Sudan is an admirable illustration of the development of an export crop to the benefit alike of the African, the investor and the government concerned. Such examples of partnership give one some ground for optimism, since they show what can be done in Africa by a few men with goodwill and vision.

Even given that goodwill and vision, partnership will not be easy. "If African nationalism becomes an effective force it will stimulate 'the will to live,' but it may destroy 'the will to co-operate.' If it fails, 'the will to live' and 'the will to co-operate' may both fade away." [1] Certainly in many parts of Africa the Blacks are increasing in numbers and rising in status. But one sometimes feels that, beneath a boastful exterior, their bewilderment increases. As Elspeth Huxley and others have pointed out time and again, we have taken so much of the color and adventure out of their lives, and put so little in its place except a relatively benevolent materialism. "We who kill the slave-raid, the juju, the leopard-cult, the human sacrifice and even, so often, the dance of the warriors, seem only to have the school band and the information room, the latrine-drive and the tax exemption form, to offer in return. . . . Life to-day in the villages lacks color and drama, the people are in danger of starvation of the soul." [2]

I should like to repeat a story I included in a book long since out of print.[3] It was told me one evening several years

[1] *Africa South of the Sahara* (Oxford University Press).
[2] *African Dilemmas*, by Elspeth Huxley (Longman).
[3] *Go East, Old Man* (Latimer House)

ago in the pleasant garden of the Dar-es-Salaam Club, facing
across the harbor, with the lights of its ships reflected cheerfully in the water. It was the story of two African brothers
who had made a living as fishermen on a river in Tanganyika
where my host had once been District Commissioner. These
two brothers, he told me, had been extremely devoted; they
never quarrelled although their lonely job left them very much
in each other's company. One day an unknown African turned
up at their hut, starving and ill, and they took him in and
nursed him back to health.

After his recovery this man suggested that the two brothers
were growing old, and that they would therefore be well advised to take him into partnership. One brother was in favor
of the suggestion but the other did not trust the newcomer,
and opposed it. For the first time in years the two quarrelled, but in the end the first one had his way; the newcomer became a member of the little firm.

The very next day the first brother was caught by a crocodile and killed, so the second knew that the newcomer was
possessed by an evil spirit. That night he killed him, as he believed it was his duty to do, and he then came along to the
police post and gave himself up. In due course, he was sen-
tenced to death, but in view of his good past record and of his
firm conviction that it had been his duty to murder this supposed wrongdoer, an appeal for commutation of sentence was
forwarded to the higher authorities. While the Native was
waiting in jail for the result of this appeal a visiting nun converted him to Christianity.

For some reason the appeal was turned down. The day before the man was to be shot he asked to see the District Commissioner. He had one last request to make—that he might be
shot while in a praying position on his knees. The D.C. told
him that regulations ordered he should be shot while standing
and facing a firing squad, and that in any case a man of his
courage and reputation should not supplicate, but should face
death bravely.

The African was obviously distressed by this decision, but

made no further protest. When they came to fetch him from his cell next morning they discovered that he had scraped away the mortar with his bare fingers and had dislodged a brick. With the brick he had deliberately broken both his shinbones and could therefore achieve his last ambition—to die on his knees in prayer to his new God.

It seems to me that three changes are needed if the development of Africa is to proceed without bloodshed. Two of them are difficult because they deal with mental attitudes, the third demands a sacrifice of national pride. We need, in the first place, to change our own outlook toward the Africans, for enough of them have now proved their ability, intelligence and integrity to make an attitude of patriarchal superiority both absurd and dangerous. It is quite true that nobody who has never visited Africa can picture the primitive way of life and thought of the overwhelming majority. But that makes it all the easier for the educated but frustrated African to misuse their ignorance, as the black politicians of Nairobi have done in the case of the Mau Mau. When an American Negro can be awarded the Nobel peace prize and Africans can do well in most of the professions, an attitude of superiority based on the color of one's skin becomes incredibly offensive and hurtful. It leaves the kind of rancor and bitterness which would make partnership in the black man's continent impossible. "Not race, not color," said Lord Milner, "but civilization, is the test of political rights."

This does not, of course, mean that white parents should welcome their daughter's marriage to a black man, or vice versa. But the objection should surely be based on their probable incompatibility, and not on sheer racial prejudice. In fact, there seems to be no real evidence to support the claim that a half-caste inherits the bad qualities of both parents. What certainly is bad is the conditions in which most half-caste children have to grow up. In the world of the moment they are misfits, and the misfit is likely to come into conflict with so-

ciety. It really is time we stopped using other people's daugh¬
ters as red herrings to distract attention from one of the most
urgent problems in the world.

But a change is also needed on the African side. One sees
little hope of genuine partnership until the Africans learn
something about the nature of civilization; that it does not
consist in the acquisition of enough book knowledge to hold
down a job in an office; that it is the development of decades
or centuries; that its roots must go deep into the land, the history, the traditions of a country; that it cannot be grabbed
ready-made from people of another race and continent. "Democracy in Africa," I read somewhere recently, "is, in the first
place, a question of agricultural equipment, of harvests, of a
rising standard of life, and, above all, of education in manual
work. Democracy is the tilling of the soil, the fight against erosion, the willingness to learn new techniques." Very useful
work in Africa is done by the Catholic White Fathers, in that
they build great churches with their own hands and with those
of their black converts. There could be no more effective way
of emphasizing the dignity of manual labor.

Because the African has no writing, he tends to believe that
all culture not gained from books is second-rate. And by trying
to absorb the alien culture of the white race, he acts without
reason, without logic, without understanding, and, most serious
of all, without close contact with his own people. Perhaps, in
this respect, the Belgians, who are so often criticized for the
materialistic nature of their rule in the Congo, are acting more
wisely than the rest of us, since they are developing a middle-
class of artisans and craftsmen out of which may grow, in the
course of time, a genuine African democracy. Perhaps the
British, who have paid greater respect than most other colonial
powers to the human personality of the African, have done
him a disservice. They may have given encouragement to the
demagogue to the detriment of the humble masses.

We are influenced, to quote J. H. Huizinga, by two inner
compulsions. "The first is the instinctive desire of every ruling
class to cling to power as long as it possibly can. The second,

constantly at war with the first, is the missionary zeal of the bearers of a dominant civilization whose innate belief in its superiority, whether valid or not, compels them to spread their gospel and recreate the subject races in their own image, regardless of the chances of success." In all British African territories to-day one is struck by evidences of this conflict, by our resulting loss of self-confidence, by the need to keep the development of our colonies, as far as possible, out of domestic politics. The differences of opinion between the political parties in Breat Britain about colonial policy are most stridently and extravagantly expressed by members who have never visited the colonies, and I believe an all-party Colonial Affairs Committee would greatly reduce the number of ignorant or prejudiced speeches in Westminster which provide so much ammunition for the extremists in Africa. So, too, would the appointment to the House of Lords of a far larger number of ex-Governors and other colonial civil servants.

Even the urbanized Africans—and they are still a very small minority of the African population—are very close to a system in which the Chiefs had unquestioned and unlimited power. They search with pathetic enthusiasm for new loyalties to replace those which our arrival has destroyed. The French have based their policy on assimilation, and, by making it a high honor to become a French citizen, have produced great French patriots with black skins. The British, on the other hand, have based their policy on the growth and development of self-government. But in practice both governments are teaching the Africans to be interested in their own history, both are developing higher education in the African territories. The Belgians are starting the Africans in the Congo on the lower rungs of the ladder toward political independence. However different their original plans and motives, the growth of African nationalism and the speed of economic development combine to face them with very similar problems. So that one wonders whether there should not be a standing conference of Colonial Ministers of all European governments with interests in Africa. For it is in the interests of both Africans and Europeans that there should be as much harmony as possible in their policies.

This brings me to an important change which would demand a sacrifice of national pride. In September 1952 the Council of Europe in Strasbourg adopted a resolution in favor of a much closer association between Western Europe and Africa. The blunt truth is that the great colonial powers no longer have either the capital or the technicians to permit the rapid development of Africa demanded both by the Africans themselves and by the rest of the world. According to Anton Zischka[4] there are only about 3,400 doctors in the whole of Africa, whereas the need is for more than 60,000, or three times as many as are studying medicine each year in the United States. The shortage of engineers, of scientists, of teachers, and of technicians of every kind is tragic, and yet there are thousands of Western Europeans, especially in Germany, who ask for nothing better than to settle in Africa. And millions of pounds of Western European capital might be made available. Perhaps the time has come to treat the development of Africa as a matter not for three or four governments that chance to have colonies there, but as an urgent task for Western Europe as a whole.

Africa has a larger proportion of tropical land than any other continent, and the white man is therefore exceptionally dependent upon the Native. With the exception of Australia, it has the lowest density of population in relation to its area, but it has over 40% of the world's water power (compared with the 15% of North America and the 12.5% of Europe) which, given the necessary capital for development, could replace the shortage of manpower. No geological survey has been made of large parts of the continent, but already it produces more than one-third of the world's supply of phosphates, 45% of its chrome, 23% of its manganese, 85% of its cobalt, 70% of its vanadium. The mere mention of copper makes one think of the Congo and Northern Rhodesia; it is uncertain whether the uranium output of the Congo will be surpassed by that of the

[4] *Afrika,* by Anton Zischka (Stalling Verlag, Oldenburg).

"slime" from the gold mines of Johannesburg, but Africa's proportion of this precious material will only be all the greater for this rivalry. Coal, tin, iron, lead, bauxite, gold, diamonds—there are few minerals of which this continent has not sensational supplies. Africa will never be the great reservoir of food we anticipated immediately after the war, for so much of the soil erosion is due to the exaggerations of its climate, and not to the folly of men, but it has great supplies of vegetable oils, cotton, timber, wool. . . .

So much for the material reasons for a great and growing interest in Africa. But to my mind that is a more forceful reason than any based merely on materialism. Why the black men have remained unaffected and unaided by the civilizations around them will remain one of the major mysteries of history. For centuries, the contact of the Africans with the outside world has been disastrous for them; owing to their helplessness, their sons and daughters have been sold into slavery in Asia, Europe and the Americas. And even to-day it is customary to excuse the unequal treatment we impose upon them by the explanation that they are still children. The more truth there is in this, the graver our responsibility, for what crime is worse than cruelty to the child?

Besides, nothing about Africa is less probable than that the African will long accept the assurance that he is too much of a child to govern himself. Rightly or wrongly, the leaders of the sixty-six million Africans in the British dependencies will not permanently accept inequality of treatment and status. They will not permanently believe that the two hundred thousand white men who control them have more than a fortuitous and temporary technical and administrative superiority over them. The argument, however true, that British rule has on the whole been beneficial will not check the desire to be rid of it. "Even beneficence can have a crushing effect upon those whose greatest needs are self-expression and self-respect." [5]

"Men are not equal in their capacity to serve the community, nor are they equal in their needs," wrote that grand old

[5] Margery Perham, *The Times*, October 28th, 1952.

man, Dr. Josiah Oldham.[6] "But they *are* equal in the possession of a personality that is worthy of reverence. They *are*
equal in the right to the development of that personality, so
far as may be compatible with the common good. And in the
determination of what constitutes the common good, they have
an equal claim that their case should be heard and weighed,
and that the judgment should be disinterested and just."

What, then, are we to expect? A black man's continent? That
would be disastrous, for it could result only from a long and
horrible period of bitterness, revolt, suppression and bloodshed. We *must* make partnership a reality, and we have little
time in which to do it. Above the entrance to Achimota College in the Gold Coast is a coat of arms consisting of vertical
black and white stripes. This, I was told, was in memory of
one of the greatest Africans of this century, Dr. Aggrey, and
to record one of his favorite sayings: "You can play a tune of
sorts on the white keys, and you can play a tune of sorts on
the black keys, but for harmony you must use both black and
white." If this book can contribute, even in the smallest degree, to that harmony, I shall have achieved one of my ambitions.

[6] *Christianity and the Race Problem.*

INDEX

243